THE AMERICAN
RELIGIOUS EXPERIENCE

THE AMERICAN RELIGIOUS EXPERIENCE

A Concise History

LYNN BRIDGERS

ROWMAN & LITTLEFIELD PUBLISHERS, INC.
Lanham • Boulder • New York • Oxford

ROWMAN & LITTLEFIELD PUBLISHERS, INC.

Published in the United States of America
by Rowman & Littlefield Publishers, Inc.
A wholly owned subsidary of The Rowman & Littlefield Publishing Group, Inc.
4501 Forbes Boulevard, Suite 200, Lanham, Maryland 20706
www.rowmanlittlefield.com

PO Box 317
Oxford
OX2 9RU, UK

British Library Cataloguing in Publication Information Available

Library of Congress Cataloging-in-Publication Data

Bridgers, Lynn, 1956–
  The American religious experience : a concise history / Lynn Bridgers.
      p. cm.
  Includes bibliographical references and index.
  ISBN 0-7425-5058-3 (cloth : alk. paper) — ISBN 0-7425-5059-1 (pbk. : alk.
paper)
  1. United States—Religion—History. 2. United States—Church history. I. Title.
  BL2525.B75 2006
  200'.973—dc22   2005024092

Printed in the United States of America

♾™ The paper used in this publication meets the minimum requirements of
American National Standard for Information Sciences—Permanence of Paper for
Printed Library Materials, ANSI/NISO Z39.48-1992.

CONTENTS

Preface   vii

1 Introduction   1

2 Calvin in New England   13

3 Piety in Pennsylvania   25

4 John Wesley and the Methodists   37

5 Jonathan Edwards, Congregationalism, and the
   Evangelical Tradition   49

6 The Amish and the Mennonites   61

7 The Quakers and the Shakers   73

8 Bacon, Swedenborg, and Transcendentalism   85

9 Catholic–Anti-Catholic   97

10 American Judaism   109

11 Anglican to Episcopal   121

12 Lutherans, Germans, and Scandinavians   133

13 Evolution of the Black Church   145

14 Baptists and Baptism   157

15 Pentecostals and the Holiness Movement   169

16 The California Missions and the Hispanic Southwest   181

17   Raids, Ghosts, and Renewal   *193*

18   Mormon Country   *205*

19   Gold Mountain   *217*

20   Pluralism and Periphery   *229*

Resources for Further Reading   241

Index   247

About the Author   255

PREFACE

The American Religious Experience is meant to serve as an introduction to American religious history. *The American Religious Experience* offers a short, accessible rendition of American religious history in which footnotes have been kept to an absolute minimum, obscure scholarly language has been eliminated, and abstraction and theological speculation have been severely limited. While focusing on Christianity in America, the book also explores the interreligious, interdenominational, and multicultural context of American religious history. The book repeatedly examines the tension between the central, dominant streams of American Christianity and those groups relegated to the periphery—groups often based on visionary traditions, emotionalized forms of religious practice, or syncretic forms that incorporate specific ethnic and racial perspectives. *The American Religious Experience* explores this tension between center and periphery primarily during the period from the American Revolution to World War I, but these dates are elastic, as certain topics necessitate addressing earlier or later developments. As an introduction, the book emphasizes clear and simple recounting of the complex elements that make up the American religious landscape. Those who wish to pursue some of the greater complexities in this field can consult any number of scholarly texts within individual religious traditions or those more in-depth works listed as resources.

1

INTRODUCTION

Mention American religious history and you are likely to get a groan and a roll of the eyes in response. One gets visions of Puritans in clunky shoes or thinks of history texts that read like long-winded sermons, stultifying the reader into submission. But that stereotype doesn't really address the reality of American religious history. Religion in America has never been worked out in isolation. Nor will an honest survey of American religious history find that it has ever been exclusively American. Instead, it has always been global and interactive. Whether one looks at the deep roots of African traditional religions in the black church or examines the Spanish legacy in America's burgeoning Hispanic population, American roots reach into foreign soil. That foreign influence is there in the Baptist beginnings in Amsterdam. It is there in the English roots of the Quakers when George Fox roamed the English countryside. Even Native American belief systems are thought to have roots that reach back to Asia, before the crossing of the land bridge or sailing expeditions to the West Coast. Thus, in many ways, today's increasingly global interaction in American religious life may reflect a return to its roots.

American religious history is a story of encounter and impact. A Spanish sailor finds himself alone in the New World. He walks from Florida to New Mexico, rising to the stature of a religious healer among the Native American tribes along the way. Cabeza de Baca returns by way of New Mexico to the Spanish colonies in Mexico, and eventually to Spain, where he writes a remarkable account of his travels.

A tall, broad-shouldered French Jesuit from Normandy masters not only the Huron language but the use of the canoe for travel on inland rivers and lakes. His Huron hosts call him Echon, which means "one who carries a load," after seeing him carry his own canoe above the falls. Echon learns

1

the Hurons' language and spends years with them, trying to convert them to Roman Catholicism. He comes to be recognized as a man of spiritual power, but his arrival among the Huron also coincides with epidemic after epidemic. Eventually, raiding Iroquois kill the priest, Jean de Brebeuf, and consume his heart so that they can gain some of his extraordinary courage. Today, Echon is recognized as a saint.

British religious exiles settle in Plymouth and are befriended by the Wampanoag and their chief, Massasoit. Through encounters with the Wampanoag, they learned to fish for lobster, to hunt ducks, geese, and turkey, to grow squash and pumpkin. As legend has it, the settlers and the Wampanoag celebrate their survival, and the settlers show their gratitude for the knowledge imparted by the Native Americans that has enabled them to survive.

These encounters, set in different times and different places, with people of different backgrounds, emphasize the cultural interaction, in the form of contact events between the Old World and New World that proved foundational in shaping American religious history.[1] A collision of cultures shapes American history—growing out of contacts between indigenous cultures native to America and European cultures whose sailing technology allowed individuals to transport themselves to American shores. These meetings also serve as forerunners, predicting the consistent diversity that characterizes American culture, history, and religion.

These encounters also bring to mind four characteristics that continue, to this day, to reflect central aspects of American religious history. First, it is interreligious—Christianity and Judaism confront Native American and African belief systems. Second, it is interdenominational—from the Catholicism of the French and Spanish to the Puritanism of the settlers at Plymouth. Third, it is multicultural—with a wide variety of national and ethnic backgrounds playing a part. And, finally, it places a premium on the experiential—experience being far more trustworthy in a frontier landscape than the most articulate abstractions from a distant homeland.

Together, these characteristics will fuel tensions that also continue to shape and characterize the American religious landscape, a tension between dual streams of authority in American religion. Among the most significant is a tension between center and periphery in American religious history. For American religion will consistently demonstrate a tension between central, mainline denominations that are home to large numbers of Americans, that utilize sophisticated political influence and consistently assert their own sense of self-importance, and smaller religious groups that appear on the periphery. These peripheral groups are often based on visionary traditions, emotionalized forms of religious practice, or syncretic forms that incorporate specific ethnic and racial perspectives but consistently challenge any monistic characterization of American religion made by larger, dominant traditions. Let's begin with an examination of the ways in which the American religious experience is inherently interreligious.

INTERRELIGIOUS

Even before the arrival of Europeans, the American landscape was interreligious. The religious beliefs of the Native Americans are not uniform, and in many ways, each cultural group has developed and practices a distinct belief system. Consider, for example, the Pueblo peoples of the American Southwest. The twenty-some pueblos in what is currently New Mexico share a stable, agriculturally based lifestyle. They share similar building techniques and grow many of the same crops. They celebrate and worship through dances—tied to the changing of the seasons and important transitions. But just among the Pueblo people there are numerous, distinct language groups. The people of Acoma, Laguna, Cochiti, and San Felipe speak Keres. The people of Nambe and San Ildefonso speak Tewa. Isleta speaks Tiwa, while Jemez speaks Towa, and the Zuni speak Zuni. Just as their languages differ, the culture of each pueblo is unique, with its own characteristics, beliefs, and religious expression.

There are even greater differences between the Pueblo people and the nomadic tribes of the area, such as the Apache, Comanche, Kiowa, and Shoshone. Some generalities may be asserted—most of these groups incorporate forms of dance in their religious practice, for example. But any sweeping generalizations about their religious belief and practice are bound to prove mistaken. The same could be said of the diversity of tribes that once populated the Northwest, the Southeast, or the Northeast. Throughout the American landscape, different groups negotiated different religious practices and beliefs, demonstrating the interreligious landscape of America long before any European settlers first came to American shores.

When those Europeans did arrive, they brought yet another group of belief systems—including those based in Christianity and Judaism. Many areas of what is now the United States show first contact between Native Americans and Europeans coming as a result of missionary encounters, as European Christians sought to convert Native Americans to their own belief system. The slave trade brought unintended travelers to American shores. African traditional religions' complex belief systems found their way to the Atlantic seaboard and up the Mississippi. Later waves of immigration brought Asian belief systems, including Buddhism, Taoism, Zen, and Confucianism.

This means that although America has often been represented as a homogenous, or religiously unified, nation, the truth is far more complex. The historical record demonstrates over and over again the need for religious immigrants to determine how to interact with those of different religious traditions. At times, it has been with open respect, tolerance, and understanding. At other times, it has been with brutality, coercion, and forced conversion. But whichever the path, the American religious landscape has always been one that required interaction between different religions. It is inherently interreligious.

INTERDENOMINATIONAL

Protestant Christians, separating from the Church of England, who came to be known as the Puritans, fled from Great Britain and made an indelible mark on the eastern seaboard. Roman Catholic Franciscan monks accompanied some of the earliest expeditions by the Spanish, seeking to convert as they explored and mapped the newfound lands of the American Southwest and West Coast. Jesuits explored the Northeast, as well as the lower Mississippi and Gulf Coast, establishing mission sites and, later, churches and schools. Anglicans financed early missionary activity in Georgia, where Methodist founder John Wesley himself was sent to serve. German Pietists, fleeing religious persecution, created communities in Pennsylvania, under the generous protection of William Penn. The nativist movement in the mid-nineteenth century sparked bitter battles between Catholics and Protestants in the cities of the Northeast and Midwest. All of this drives home the point that the American religious landscape is one that is inherently interdenominational.

The United States never had a national church, like the Church of England. No single Christian denomination has ever been allowed to claim the entire land. Instead, a multitude of Protestant denominations have flourished, and the Roman Catholic tradition, while theoretically unified, houses a broad range of differing regional practices, ethnic backgrounds, and languages.

In Europe, differences between denominations had often been suppressed, with traditions separated, divided by different villages or regions. In America, settlers were thrown into intimate contact with individuals from other denominations. In many frontier towns, believers from widely different strains of Christianity worshipped together, in one church, long before time and economic resources permitted the construction of separate houses of worship.

Denominations did not always get along well together. Protestant publications such as the *Anti-Romanist*, the *Protestant Vindicator*, and *Priest-craft Exposed* warned citizens of Catholic priests intent on "worming" their way into the religious lives of their "unsuspecting victims." Protestant ministers became leaders of anti–Catholic association in cities across the United States, their antagonism growing out of the pressures created by wave after wave of Catholic immigration. Nativists, or members of the No-Popery movement, painted Roman Catholic hierarchy and structure as direct threats to American democratic institutions. Tensions grew so great that on August 11, 1834, a group of forty or fifty men stormed an Ursuline convent and school at Mount Benedict, Massachusetts, and burned it to the ground.

After founding the Church of the Latter-Day Saints, Joseph Smith encountered similar hostilities. Persecution at the hands of those who did not share his religious perspectives led him to take his followers west to Missouri. But, once again, their neighbors found Smith's mix of Christian and non-Christian beliefs threatening. Hostilities broke out between settlers who feared the Mormons' growing political and economic power and the ever-growing numbers of Mormon believers. The Mormons moved east and founded a city near Quincy, Illinois, in 1839. In five years, the town had grown to ten thousand, and the Mormons boasted thirty-five thousand believers. After Smith announced his intention to run for president of the United States, in 1844, hostilities erupted. Smith was jailed in Carthage, Illinois, along with his brother. A crowd, enraged over the Mormon practice of polygamy, forced its way into the cell. Both Smith and his brother were killed by the mob.

While Thomas Jefferson's separation of church and state guaranteed a plurality of religious traditions, it offered no roadmap for how to achieve a peaceful and productive pluralism. That was left to the impassioned believers of conflicting traditions to sort out among themselves. Often, they managed to do so peacefully. Sometimes resolution came only in the aftermath of brutal violence.

MULTICULTURAL

American religion is not only interreligious and interdenominational, but it has always been multicultural as well. Native Americans inhabiting the area that became the United States came from widely differing cultural groups, spoke different languages, and engaged in different cultural practices. Some were nomadic, following the large herds of buffalo and antelope across the plains. Others lived in pueblos or fixed communities for generation after generation. Some lived inland and survived by hunting and gathering. Others lived on the coast and incorporated sophisticated fishing techniques and exquisite basketry into their lives by the water.

Nor did subsequent immigrants to America come from one specific nation or culture. Even before the widely recognized contact encounters between Spanish explorers and Native Americans in the Caribbean or on the mainland, Vikings, it is thought, had landed along the northern Atlantic coast and built settlements, which they later abandoned. And long after the Spanish began to map the New World, explorers and traders from other nations began to explore the waterways and rivers, to chart the coasts, to name cities and areas in their own languages, often for places sorely missed in their homelands. The names of the American landscape stand as mute testimony to the inherently multicultural aspects of its historical and religious development. From New Amsterdam to New Orleans, from Rome, Georgia, to La Ciudad de Nuestra Dama, la Reina de los Angeles, more commonly known as Los Angeles, the imprint of differing cultures has been cast across the country.

Immigrant cultures brought with them different religious practices and traditions. The strains of German pietism were etched into the hills and river valleys of Pennsylvania. The echoes of traditional African religions were widespread among the African Americans in the South. The dark power and majesty of Spanish Catholicism was writ large across the American Southwest and dominated the California coast. The steady drumbeat of successive waves of Asian religions has left a Pacific rim studded with temples and houses of prayer. Thus, in population, in the names of the land, and in the religious traditions practiced, the American religious landscape bears a multicultural mantle, adding to the rich diversity, and also to the inherent tensions, of a multicultural, pluralistic society.

EXPERIENTIAL

A final aspect characterizes American religious history, and that is the many ways in which American religious history values the experiential. The origins of this preference for experience over theory or doctrine can be seen in the earliest days of American history. Native American religions, with their oral traditions, passed on the collective experience of a people, and the experience of preceding generations was closely woven into the cultural and spiritual lives of the current generation. African Americans also employed oral traditions, but those who survived the Middle Passage found themselves in the context of slavery, where their own religious histories were outlawed and driven underground. Geographically and historically disenfranchised, they developed the Invisible Institution, practicing slave religion in secret, below the level of detection by those in power. In a landscape where one's doctrine is outlawed, experiential sources of religious authority come to the forefront. To maintain their own, and not the master's, religion, African slaves came to rely even more on known, if unwritten, experience.

Europeans settlers on the various American frontiers also had reasons to put experience in the forefront. Without the shared experience of the Native Americans they encountered, many of the earliest European settlers would have starved to death in a relatively short time. Carving a comfortable living out of an inhospitable environment meant that settlers had to learn quickly what worked in that new context. In a staid European town or village, the prevailing power structure and incremental stratification of society was important. One had to show proper deference to those in power. On the frontier, such gradations were erased. A new nobility was born, and it was one based on experiential knowledge of how to survive on that same frontier. Perhaps the same reliance on experience shares roots with the consistent subcurrent of American anti-intellectualism. It was not grand theory or abstract ideas that mattered in the American landscape but the hard-won information born of experience.

This same valuation of experience in more pragmatic areas carried over to American attitudes toward religion. Americans resisted and suspected the many gradations and grand hierarchical structure of the Roman Catholic Church. They had little use for abstractions in theology or religious theory. What they could know and value was direct religious experience, which has always been valued to a greater extent and in a different manner in the American religious landscape.

That trust in religious experience may have lain behind the fascination with Native American forms of worship, the fascination with the dance, and the pipe, and the mysterious beliefs of their religious cultures. But it also erupted in the landscape of American Protestantism and American Catholicism and continues to shape American practices to this day.

The quest for understanding of religious experience led Jonathan Edwards to write about its expression in his 1737 work *A Faithful Narrative of the Surprising Work of God*. In response to Edwards's heartfelt sermons, people made unusual noises, went into trances, reported profound conversions, and seemed often permanently changed. With the arrival of the English Methodist George Whitefield in 1740, the Great Awakening was born. Traveling as an itinerant preacher, Whitefield proved extraordinarily charismatic. In Boston, fifty thousand came to hear him, and thousands gathered in other spots along the eastern seaboard. In response to his preaching, people began weeping and crying aloud, speaking in tongues, or wailing to one another. He was quickly branded an "enthusiast," and his demonstrative followers became suspect as somehow fraudulent, as those who had somehow failed to grasp the essentials of "real religion." By 1746, Edwards was laying out his own understanding of the differences between genuine and spurious religious experience in his classic *A Treatise on Religious Affections.*

The First Great Awakening left in its wake the beginnings of American revivalism and the American holiness tradition, as well as of a larger American tradition that encouraged exploration of personal religious experience. Experience is explored in the embodied worship of the American gospel tradition, in the cathartic experience of the Pentecostal, and in the profound reverence that follows Marian visions. It is personal experience that brings deep personal meaning to Roman Catholic monastic practice and communities like the Ephrata Cloister. Personal religious experience vouches for the miraculous healings of Mary Baker Eddy and the Church of Religious Science and brings new members to today's megachurches. The American religious tradition has always seemed more comfortable with profound religious experience and more willing to help those who report such experience to integrate it into their lives. This continues to leave a divided legacy in terms of authority in the American religious landscape.

DUAL STREAMS OF AUTHORITY

Recognition of this divided legacy has led theologian José Comblin to suggest there have long been two streams of authority in the church.[2] While many people equate religious authority with the visible structures that propose doctrine and enforce it, Comblin suggests the landscape is more complex than that. He posits that there are actually dual streams of authority. The first stream of authority is the hierarchical, episcopal, and doctrinal stream with which most people are familiar. This is the visible stream of religious authority that runs our churches, prints our hymnbooks, proposes and enforces doctrine, and is respected by the majority of the population as the leadership of the church.

Comblin suggests it is a mistake to consider that the only form of authority, however. The second form of authority is what he refers to as the mystical, prophetic, and liberatory. This stream places its authority not in the position held within the visible church structure but in the experiential realm, which Victor Turner refers to as the "liminal." Mystics become mystics through personal encounters with God and the development of their relationship to the divine. Prophets hear God's call and accept the responsibility of leading their people to justice. Liberation is the fruit of God's promise and the goal of those who suffer oppression, ostracism, enslavement, or disenfranchisement.

Comblin goes on to suggest that these two streams of authority, while initially seen as conflicting, actually need one another. The episcopal, hierarchical, and doctrinal stream of authority runs the risk of becoming rigid and too far removed from personal religious experience. It needs the fresh infusions provided by those with heartfelt and immediate religious experience, as they interpret their experience in light of established traditions. It is those figures who reinvigorate religious belief and practice for the larger population of believers, who bring fresh accounts of their encounters with God and reawaken belief in all of us.

Similarly, the mystical, prophetic, and liberatory stream of authority runs the risk of being lost in time, of never surviving longer than the life of the individual mystic or prophetic figure. These figures rely on the institutional church to keep their stories alive, to embed them in an ongoing tradition, and to sort out the doctrinal implications of the religious experience and insights they have brought to the church. Without that grounding in the larger society and institutional framework, their stories are at risk of being regarded as spurious and flighty, as mere personal aberrations instead of prophetic or mystical encounters with God, recorded and sustained in a larger tradition.

The tension between these two streams of religious authority is very alive in the American religious landscape and has long characterized different elements of the American religious experience. European and other traditions have been imported, and their distinct religious hierarchies have been carefully assembled or replicated in the American religious landscape. They have built churches, formed networks of governance, established ranks and responsibilities, and defended the interpretation of doctrine in American society.

But in America, the elevated role of religious experience, the guarantee of religious freedom, and the diversity of the American landscape have also given rise to countless smaller religious organizations. We find visionary traditions born out of the mystical or prophetic insights of a founder, schismatic sects that pull away from larger congregations, and ethnically based groups that help keep specific cultural streams alive despite the rigors of immigrant life.

CENTER AND PERIPHERY

The tension between these two streams of authority is also replicated in a tension between center and periphery in the American landscape. The presence of mainline denominations is so widely recognized in American culture that it is easy to think of American religious history as made up only of Roman Catholic, Episcopalian, Baptist, and Methodist history. Instead, these larger, mainline denominations only form the central stream of American religious history. Their dominance can obscure the presence of smaller religious traditions—visionary traditions, ethnically based traditions, progressive traditions not recognized in the mainstream, or smaller, religiously based communities. It is important to remember this tension between the center and these smaller peripheral groups.

In architecture the old adage was "form follows function." More recently, some have revised that to "form follows funding." The same applies to religion. To a great extent, the visibility of the older, mainline denominations may be more the result of generations of relative financial security than of the accuracy or importance of their beliefs and positions.

Mainline Protestant denominations have had centuries to build colleges and seminaries, to endow teaching chairs, to build elaborate institutional infrastructures. Those colleges and seminaries produce scholars and religious leaders who will engage in print and media with the tradition in which they've been trained, keeping it a visible and living tradition in the American landscape. Elaborate institutional infrastructures supervise formation of candidates to carry on the tradition, keeping it viable in a changing American landscape.

Roman Catholic religious orders and diocesan structures have largely been entrusted with the same tasks in the Catholic landscape. They have built churches, convents and monasteries, seminaries, and theologates and undertaken the systematic training of members of the priesthood, religious orders, and the laity. The Sulpicians traditionally trained members of the diocesan priesthood, encouraging uniformity in the training and orientation of members of the priesthood. The U.S. Conference of Catholic Bishops meets regularly to insure consistency in doctrinal positions and to respond to national needs. A solid infrastructure of development and fund-raising continually funds such efforts, making sure that the American Roman Catholic tradition continues, and the church flourishes.

Smaller religious movements or congregations have few of these privileges or resources. Often, they are seen as of dubious quality simply because they are new on the American scene or because they lack physical visibility in terms of established churches, schools, and seminaries. An honest appraisal of American religious history recognizes the role of many of these smaller communities, as well as the need to respect their traditions and beliefs, and remains vigilant about their contributions to the rich diversity of American religious history. The tension between center and periphery need not result in arbitrary determinations of quality or truth of vision.

CONCLUSION

The encounters between Europeans, Africans, and Native Americans that provided the roots of the American religious experience also bring to mind the four characteristics that continue, to this day, to reflect central aspects of American religion. As noted above, the landscape of the American religious experience is interreligious. Native American beliefs meet Christianity and Judaism. Islam and Buddhism play greater and greater roles. It is interdenominational. Catholics dominated the lower Mississippi, the Southwest, and the West Coast. Puritans and Congregationalists cut a wide swath in New England. Lutheranism followed Scandinavian and German immigrants to the Midwest. Baptist, Methodist, and African Methodist Episcopal Zionist traditionally had their greatest number of members in the South. The landscape of the American religious experience is fundamentally multicultural. With an ever-increasing variety of national and ethnic backgrounds represented, it is becoming more diverse, not less so. Finally, American religious history has always valued the experiential. Americans on the frontier found experience far more trustworthy than dogma, and, to a great extent, Americans retain a fascination for extreme forms of religious experience. The tension between the immediacy of the mystical, prophetic, and liberatory dimensions of religion and the dogmatic, hierarchical, and episcopal structures that sustain it over time continues to radiate and curb the dominance of either stream.

Collectively, these characteristics continue to fuel the dynamics that shape and characterize the American religious landscape, the tension between dual streams of authority in American religion, and the tension between center and periphery in American religious history. American religion continues to evidence a tension between central, mainline denominations that are home to large numbers of Americans, that utilize sophisticated political influence and consistently assert their own sense of self-importance, and the smaller religious groups that consistently crop up on the periphery. Visionary traditions, emotionalized forms of religious practice, or syncretic forms that incorporate specific ethnic and racial perspectives consistently challenge any monistic characterization of American religion made by larger, dominant traditions.

The result is a landscape and a history that is extremely rich and vibrant but fraught with tension and past pain. It has periods of sun, when the altruism and determined optimism of the religious landscape seems to permeate the American psyche. But it also has periods of shadow, when religious justification erupts in violence and radical discrimination. An honest assessment of our own religious heritage is unafraid to confront both sun and shadow, both the best and worst of our religious legacy, and to acknowledge both the strengths and the vulnerabilities that emerge from such a landscape. Let us turn now to an exploration and celebration of some of the diverse streams that contribute to the inestimable richness of the American religious experience.

NOTES

1. The entire Western Hemisphere is rightly considered America. Certainly, neither North America nor the United States of America can claim the name exclusively for its own use. However, for the purposes of this text, we will use the terms *America* and *American* to refer to the peoples and history of the United States. This is in no way meant to minimize or distort the role the rest of the Americas have played in larger historical developments or in contemporary life but is adopted mainly for readability and to avoid consistent distractions based in ongoing need for clarification within the text.

2. José Comblin, *Called for Freedom: The Changing Context of Liberation Theology* (Maryknoll, NY: Orbis Books, 1998).

2

CALVIN IN NEW ENGLAND

When most people think of American religious history, what first comes to mind is a picture of the Puritans—individuals dressed in black or drab colors, with severe white collars. The men are probably wearing breeches and have hats anyone would consider odd by today's standards. The women might have gray dresses and white bonnets, with long strings on both their bonnets and aprons. The severe dress and absence of color associated with the Puritans reflects their adherence to Calvinism, the belief that traveled across the Atlantic to leave a lasting impact on American culture and, particularly, on the culture of New England.

John Calvin (1509–1564) was born Jean Cauvin to a French, upper-middle-class family. Originally, he believed he was destined for the priesthood and undertook studies at the University of Paris to prepare himself for the clergy. Once there, Calvin was exposed to the thinking of Martin Luther and found himself increasingly moving toward alignment with the major tenants of Protestant thought.

Having learned Greek and Hebrew, Calvin came to believe in a literal reading of Christian scripture. Following the Lutheran idea of *sola scriptura* (only scripture), he rejected a reliance on church tradition and sought to interpret only what was explicitly stated in scripture. As his thought developed, he came to believe that the church was not the only institution that should be guided by a literal reliance on scripture. Given his training as a lawyer, it is perhaps unsurprising that he decided other social institutions, including political organizations and even the larger society, should also be founded on a literal reading of scripture.

Calvin structured church leadership at four levels: pastors, teachers, elders, and deacons. The pastors were given the fullest level of authority in the religious lives of their followers. Teachers were those who conveyed doctrine.

Elders were men chosen to set the standards of Christian life in the community, to oversee the lives of everyone in the city, and to insure conformance to scripture. Finally, deacons concerned themselves with acts of charity, watching over the sick and infirm, the widow and the orphan.

Calvin settled in Geneva, Switzerland, but initially the people of Geneva resisted Calvin's strict religious perspective. In 1538, he was asked to leave the town. Calvin spent years in exile, writing biblical commentaries and working on his masterwork, *The Institutes of the Christian Church*. In *The Institutes*, he not only developed the central tenets of Calvinism but argued for the accuracy of his own theological positions as he constructed a social, political, and theological philosophy.

In addition to the elaborate interrelationship between church and civic structures, Calvin argued for the doctrine of predestination. He felt that certain individuals were "predestined," or "elected" by God and only the elect could be guaranteed salvation. This was a doctrine originally proposed by Augustine of Hippo (354–430 CE), but Calvin adopted it and, in many ways, carried it to its logical conclusions. Calvin proposed a theory of salvation in which "the elect," or the "living saints," were guaranteed salvation. Churches were called to recognize these individuals and offer them salvation. Through membership, they might join other members of the elect within the safe confines of the church.

Whatever the reasons, the people of Geneva had a change of heart, and Calvin was asked to return. By the 1550s, Calvinist thought and belief dominated the landscape of Geneva. Protestants driven out of their own lands began to emigrate to Geneva, which became a center of Protestant thought and culture. By the seventeenth century, Calvinism had become the dominant form of Protestantism.

Calvinism came to America as an unlisted passenger on the *Mayflower*. In England, the Puritans proposed adherence to the thought of John Calvin as an alternative to participation in the Church of England. By the 1600s, so many Puritan colonies were established along the eastern seaboard of America that some historians refer to one period of Puritan influx as "the great migration." In 1626, Puritans settled in Salem, Massachusetts, not far from Boston. The Massachusetts Bay Company was granted a charter and established a colony nearby. By 1630, large numbers of Puritans began immigrating to the United States. An estimated thirty thousand settled in seven planned Puritan towns in that year alone, and twenty-seven vessels loaded with Puritans left England for Massachusetts.

In order to establish a Massachusetts town, a select few of the male leaders of the group requested a charter from the governor of the colony. They had to demonstrate to the governor that they had the needed skills for the town to survive and that they had already obtained the services of a minister. Once the charter was granted, they set up the community with clear criteria for who was eligible for citizenship. The founders then proceeded with the building of a church, the distribution of land in the area, and the election of leaders. By 1645, twenty-three Puritan churches had been established, and ministers flocked to serve them. In one eleven-year period, sixty-five Puritan ministers came to the colony.

Calvinism was arguably the dominant form of religion in the American colonies, and some historians have estimated that about two-thirds of the colonial population was trained in Calvinistic denominations or Calvinistic thought. These included Scottish Presbyterians, English Puritans, German and Dutch Reformed Christians, and French Huguenots. As a result, in New England, Calvinism became the dominant religious perspective throughout the Colonial period.

Many of the prominent early figures in the Colonial period were openly identified with Calvinistic thought. These included John Endicott, the first governor of the Massachusetts Bay Colony; John Winthrop, the second governor of the Massachusetts colony; Thomas Hooker, who founded Connecticut; and Roger Williams, who founded Rhode Island. William Penn, who founded Pennsylvania, was associated with the French Huguenots, also considered Calvinists.

Basic Calvinist beliefs shaped the spiritual life of many of the towns that dotted the New England landscape. Individuals were predestined for heaven or hell, and only the elect would know salvation. The flesh was the source of sin. One should confess one's belief before the congregation and be accepted into the church in order to be a respectable member of society. Church officials developed close ties with civic officials. They assessed tithes, or mandatory donations to the church, and issued blue laws.

Blue laws were called that because originally they were printed on blue paper. Connecticut blue laws, for example, stated that no one could vote unless he was a member of one of the churches "allowed in the dominion." Freemen were required to swear allegiance to God and Jesus. No food or lodging should ever be given to a heretic—or those not belonging to the prescribed churches. Anyone wearing clothes trimmed with gold or silver would be heavily taxed. And fines would be assessed on anyone who carried dice or cards.

Calvinists were a prominent force in the political scene and played such a large part in the American Revolution that King George III laid all the blame for the Revolution on the Presbyterians. In England, the war was commonly referred to as the "Presbyterian Rebellion." So, it is unsurprising that the grim, serious nature of Calvinistic thought came to be associated with the earliest stages of American religious history in the Colonial period. Nor is it surprising that Presbyterian schools, along with their Calvinistic fellow travelers, the Congregationalists, produced some of the greatest thinkers and writers associated with American religious history in the late eighteenth and early nineteenth centuries.

The congregations of the churches ruled social and political activity in New England towns. Because of this, members of the churches sometimes came to be called Congregationalists. John Cotton (1584–1652) became a member of the Massachusetts Bay Colony in 1633. He described his views of Congregationalism in the "True Constitution of a Particular Visible Church." His work was widely read in America and back in England. Influenced by their reading of the work, five members of the Presbyterian Westminster Assembly signed "An Apologetical Narration" in 1643, a document that would later be described as the "manifesto of all Congregationalism."

Congregational communities had mixed relations with Native Americans living in the area. Their towns and communities displaced the tribes that had traditionally inhabited the lands upon which they were built. Initial contacts were largely kind and charitable on both sides. Later, as Native American experienced wave after wave of disease, including smallpox and measles, and some settlers demonstrated increasingly aggressive behavior, wars began for the possession of land. Even as relationships between settlers and Native Americans deteriorated, some Europeans were driven to pursue greater understanding of the tribal societies.

One such early figure was John Eliot (1604–1690). Born in England, Eliot was the son of a middle-class farmer. Little is known of his early life, but in 1629 or 1630, he was employed at a school led by Rev. Thomas Hooker. Hooker seemed to have influenced Eliot to become a Puritan. After his conversion, few avenues were open to him in England, so Eliot turned to the relatively free and open religious landscape of America. From 1632 until his death, Eliot taught at the church of Roxbury, Massachusetts. Within ten years, he had decided that his future lay in working as a missionary to the Indians and, by 1646, had taught himself enough Algonquian to preach in it.

Eliot's language skills were to have wide ranging effect. He hired a Massachusetts Indian, Job Nesutan, to help him. Nesutan tutored him in his language and served as his chief assistant in his missionary efforts with the tribes. With Nesutan's help, Eliot was able to translate the Bible and other religious works into the Algonquian language. By writing down the Algonquians' language, he led them to literacy, impacting subsequent generations of the tribe. He was also the editor of the Bay Psalm Book of 1640, considered the first book of any kind printed on American soil. Eliot also became a model to devout men who came after him, demonstrating a way of life and a determination in his missionary work with Native Americans that would catch the attention and inflame the hearts of subsequent generations of Calvinists.

Arguably the most influential figure associated with Puritan thought is Jonathan Edwards (1703–1758). Edwards grew up in the culture formed by the blue laws of Connecticut. He spent his childhood in a Puritan evangelical household in East Windsor, Connecticut. His father was a Congregationalist minister. His mother was the daughter of a Congregationalist minister, and he was the only boy in a family with eleven children. He entered Yale at the remarkable age of thirteen as a child prodigy. There, he was introduced to the thought of John Locke and Isaac Newton and began to seek ways to synthesize their thought with his own orthodox Calvinism.

At twenty-three, Edwards became the pastor of a church and congregation in Northampton, Massachusetts, that had previously been led by his grandfather, Solomon Stoddard. His powerful preaching produced dramatic results, and he focused his attention on the intense religious experiences he witnessed. Over time, he came to be considered a "theologian of the heart." His publication of "A Faithful Narrative of the Surprising Work of God" brought him fame in 1738. It became a model by which other pastors structured revivalist meetings in their churches.

Collectively these revivals came to be known as the "Great Awakening." As more conservative Christians and theologians began to criticize these highly emotional forms of religious practice, Edwards became an apologist for the movement and, in the process, developed some of the works for which he is most famous. These include "The Distinguishing Marks of a Work of the Spirit of God" (1741), "Some Thoughts Concerning the Present Revival" (1742), and his best-known work, "A Treatise Concerning Religious Affections" (1746).

Among the younger men Edwards encountered in his work was David Brainerd (1718–1747). Brainerd was a sickly, frail young man who was determined to become a missionary. He attended Yale but never graduated, having been expelled for too clearly stating his opinions of one of the faculty. In 1743, Brainerd began missionary work in Kannameek, New York, then pursued further missionary work in Crossweeksung and Cranberry, New Jersey. Throughout his encounters with Native Americans, he kept a diary of his experiences, noting his prayer life, his religious experience, and his successful conversions.

Brainerd's diary had a profound effect on those who read it. Some even considered reading the diary a life-transforming experience, and many exposed to it dedicated their lives to service as missionaries or evangelists. In 1747, at twenty-nine years of age, Brainerd succumbed to tuberculosis, dying in Edwards's home. The same year, Edwards wrote "Character of David Brainer," praising his intellect, eloquence, and ability to express himself. He also remarked on Brainerd's ability to preach and his solid understanding of human nature.

Edwards was deeply impressed by Brainerd's diary and deeply moved by his death. Following Brainerd's death, Edwards decided to edit and publish the diary. It was released as "The Life of David Brainerd" in 1749. The timing proved fortuitous, for the following year Edwards would be dismissed as head of his congregation in Northampton.

Increasingly, Edwards's views came into conflict with those held by members of the congregation. Massachusetts had adopted a controversial policy known as the Half-Way Covenant in 1662. This covenant allowed the baptism of children into congregations when their parents were not members, provided that their grandparents had been members in good standing with the church. Just who was admitted to membership was an important decision and highly politicized, as males baptized received the right to vote at town meetings.

Edwards felt that the Half-Way Covenant, as a policy of admission, was too permissive. In taking that position, he differed in interpretation from his grandfather, Solomon Stoddard, under whom he had first worked at Northampton. Edwards also emphasized the need for a conversion experience before admitting one to communion, hardly surprising given his ongoing interest in the affective dimensions of religion and the power of revivals. Many New England clergy who supported the revivals of the Great Awakening supported Edwards's position. But it brought the ire of some of the older, more established members of the congregation who were more staid in their views. One group that opposed the revivals, the Boston advocates of free will, presented arguments that would eventually lead to the Unitarians' branching off from Congregationalism and their establishment as a separate denomination.

Edwards's perspectives on discipline and the Half-Way Covenant were contested, and he was dismissed after serving as pastor for twenty-three years. This proved providential in terms of his later work. Inspired by Brainerd, Edwards moved to a mission post, where he could minister to a small English congregation and serve as a missionary to the Mohicans and Mohawks. During that period, he wrote some of his most important books, exploring the relationship between determinism and freedom.

Overall, Edwards is seen as someone who was almost prescient in his ability to anticipate directions American culture would take. He pioneered the psychology of religion, was considered a master of rhetoric, and is still revered for his preaching ability. He anticipated elements of transcendentalist thought by presenting nature as a source of revelation and made significant doctrinal contributions in the exploration of free will. He was able to formulate great synthetic work in science, philosophy, and religion and to integrate Reformed theology and Enlightenment philosophy.

In 1757, Edwards accepted a position as president of the College of New Jersey, the institution that would later become Princeton University. Leaving Stockbridge, Massachusetts, Edwards relocated to Princeton. He was there only a few months when he agreed to be inoculated against smallpox in the form of a relatively untested vaccine. He died from related complications in March 1758. Only fifty-five when he died, in his relatively short life, he made a huge contribution to American religious history and to our understanding of the role of emotion in religious experience.

Over two centuries later, perhaps the denomination most often associated with Calvinism is Presbyterianism. Some of the earliest immigrants to New England were Presbyterians, and as early as the 1630s, they had founded congregations along the East Coast and begun to push into the wilderness. The Huguenots, the name given to Calvinists in France, focused their early immigration on what was then known as the New Netherlands. The earliest group, sent by the Dutch West India Company, set out in 1623. They founded the city they called New Amsterdam, which we know as New York. In France, the Huguenots came under increasing levels of persecution, and as their trials increased in the Old Country, more and more began to undertake the voyage to the New World of America. Soon, they had established communities in South Carolina, Virginia, Maryland, Massachusetts, and New York.

Orthodox Presbyterians organized their faith around the recognition of two critical documents, both dating from 1647. The first was the *Westminster Confession of Faith*. The document explains the relationship of scripture to God, creation, and human sin. It emphasizes the role of God in salvation and lays out the Presbyterian positions on Christian life and worship. It concludes by reiterating the anticipation of Christ's return. The second critical document written at the Westminster Assembly in 1647 was the *Catechisms.* Of the two catechisms drafted by the assembly, one is referred to as the "Larger" and one as the "Shorter." The catechisms lay out precisely what a church member needs to know in order to become a member in good standing.

More formal organizational structure for the Presbyterian Church in America came in 1706, when eight Presbyterian ministers gathered together in Philadelphia. They organized the Presbytery of Philadelphia, the first in America. Ten years later, they would elevate it to a synod, when their organization of religious life, regular worship, preaching, and teaching brought more and more churches into the fold. Once the synod was developed, they began to develop internal training for leadership and education. They also organized missionary efforts and charities. By 1788, the growth and increasing sophistication of the Presbyterian community brought about the formation of the General Assembly of the Presbyterian Church in the United States (PCUSA).

Calvinism came to inform not only the Puritans but several of the mainline denominations we recognize today, including Congregationalism, Presbyterianism, and Unitarianism. In many ways, the influence of Calvinism was not limited to those who believed in and supported Calvinistic doctrine. Many new religious movements emerged out of a rejection of the more austere aspects of Calvinism and its strong sense of the fallen nature of the human being. One common mnemonic device for remembering the basic tenets of Calvinism is use of the word TULIP. The "T" stands for "total depravity," emphasizing the dark view of human nature that Calvinism embraces. The "U" stands for "unconditional election," emphasizing that there is no way we can "earn" God's grace or our salvation. God alone has the power to decide who is among the elect. The "L" represents "limited atonement," the idea that Christ died to commute the sins of the elect, not those of everyone. The "I" stands for "irresistible grace." No one can resist the grace of God when the elect are called into salvation. Finally, the "P" stands for "perseverance of the saints." Saints or living saints are people whom God has graced with election. They are guaranteed salvation, regardless of their actions here on earth. Each member of the Trinity plays a part. The Father elects. Christ, as Son, grants redemption. The Holy Spirit brings salvation. Those who have achieved such salvation can be assured of having it for all eternity.

Much of the subsequent development of American religious history, both in terms of those who build on the primary streams of American religious thought and those who are part of small visionary traditions, comes as a reaction to Calvinism. Some, like John Wesley, who will be addressed in chapter 4, rejected elements of Calvinism. Wesley went on to form Methodism, which is considered one of the mainline congregations in America today. Others who rejected Calvinism went on to form smaller religious groups or traditions. Many of them were visionaries whose mystical encounters with the divine no longer permitted them to embrace some of the negative views of humanity found in Calvinism. How Puritanism came to be both expressed and resisted in the New World is as important for understanding American religious history as understanding the basic nature of Calvinism and its widespread influence.

It is somewhat ironic that the figures for whom these religious perspectives are named were often not the original sources of the ideas associated with them. Many of the ideas promulgated by Calvin date back to the fifth century, and can be found in the work of Augustine of Hippo. Augustine was forced to define his thinking on free will when challenged by questions posed by a British thinker named Pelagius. Late in Augustine's life, questions of free will again arose when Julian of Eclanum and his followers raised Pelagian arguments. As a result, Augustine developed some of the core ideas associated with Calvinistic thought, including predestination, and clarified his views on the role of grace.

Similarly, ideas associated with Arminianism, one stream of opposition to Calvinism can be found in the much earlier work of Clemens Alexandrinus, or Clement of Alexandria. Clement was a Greek convert to Christianity who addressed Gnostic belief systems of his day and the influence of pagan philosophy. Arminianism takes its name from a Dutch seminary professor, James or Jacobus Arminius (1560–1609) and is often associated with the revival of an ancient heresy known as semi-Pelagianism. The Pelagian view, which grants much greater power to human agency in securing salvation, runs counter to the Augustinian position, which relies more heavily on divine grace.

Calvinist doctrine, building solidly on Augustine, emphasizes the role of God in the salvation of the individual. God alone decides who shall be saved, and salvation is God's work. We humans cannot assure our salvation by our own efforts. Most people today envision a relationship with God in which human agency and the willingness of the human subject to cooperate with God play a larger role. God still is the one who offers salvation, but our actions play a large part in determining whether salvation will be granted to us as individuals, and that often includes being willing to confess our sins and to recognize Christ in our lives. This is a more Arminian perspective.

Arminius was a professor of divinity at the University of Leiden and a minister in the Reformed Church in Amsterdam. Few of his own writings survive, but we have portraits of him through the eyes of his fellow Calvinists. He was known to be particularly well versed in Augustine's thought and frequently referred to him in his work. However, when Arminius more closely examined Augustine's positions on predestination and free will, he could not fully support the interpretations that Calvin had come to on these issues. Although many associate Arminius with Pelagianism, as noted above, he himself denounced Pelagius as a heretic. Arminius entered into four significant disputes with other theologians, and differences in his views of predestination emerged. Specifically, Arminius outlined five areas in which he disagreed with Calvinism. First, he believed in conditional predestination, where selection of the elect is "conditioned" by God's knowledge of each person's belief. Secondly, he proposed universal atonement. God died not just for the elect but for all humankind. Third, faith can save us. Without Christ we can do little, but practicing faith manifests better outcomes in our spiritual lives. Fourth, grace is resistible. An individual must cooperate with grace. Fifth, our perseverance is not certain. There is no scriptural support for the idea that once one has received saving grace, one is not capable of later losing it.

Arminian thought was to have a strong influence on a number of religious groups in America. Perhaps the best known is the Methodists. Wesley spoke out for Arminianism and even named his journal for it. Arminianism can also be found in Episcopalian thought, among the Mennonites, some of the Baptists, the Nazarenes, the Pentecostals, and the Holiness Movement.

One of the early groups to embrace Arminian perspectives was the first Baptists, as addressed in chapter 14. This group was led by Thomas Helwys (1550–1616), who was a leader of the Puritans in England. Helwys organized a Separatist group and later determined that his group should emigrate to Amsterdam. There, he helped to build and organize the first Baptist church with John Smyth.

Smyth was already undertaking certain religious practices radical for that time. Smyth had rejected infant baptism and rebaptized his entire congregation. As a result, his congregation became an independent Anabaptist church. In 1610, Smyth tried to join his church to the Dutch Mennonites. Helwys and a dozen other left the congregation as a form of protest.

Helwys agreed with the Mennonites and the Anabaptists in the rejection of infant baptism but rejected any affiliation with these groups. The new group was called Baptist by its critics and not Anabaptist. The name stuck.

In 1612, Helwys returned with a small group to England and settled outside of London. He wrote a tract called "A Short Declaration of the Mystery of Iniquity," in which he challenged the power of the king over the mortal soul of his subjects. As a result, he was imprisoned in Newgate, where he died in 1616. Later, the same congregation would move toward baptism by full immersion, so commonly associated with the baptism tradition today. Some consider his church the "mother" of all of the General Baptist churches in England. He emphasized direct reading of scripture and refused to let speakers use translations or printed material to assist in their interpretation. He rejected use of the King James Bible and all forms of singing during church services. Thus, we see many of the elements today associated with the Baptist tradition—emphasis on baptism and the Word, direct interpretation of scripture, and limitations on certain behaviors. That tradition would grow in size and influence in the fertile soil of America.

John Wesley (1703–1791), often considered the founder of the Methodists, also defined himself, in part, by his rejection of Calvinism and was heavily influenced by Arminianism. Much of Wesley's knowledge of Arminianism came through his friendship with John Fletcher (1729–1785). In 1773, Wesley hand-picked Fletcher to be his successor in the Methodist movement, and Fletcher defended Wesley's theological positions and emerged as a spokesman for Wesleyan Methodism.

Fletcher was the vicar of Madeley, Shropshire, England, and considered a man of devout faith, significant learning, and discipline. While Wesley is associated most with traveling and spreading the news of the Methodist movement to wide-ranging communities, and while his brother, Charles Wesley (1707–1788), is best known for writing Methodist hymns, Fletcher is the one who developed the theological and doctrinal foundations of Methodism, through his ability to interpret, defend, and explain the ideas behind the movement.

Fletcher was considered one of the best scholars of the work of Arminius, well trained in the interpretation and exposition of Arminius's theology. His work "Checks to Antinomianism" has led him to be considered by many the "first systematic theologian of Methodism." But Fletcher brought with him into Methodism Arminius's rejection of the basic tenets of Calvinism. And these elements had a profound influence on the man widely regarded as the founder of Methodism, John Wesley. Wesley considered Fletcher's "Checks" to be a significant contribution to his own thought and considered Calvinism the "antidote" to Methodism, or what he termed "heart religion."

When Methodism shifted from England to America, Fletcher's writings were brought over along with Wesley's. As early as 1791, an American edition of Fletcher's "Checks" was published. In the 1827 Methodist Illinois Conference, Fletcher's book and the Arminianism it built upon were recommended reading. Thus, today, much of what we associate with the identity of American Methodism is implicitly built on a rejection of certain Calvinist doctrines.

The extent of Calvin's influence in American religious history cannot be underestimated. Calvin has affected millions of Americans through an embrace of his belief systems and practice of those traditions most closely associated with him, including Presbyterianism and Congregationalism. But Calvin, too, has provoked many to reject his beliefs and, in that manner, has spurred on the development of many diverse groups that might otherwise have maintained narrower congregational identities. Throughout American history, Calvin's influence has continued to spread, both among those who have embraced his thought and those who have most vehemently rejected it. He remains a critical player in the landscape of American religion today.

3

PIETY IN PENNSYLVANIA

Calvinism was not the only European tradition of Christian faith to be imported to America. As we shall see in upcoming chapters, numerous spiritual perspectives were the unnamed passengers on the ships that regularly crossed the Atlantic. Another European religious movement that became highly influential in the American landscape was German pietism.

Pietism began as a Lutheran movement in the seventeenth and eighteenth centuries. Its focus was not on the nuances of doctrinal interpretation or the abstractions of theological method but rather on the sincere and heartfelt devotion of the believer. With a pietism informed by the movements of the heart, the believer would lovingly engage in works of charity and be more concerned with the practical than the intellectual dimensions of pastoral work.

Most consider Philipp Jakob Spener (1635–1705) the founder, or "father," of pietism. Spener was a Lutheran minister in Frankfurt am Main, Germany. In the late 1660s, he encouraged the moral reform of the city and began to call laymen to meet regularly to support one another in their faith. In 1670, he began a *Collegia pietatis,* or pious assembly, and encouraged biweekly meetings. The "students" of the college were to come together to pray, to read scripture and ponder its place in their daily lives, and to share what they learned from that week's sermon. Spener hoped that the discipline of and the intimacy formed between group members would carry over to the larger church, strengthening the body of the church and the faith of the individual believer. He hoped an added benefit would come from the abandonment of dissolute habits, from men spending less time throwing dice, playing cards, or drinking in the taverns. Soon, a number of devout, conservative Christians were meeting regularly and working to improve their spiritual lives.

Not everyone supported Spener's work. Lutheranism had long endorsed the universal priesthood of all believers, the idea that all believers are called to some form of ministry. Spener's collegia was founded, in part, in that spirit. But some saw the systematic formation of members of the laity as a threat to the institutional structure of the church. The independence and increasingly developed roles given to the laity in Spener's collegia threatened the prevailing prerogatives of power, and critics soon emerged.

In 1675, Spener was asked to write a preface for a book of sermons by Johann Arndt (1555–1621). Arndt had written a widely popular book on Christian faith called *True Christianity*, which Spener had clearly read. Spener used the preface to address some of the criticisms leveled at him and his institution, to outline his own basic beliefs, and to explain why he thought spirituality was in decline in Germany. The preface became so popular that it was eventually offered as a separate book.

In a work, later known as the *Pia desideria* (*Pious Wishes*), Spener offered six proposals for reform of the church. He called for more focus on the Bible and better integration of the use of scripture. He urged a renewal of a "spiritual priesthood," as understood in the priesthood of all believers. Spener called for new emphasis on Christian practice and not simply on knowledge of the faith. He wanted believers to practice moderation in religious disputes and to demonstrate a willingness to pray for those who were not believers or were straying into sin. Spener demanded a reform in the education of the clergy that would emphasize training in devotion as well as academics. Finally, he urged improvement in the quality of preachers' sermons and asked preachers to create sermons that were of interest to the common people, not abstractions on theological doctrine.

Two difficulties emerged for the movement of pietism after Spener's proposals were published. First, many theologians and members of the clergy opposed them because of Spener's vocal opposition to faith that was solely intellectual or academic. Second, some lay members saw Spener's position as one that justified their leaving established churches altogether.

By 1686, the embattled Spener left Frankfurt for Dresden, but controversy followed him there as well. Five years later, he moved on to Berlin, where he helped to found the University of Halle. Spener recommended a young man who had deeply impressed him for the faculty, August Francke. In some ways, Spener and Francke's relationship mirrored the relationship of Martin Luther (1483–1546) and Philipp Melancthon (1497–1560). Spener, like Luther, had the heartfelt experience that launched the movement. Francke, like Melancthon, was the one who institutionalized the movement and, thereby, insured its survival over time.

Francke added his considerable academic credentials to the Pietist movement and brought it considerable more credibility in the process. He established a number of enterprises that became the public face of the movement—an orphanage, a widow's home, a bookstore, a hospital, and a library, among others. In 1687, Francke underwent a profound conversion, adding a greater spiritual depth to his organizational abilities and his academic knowledge. He became deeply invested in evangelism and missionary work and encouraged the university to put more and more of its resources into support of missionary work. Groups like the Moravians would be strongly influenced by Francke's emphasis on the role of the missionary in the church. The Moravians, in turn, would deeply influence John Wesley as he developed the central beliefs that inform Methodism.

The Moravians and the early Pietists had more in common than an interest in missionary work. The man whom many consider the founder of the Moravians, Count Nikolas Ludwig von Zinzendorf, was Spener's godson. He was also one of Francke's pupils. But, actually, the origins of the Moravians go back further than the seventeenth century. They were first organized in 1457.

The name Moravian comes from areas in the Czech Republic known as Moravia and Bohemia. Greek Orthodox missionaries converted the areas to Christianity in the ninth century, but over several centuries, the area came under the jurisdiction of the Roman Catholic Church. John Hus (1369–1415) was one of a number of reformers who called for the Czech people to dissociate themselves from the mantle of Roman Catholicism. He led a protest movement denouncing practices of the clergy and the Roman Catholic hierarchy. As a result, Hus was arrested and subjected to trial. Accused of heresy, he was burned at the stake in 1415.

The Moravian Church sprang from followers of Hus. In 1457, a group of his followers met at the village of Kunvald in Bohemia and founded a church, naming it the *Unitas fratrum* (Unity of Brethren). Decades before Martin Luther's ninety-five theses were hammered to the door, the Moravians established their own form of reformation, and, today, they consider themselves the oldest Protestant church in existence. They organized and, within a decade, defined three levels of ministry based on the traditional Christian classifications: deacon, presbyter, and bishop. Over the first fifty years, the growth of the church was extremely successful; it grew to two hundred thousand members in forty parishes. This success threatened some, and persecution increased. In the course of the Thirty Years War, the greatest level of persecution developed, and the church went through dark days and trials. As a result, thousands of Moravians fled with their families.

The renewal of the Moravians came about through the intervention of Zinzendorf, a nobleman from Saxony. Zinzendorf had graduated from the University of Wittenberg. In 1722, a number of Moravian families had sought refuge on one of Zinzendorf's estates. Zinzendorf encouraged them in the practice of their faith. Zinzendorf also put his considerable economic and academic resources at the disposal of the faith.

Zinzendorf never became a Moravian. He remained loyal to his Lutheran godfather, Spener. But, oddly, he allowed himself to be consecrated as a bishop in the Moravian Church. More essentially, his religious tolerance created a space in which the renewal of Moravianism could flourish. In the late 1720s, he had about three hundred refugees on his land in the village of Herrenhut. Zinzendorf called together refugees of different backgrounds and challenged them to display greater evidence of the Christianity they professed to believe in. Zinzendorf helped develop a plan for Christian education in the schools and a plan for development of business interests in the town. Herrenhut became recognized as a center for the Moravian faith.

By the 1730s, the Moravians had begun to undertake missionary work seriously. One group of missionaries was sent to minister to the African slaves in the West Indies. Another group was sent to Greenland to mission to the Eskimo. They tried, unsuccessfully, to establish a Moravian mission in the colony of Georgia (1735–1740). After the failure of the Georgia mission, Moravians moved to Pennsylvania, living first on the estate of George Whitefield, and later on five thousand acres of land they purchased from Whitefield's manager. There, they established the communities of Bethlehem and Nazareth, which became springboards for other settlement congregations in Pennsylvania, New Jersey, and Maryland.

In 1752, Moravian bishop Augustus Spangenberg (1704–1792) traveled to North Carolina in search of an additional tract of land. The party he led eventually established a town named for Zinzendorf's estate in Austria, Wachau, which came to be known as Wachovia. Areas including Winston-Salem also began as Moravian settlements in North Carolina, and Bethlehem and Winston-Salem became the centers of the northern and southern provinces of the Moravian Church.

The Moravians not only influenced the American religious landscape through their mission work and the establishment of their church in America. They also influenced other dimensions of the American religious scene. Perhaps most notable is their influence on the founder of Methodism, John Wesley.

Wesley first encountered the Moravians when he was sailing across the Atlantic to undertake his own mission work. The Moravians were traveling to establish their own ill-fated mission in Georgia. In the winter of 1736, the ship in which Wesley and the Moravians were traveling became caught up in severe storms. They may well have caught the tail end of a hurricane. But while the English passengers wailed and cried and worried, the Moravian women and children sat quietly and peacefully through the storm. Intrigued, Wesley asked one of the Moravian men why his people were so unafraid. "We do not fear death," they replied.

Wesley was deeply moved by the courage displayed by the Moravians, especially the women and children. He grabbed every opportunity to speak with the Moravians for the remainder of the voyage, to learn more about their beliefs, and the deep certainty their faith brought them. While he admired the Moravians, he seemed to have no such certainly about the disposition of his own soul. Later, when he returned to England, he would again seek the advice and inspiration of the Moravians. Back in London, he sought out Peter Bohler, a leader of the Moravian Christians. Bohler suggested that Wesley would experience justification as a kind of abrupt conversion experience, a certainty that would come to him suddenly and unbidden. Wesley knew his brother Charles had already had such a conversion experience, when he was recovering from an illness under the care of the Moravians.

Wesley's conversion came in the form of his famous Aldersgate experience. On May 24, 1738, Wesley went to the Aldersgate area of London to hear a reading of Martin Luther's "Preface to the Book of Romans." Wesley had been rather unwilling to attend this particular meeting but was encouraged to do so and finally relented. Luther's text addressed the work of God in the heart of the believer through faith in Christ. Wesley had an experience that he later described in his writings when he said, "my heart felt strangely warmed." More importantly, this "warming" of the heart brought with it an assurance that his sins had been forgiven and that Christ had willingly assumed the mantle of his sin. Later, Wesley would build a theology that recognized both the justification of such an abrupt conversion experience and the sanctification that often comes only through the practice of religious life over long periods of time, the ongoing practice of faith described in Arminianism. Wesley would combine both Arminian and Moravian influences with his own Anglican tradition to formulate the framework of the Methodist tradition.

When the Moravians moved to Pennsylvania to live on the estate of George Whitefield, they followed a pattern marked by numerous religious groups. Pennsylvania became a haven for groups of widely different religious practice and perspective because it was one area where those of different religious outlooks were "in no ways molested or prejudiced." The religious freedom of such Pietists groups in the Pennsylvania landscape was largely the work of its founder, William Penn (1644–1718).

Penn was an Englishman, born in London and educated at Oxford. In his twenties, he became enamored of the Society of Friends, the Quakers (addressed in greater depth in chapter 7). Penn was surrounded by Puritan influences in his early life and seemed ill suited for the Calvinist austerities and dark view of humanity. At twelve years of age, Penn had some sort of illuminative experience, accompanied by a strong sense of the presence of God, of great comfort, and of the importance of communication between God and the individual soul.

While studying at Oxford, he began to resist Anglican statutes. He encountered numerous punishments for his beliefs, and his family became highly critical of his activities. At twenty-three, Penn converted and became a Quaker. With the newfound zeal of a convert, he began to make public statements about freedom of religion and freedom of conscience. As a result, he found himself in prison. Only his father's influence and his family's high social standing enabled them to secure his release.

Once he was released, Penn became a Quaker minister and, with great fervor, hoped to convert his native land to his newfound belief. He denounced clergy who did not conform to his view of a Christian life. Although challenged in his religious views, he refused to recant and was once again arrested and imprisoned. Once again, his family, through their influence and connections, managed to get him released.

Penn knew firsthand the persecution of various religious groups at the hands of civil authorities and became convinced that the imposition of civic force on religious affairs was inappropriate. His objections found voice in a treatise, "The Great Case of Liberty of Conscience." But England showed little intention of liberalizing its treatment of smaller religious groups in the near future, and Penn began to cast around for other possible solutions.

Penn's family connections provided one. His father was a knighted British admiral and, as a result of his naval exploits, was owed a great deal of money by King Charles II. Penn's father died in 1670, and in addition to a significant amount of money, Penn inherited his father's claim. Rather than part with hard currency, Charles paid the debt by giving Penn a huge piece of land in the colonies. This would provide the opportunity for him to put his ideas about religious tolerance into action. The colony of Pennsylvania came into being in 1681, and Penn would make the area into one that forbade religious persecution and mandated religious tolerance. Written into the 1682 Frame of Government would be the requirement that all persons living in the area acknowledge God and live "peaceably and justly" with one another. There would be no more persecution of small religious groups by civil authorities or by larger and more dominant religious communities.

In addition to mandating a spirit of cooperation in religious affairs, Penn also sought to have a much better relationship with the Native Americans who inhabited what is now known as Pennsylvania. He sent envoys ahead to communicate with the Delaware Indians, asking for their love and their consent in his plans. Penn ordered those who represented him to be just and fair in their interactions with the Native Americans and eventually developed a treaty with them.

The capital of this land of religious harmony would be Philadelphia, the city of brotherly love. Penn designed broad avenues in a careful civic design. Soon, the streets of Philadelphia would be lined with churches of diverse religious groups, and the landscape of Pennsylvania would bloom with communities following diverse religious traditions. Penn's own Quakers were the first to take advantage of the remarkable historical opportunity that Pennsylvania represented, and many of them settled in Philadelphia. Lancaster County attracted Anabaptist groups, including the Amish and the Mennonites. German Lutherans and German Reformed Church members began to settle in the countryside, to carve out farms and townships. Other groups came in their wake: Presbyterians, Baptists, African Methodists, Catholics, and Anglicans. German Pietist Conrad Beissel (1690–1768) and his followers began to establish a visionary community outside of Lancaster, which came to be known as the Ephrata Cloister, described in greater detail below. With a wealth of different Protestant traditions established, the area began to emerge as a hot spot for Lutheran, German Reformed, and Presbyterian theology and practice.

By the late eighteenth century, Pennsylvania was known not only for being a center of Protestant thought but for being a center for pacifism as well. The large numbers of Quakers that were among the earliest settlers in Pennsylvania were known for the pacifism that was among their most strongly held religious beliefs. Quakers were not the only group that practiced pacifism, and other groups that held it among their beliefs began to be attracted to Pennsylvania. These included the Anabaptists—the Amish and the Mennonites—as well less well-known groups, such as the Schwenkfelders and Dunkers.

Along the western frontier of the colony, Presbyterians began to settle in large numbers, founding churches and bringing their work ethic to the tough job of carving out a life on the frontier. Welsh Baptists settled near Philadelphia and, by 1707, had founded the first interchurch fellowship of

Baptists in America. Roman Catholics, often persecuted in other colonies for their "papist" beliefs, felt comfortable in Pennsylvania and began building churches. Jews, too, found the landscape of religious tolerance and diversity a welcome change from the pogroms they had faced in Europe, and many began to settle in Philadelphia. A group of free blacks founded their own church in Philadelphia in 1794. It was the seed of the African Methodist Episcopal Church and the beginning of religiously autonomous congregations for African Americans.

Anglicans, shorn of the comfort that came from close connection with the English crown and unused to a landscape of such diversity, settled in small numbers, but they also added to the diverse landscape of Pennsylvania. The Anglican Christ Church was founded in Philadelphia in 1695, and another, in Oxford, in 1698. By 1715, nine more Anglican churches had been established in the areas around the city. Anglicans would later play a role in the founding of the College of Philadelphia, now known as the University of Pennsylvania. Initially, the Anglicans were a small minority in the colony, but by the end of the eighteenth century, many of the wealthier Quakers in the Philadelphia area converted to Anglicanism. William Penn's heirs were among those who did so.

One of the boldest religious experiments to take place in the fertile religious ground of Pennsylvania was clearly the work of Johann Conrad Beissel (1690–1768) and the Ephrata Cloister. Beissel had direct ties to the German Pietist movement. In fact, for a time, Beissel joined a spiritual community founded by Philipp Jakob Spener (1635–1705). Beissel's early life was not easy. He was born into brutal poverty, in a household without a father. His mother died when he was seven, and he was left an orphan. For some years, Beissel wandered and led a life of dissipation. His encounter with Spener and his followers had a profound, transformative effect on the young man, and Beissel began a spiritual journey of prodigious proportions.

As noted above, Spener and his companions were working toward the transformation of Lutheran interpretations of religious practice. As a group, they emphasized the interior dimensions of religious life. Spener encouraged his followers to come together to pray, to read scripture, and to share their interpretations of scriptural passages. Through such practices, Spener hoped that the discipline of and intimacy formed between group members would carry over to the larger church. Strengthening the body of the church, as well as the faith of the individual believer, over time would result in a cleansing and renewal of the larger church.

Entering into the group, Beissel absorbed an orientation toward religious life that emphasized the interior, contemplative dimension. He ab-

sorbed a renunciation of material goods, combined with an interior training and asceticism. His contact with the Pietists whetted his spiritual ap-
petite, and, soon, he was connecting with other groups that emphasized interior knowledge or mystical approaches to spirituality. He learned of Jakob
Bohme (1575–1624) and the Society of Philadelphia, of the Inspirationists,
whom today we might characterize as charismatics. He began to study mysticism in other religious frameworks. He wandered through the teachings of
the Kabbalah, of the Rosicrucians, and of the Gnostics.

When William Penn undertook his "holy experiment" in Pennsylvania, numerous persecuted groups migrated to Philadelphia and the surrounding countryside. Beissel traveled alongside them. He arrived in Boston
in 1720. In the early days after his arrival in America, Beissel associated with
the German Baptist Brethren and a congregation near Lancaster, Pennsylvania, in the Conestoga territory. Increasingly, his own vision of the spiritual life created friction with the group, and, so, Beissel left. His initial plan
after leaving the congregation seems simply to have been to find a place
where he could undertake the life of a hermit. He sought to devote his life
to contemplation and prayer as a solitary. But others were drawn to him by
the force of his pure spirituality. Beissel would move deeper into the wilderness to escape their attentions, but, inevitably, they would follow. Eventually,
Beissel accepted that he would have to provide some form of leadership for
the group, and a community began to form. That community came to be
known as the Ephrata Cloister.

In 1732, when Beissel established Ephrata, members of the Brethren
began leaving their church to join him. As Beissel personally directed the
development of the community at Ephrata, it began to prosper and grow.
Beissel, it seems, had extraordinary gifts in terms of persuasion and personal
charisma, for he was able to convince increasing numbers of followers to
join him in his noble experiment. More and more Brethren congregations
assimilated into the Ephrata Cloister.

Life at the cloister was quite austere. Members were vegetarian, for the
most part. Lamb was served, but only at communion, and was the only meat
allowed. The colony became self-sufficient. In addition to vegetable gardens,
fields of grain, and orchards, they built a sawmill, gristmill, paper mill, and
printing press. They also grew flax, had a flax cutter, and manufactured
clothing. Much of their time was devoted to the daily tasks involved in
maintaining this infrastructure of the colony.

Life was austere in other ways as well. Members of the group wore
white hooded cloaks, similar to members of the more austere monastic orders. They slept on wooden benches with wooden blocks for pillows. They

practiced celibacy, since Beissel believed celibacy was necessary to maintain communication with the divine. When chores were finished, in the evening hours, the group gathered to sing in chorus. They came to be known for their music. Beissel wrote hundreds of songs. The five-part harmonies practiced in choir came to be widely admired.

Eugene Taylor remarks, "[T]he first of its kind in the New World, Ephrata has been characterized as a missing link between the monastic communities of Europe and the great American experiments in utopian communalism."[1] Beissel seems to have been extremely well versed in monasticism and incorporated many elements into the community. Women who came into the community were deemed spiritual virgins, regardless of their physical status in terms of virginity. Single men became members of the Brotherhood of Angels. Married couples were permitted to keep their household goods and to settle in one part of the colony. Others were allowed to pursue the life of the hermit, called "The Solitary," and to live in isolation from other community members. Community members were expected to demonstrate a profound conversion as their souls awakened to an intense relationship with the divine. Such experiences not only confirmed the holiness of the individual in question but also served as an inspiration for other members of the group.

Many of the practices that members of the community engaged in were disturbing to their more conservative neighbors. They observed the scriptural Sabbath on Saturday, not Sunday, and, so, were often chastised for working on Sunday. They made long processions to midnight prayer services, chanting. They publicly announced their own sins and encouraged others to do the same. For one period, they shaved their heads.

Beissel ruled over all with the sheer force of his personality. As he had done on the other side of the Atlantic, he continued to seek out new information about mysticism or different approaches to the interior life. He visited groups such as the Keithian Quakers, the Sabbatarians, and the Labadists. Some reports suggest that he also knew practicing Rosicrucians. True or not, it is clear that Beissel retained a hunger for spiritual knowledge and for new approaches or practices that could be incorporated into his living monument to God.

Some reports paint a darker picture of Beissel. Some of the Brethren clergy saw him as a kind of "raider" who plundered members from struggling congregations. His success in attracting married women, and the frequency with which they left their families, raised eyebrows. He seemed to brook little opposition—those who opposed him usually just left the community. Some community members chafed at the restrictions Beissel imposed and the austerities he demanded and left, bitter and disillusioned. Some saw the colony itself as a means by which Beissel garnered attention for himself and saw him as lacking in fundamental humility.

The Ephrata Cloister picked up many of the elements of traditional Roman Catholic monasticism. They lived together as an altruistic community, striving to live a communal Christian life in accordance with scripture. They participated in daily prayer and hard physical labor—the two fundamental Benedictine dictums, *ora et labora*. They wore robes much like those worn to this day by the Trappist and Benedictine orders. They strived for perfection in the interior life and for a harmonious Christian community in the real world. But without the deeper sense of tradition found in Roman Catholic monasticism, the Ephrata mystics could not survive generation after generation.

The Ephrata Cloister was more a cult of personality than the beginning of a new religious tradition. Like other organizations following the guru curve, it did not long survive the loss of its founder. While Benedict of Nursia was able to found twelve monasteries of twelve men and to establish a broader cultural phenomenon than just one community, Beissel was never able to follow that model. Attempts to establish a second community at Snow Hill were only successful for a relatively short period of time, and then membership declined. After Beissel's death, Ephrata, too, went into a process of decline.

Perhaps Ephrata's inability to survive in the long run was the result of Beissel's charismatic personality and his inability to share the role of principal authority in the community. Unlike Luther, he had no Melancthon to attend to the institutional aspects of a growing religious community. Unlike Wesley, he had no Fletcher to ground the belief system in terms of doctrine. To use José Comblin's categories, as described in chapter 1, Beissel excelled in the mystical, prophetic, and liberatory stream of authority, but not in the episcopal, hierarchical, and doctrinal one. And it is the latter that insures the teaching of the mystic will be carried on into future generations, will be remembered and revered, and will become part of a larger, ongoing tradition.

But Beissel's community at Ephrata did leave a legacy that could serve as inspiration to later utopian communities across the American landscape. Subsequent generations would try similar altruistic experiments, with varying degrees of success. Beissel, along with the Moravians, the Mennonites, and the Amish, also brought many of the key elements of German pietism to America. He did model a bridge between the contemplative orders of Roman Catholic tradition and idealistic Protestant communities that embrace a communal life based strictly on scripture.

In 1941, the Pennsylvania Historical and Museum Commission assumed ownership of the lands and buildings that once housed the Ephrata Cloister. Today, one can visit the grounds and walk among the buildings erected by the community. One can visit, too, the final resting place of Johann Conrad Beissel, where his elevated tomb stands high above the surrounding graves, a testament to his inability to rein in and to share his own remarkable spiritual authority with other members of his community. One can still see the evidence of one of the most dramatic examples among many of piety in Pennsylvania.

NOTE

1. Eugene Taylor, "Puritans and Mystics of the First Great Awakening," in *Shadow Culture: Psychology and Spirituality in America* (Washington, DC: Counterpoint, 1999), 33.

4

JOHN WESLEY AND
THE METHODISTS

One of the most influential figures in American religious history, John Wesley (1703–1791), actually spent very little time on American soil. He spent the majority of his life on the soil of his native land, England, but started a religion that would quickly take up residence across the United States, build churches throughout the country, and construct numerous colleges and universities.

Wesley was born on June 17, 1703, to a large family. Wesley was the fifteenth of nineteen children, and one of eight who survived infancy. His father, Samuel, was an Anglican priest who struggled with debt, trying to support his large brood. At one point, Samuel was actually arrested and consigned to debtor's prison, but a concerned archbishop rallied the local clergy in his support, and they paid off enough of his debts to secure his release. The family continued to live close to the margin. One church official even asked Wesley's mother, Susanna, if she had ever "wanted for bread." With Samuel often absent, attending to ministry or in prison, Wesley's mother assumed much of the authority in the family and oversaw her brood in a disciplined fashion. She developed "bylaws" for the family that spelled out clearly the responsibilities of the child in terms of obedience, propriety, and the enforcement of moral character.

In February 1709, when Wesley was five, a fire swept through the rectory in which they lived. While other family members woke up and fled outside, Wesley slept through the commotion. Wesley's father thought his son was lost to the flames and commended his soul to God, but Wesley was seen at a window and neighbors came up with a lifesaving idea. One man stood on the shoulders of another, creating enough height to reach the child in the second-story window. As soon as the child was out of the window, the entire structure collapsed in flames. His mother, Susanna, later came to see this as an example of the providential care of God and decided that she would be "more particularly careful" of the soul of John Wesley.

In 1720, at the age of seventeen, Wesley was admitted to Christ Church, Oxford University. During his time at Oxford, he was introduced to two works that played an important role in shaping his spiritual priorities. The first was Thomas à Kempis's *Imitation of Christ*. From Kempis, Wesley learned the importance of emotion in religion and the necessity of serving God not only with the head but with the heart. The second was Jeremy Taylor's *Rule and Exercise of Holy Living and Dying*. This text, written by a seventeenth-century Anglican cleric and chaplain to King Charles I, also emphasized the purity of one's intention before God and the "tempers" of the heart. Thus, Wesley came early to an appreciation of the way in which affection contributed to spiritual growth and Christian perfection.

It was also at Oxford that Wesley decided to pursue holy orders. His father initially opposed the idea, but then came around to supporting the process. Wesley was ordained in the Church of England in 1728. While at Oxford, he had met regularly with a group of young men who prayed and studied together and had sincere conversations about their religious belief and spiritual development. The group went by many names: the Holy Club, the Godly Club, and the Bible Moths. Four years later, one man would remark that a set of "Methodists" had sprung up. Not all historians agree on this as the origin of the term "Methodist," but whatever the precise origin, the name stuck; the group came to be called the Oxford Methodists, and, over time, the movement associated with John Wesley came to be called Methodism.

Among the young men drawn to the Holy Club was George Whitefield. The impoverished son of a widow, Whitefield was struggling to continue his studies. Wesley's brother Charles loaned Whitefield a book, *The Life of God in the Soul of Man*, which had a profound effect on him and eventually led him into a powerful conversion experience. Plagued by poverty and ill health, Whitefield took his time completing his degree, but complete it he did. In June 1736, he was ordained a deacon in the Anglican Church. After his ordination, he began his ministry by preaching in jails, addressing what one might truly call a captive audience.

Wesley had continued his studies at Oxford, as well as his meetings with the Oxford Methodists, but cast about for a new direction. He was looking for a position as a cleric but turned down an offer from his father to take over his position at Epworth. While on a visit to London, he met Rev. John Burton, who encouraged him to become a missionary to America. Something about the proposition caught his attention. Burton introduced Wesley to the governor of the colony of Georgia, James Ogelthorpe, who also urged the serious young man to consider missionary work in America.

Wesley's brother Charles had also been ordained recently, and, so, the two brothers decided to venture out together to the Georgia mission field. On the voyage to Georgia, Wesley had his first encounter with the Moravians (described in chapter 3). Impressed by their devotion and their lack of fear in the face of impending death, Wesley studied the Moravians closely and was deeply affected by their spirituality. Ultimately, both Wesley's missionary work in Georgia and the Moravians' attempt to establish a community in Georgia would fail, but at the outset of their travels, they had much in common as they prepared themselves for their respective missions.

Wesley had envisioned himself as a noble missionary to the Native Americans, converting the Indians to the saving light of the Christian faith amid primitive surroundings and hardship. Instead, he was assigned to pastor a congregation in Savannah, Georgia. It wasn't long before Wesley's emotionally driven preaching, restrictions about who could participate in communion, and strict interpretation of certain religious practices clashed with the perspectives of various members of the community. Some even considered him a "papist in disguise."

In August 1736, Wesley became ill. His nurse was a pretty, dedicated young woman named Sophia Hopkey. Over time, Wesley developed a kind of infatuation with the young woman, to the extent of asking her to marry him, although she was apparently promised to another man in the community. Wesley struggled with his desire for the comely Miss Hopkey, fearing that love for a wife would displace his love for God. While he struggled on with his ambivalence about marriage, Hopkey agreed to marry another man. Wounded by her decision to marry and feeling he had been deceived, Wesley became intent on finding fault with the newly married young woman and publicly humiliated her when he barred her from taking communion.

Hopkey's uncle, Thomas Causton, called for a grand jury investigation, and ten indictments were issued against Wesley in 1737. After one year and nine months in Georgia, Wesley gave up his position and prepared to return to England. On his return voyage in January 1738, he reflected on his experience and found his own spiritual response lacking. He realized that his pastoral style had been insensitive. He felt his response to Sophia after her marriage had been less than loving. He reflected on the pure faith he had witnessed in the Moravians and, yet, could not claim the same fearlessness in the face of death. Again, he found his own faith lacking. It was a greatly chastised and humbled John Wesley who returned to England after his numerous failures in America.

Shortly after his return, Wesley met Peter Bohler, a Moravian missionary. Wesley was much impressed by their spiritual exchange and by Bohler's views. A month later, he came across Bohler again. Bohler offered numerous suggestions on how Wesley might deepen his faith and offered his own insights into the nature of abrupt conversions. Later, Bohler formed a little religious group on Fetter Lane in London and invited assorted clergy as visiting preachers. Little by little, Bohler brought Wesley to a more Lutheran-Moravian understanding of grace and the nature of faith.

On May 24, 1738, Wesley traveled to Aldersgate Street to hear a reading of Luther's "Preface to the Epistle to the Romans." In the course of the reading, Wesley reported that he felt his heart "strangely warmed." In light of this experience, his trust in Christ deepened, as did his understanding of the nature of salvation. The experienced deepened and confirmed Wesley's faith and expanded his understanding of conversion. Wesley is one of the few theologians to address explicitly both an abrupt form of conversion, which he calls justification, and a more gradual form of conversion, which is most often designated sanctification, in his theological framework.

In the fall of the same year, Wesley met George Whitefield in London. Whitefield was known for his extraordinary ability to preach and to move his listeners in profound ways. Whitefield also advocated "field preaching," preaching to a gathered crowd outside, exposed to the elements. Whitefield's tendency to arouse highly emotional responses from his audience had gotten him barred from preaching in a number of churches, so there may have been an element of pragmatism in his endorsement of field preaching.

Whitefield's beliefs were decidedly more Calvinistic than Wesley's, and, ultimately, the two became estranged because of their differing views on grace. But the coming together of these two men brought in the final element often associated with Wesley, Whitefield, and the events that followed. They had the interiority of such experiences as Aldersgate, along with the public response of field preaching. They had an emerging theology, a distinction between justification and sanctification, a number of clergy eager to carry their message, and listeners eager to hear. The elements of a revival were in place.

The numbers that Whitefield preached to were astonishing, even by today's standards. He is thought to have preached to twenty thousand people at Moorfields and Kennington Common. He crossed the Atlantic thirteen times and played an important role not only in the development of Methodism in England but also in the Great Awakening on American soil.

One estimate suggests that he preached eighteen thousand sermons throughout his life, at an amazing rate of five hundred a year.

Whitefield's impassioned sermons in America helped to fuel what is known as the Great Awakening. Jonathan Edwards reported that after Whitefield had preached in his area, people were much more engaged in religion. A short time later, he wrote of a genuine "awakening" and of new cases of conversion. Whitefield was considered the leader of Calvinistic Methodism and emphasized the role of religious experience in forming and sustaining spiritual life.

Often, local ministers were not as welcoming as Edwards had been. Many viewed traveling preachers like Whitefield to be a form of competition, directing much needed funds away from their offering plates. Many, too, did not welcome the emphasis on "enthusiasm," or the role of religious experience and emotional response demonstrated by new converts. Some thought it undermined a rational, or more reasonable, approach to religion and that the conversions would prove to be only temporary.

But Whitefield's Calvinistic Methodism ran nicely parallel to Edwards's Calvinistic Congregationalism on key points of Calvinistic doctrine. Neither sat well with the theological forms that were developing in Wesley's Methodism. From theological disagreements between Wesley and Whitefield, the key elements of Methodism began to be distinguished from Lutheranism, Moravianism, and the Anglican tradition from which it sprang. After meeting with Count Nikolas Ludwig von Zinzendorf, the patron to the Moravians described in chapter 3, Wesley clarified his position on the distinction between justification and sanctification. The count felt that the moment a believer was justified, he was sanctified in every way. Wesley felt too strongly that the Christian life involved ongoing growth in faith, requiring the much slower process of sanctification. Making clear the differences between his own theological beliefs and those of the Moravians, he also clarified his belief in relationship to key elements of Calvinism, rejecting unconditional election, irresistible grace, and the perseverance of the saints, as discussed in chapter 2.

Over the next few years, the organizational structure of Methodism began to emerge. Wesley developed the Methodist class meeting, "bands" of Christians, and "select societies." By 1744, the first Methodist conference was held, and Methodists began to define how precisely they would spread the message of Wesley's "real" Christianity.

Modeling himself, in part, on Whitefield's success, Wesley traveled the English countryside, preaching, organizing class meetings, and advocating for the poor. His travels took on a decidedly evangelical cast, and he developed friendships with numerous evangelical Anglican clergy. In August 1748, he fell ill on his travels and was nursed back to health by a woman named Grace Murray. He seemed to have a soft spot for women who nursed him, for once again, as with Sophia Hopkey, Wesley proposed to his lovely nurse, and the following year they signed a betrothal contract. Since he continued to travel to meet the needs of his growing movement, Wesley entrusted the care of his fiancée to a man named John Bennet. But when Wesley returned to claim his bride, he found that she and Bennet had become emotionally involved. Wesley delayed, hoping still to marry Miss Murray, but felt he had to tell his followers of his intentions. His brother Charles intervened. Charles Wesley took Miss Murray to Newcastle and saw to it that she married Bennet. The experience that proved so painful during Wesley's sojourn to Georgia had taken place all over again.

He may have been twice bitten, but this did not prevent Wesley from pursuing marriage. Shortly thereafter, he proposed to Mary Vazeille, the widow of a London trader. They married in February 1751. The marriage did not prove to be a happy one. Mary Wesley was jealous of all the time her husband spent away from her and of the many women he interacted with in the course of his work. Additionally, Wesley faced a great number of professional concerns. He was often criticized for his religious practices, especially his preference for letting lay persons preach.

Wesley distinguished between an "extraordinary ministry" and an "ordinary ministry." While he felt only the ordained should be permitted to administer sacraments, he felt that lay persons could do a competent job of interpreting scripture and preaching.

These distinguishing elements—lay preaching, participation in class meetings, and societies—led to the perception of the Methodists as an aberrant group within the larger confines of the Anglican Church. By the 1750s, Wesley was busy defending his position as an Anglican priest and his role in the larger church. By 1753, these pressures had taken their toll, and Wesley became seriously ill. Fearing impending death, he actually composed his epitaph. He used the time while he was recovering to develop further his theological writings and materials for teaching Methodism.

By the 1760s, Wesley became increasingly focused on the second form of conversion, the gradual process by which one achieves the higher levels of holiness, which he termed sanctification. In 1766, he produced a book on the subject, *A Plain Account of Christian Perfection*. He began to feel that only those actively pursuing a life of Christian perfection should be preaching or working in the field. Wesleyan spirituality thus took on a dynamic quality, an ongoing process of becoming in which one could never fully rest on one's laurels. Justification could transform the relationship of the believer to God, but it could not complete it. For that, the slow process of sanctification was needed. And it is through sanctification that the "dispositions of the heart" are changed, where the love for holy things grows in the life of the believer, and the temptation of the unholy slowly withers and declines.

In the 1770s, Wesley began to admonish his followers to demonstrate more of those dispositions in terms of their relationship to the material world. He preached sermons like "The Use of Money" and began to examine the morality of taxation, inspired in part by the rhetoric of the American Revolution. The success of the American Revolution would bring other troubles to Wesley. Wesley saw Methodism as a stream that could remain safely within the larger stream of the Church of England. Wesley never did formally leave the Anglican Church; nor did he seem to feel it was necessary to do so in order to be Methodist. But political events forced decisions to be made that were not anticipated.

Following the American Revolution, the Church of England, with its clear ties to the British crown, refused to ordain ministers to serve in America. Believers in America were effectively cut off from future spiritual leadership. Since the Church of England would not ordain ministers for the Americans, Wesley took it upon himself to do so. In 1784, he wrote the treatise "To Our Brethren in America" and reasoned that he was now at liberty to follow the guidance of "Scriptures and the Primitive Church." Following that, he participated, as a bishop, in the laying of hands on Thomas Coke at a 1784 conference. In his private diary, he refers to Coke as having been ordained. Coke was also given instructions to "ordain" Francis Asbury as general superintendent once he returned to America. By doing so, Wesley found himself in schism with the Church of England. As a result, the first Methodist church was chartered on February 28, 1784.

The "ordinations" of Coke and Asbury brought numerous problems. Charles Wesley disagreed with his brother on this matter and made his disagreement well known. Asbury, in America, quickly adopted the title "bishop," preferring it to "superintendent." Wesley quickly wrote to chastise Asbury but seems to have had little effect. Asbury was convinced that no one living in England could fully understand the complexities of running a religious enterprise on American soil and continued to go his own way.

Wesley, back in England, found that divisions had a way of multiplying. While he made it clear that he had no desire to leave the Church of England, he kept undertaking actions that furthered the schism. He maintained that he had not varied from the Church of England in terms of doctrine but only in terms of discipline, using such techniques as open-air preaching, lay preachers, and the holding of conferences. The following year, though, he ordained ministers for Scotland. Initially, he rationalized that the situation of Scottish ministers was parallel to that of the ministers he ordained for America. Both groups would be operating outside of England. By 1788, he was ordaining ministers to serve in England as well. Overall, he ordained more than twenty-five ministers for work in Scotland, England, and America. He was never officially censured by the Church of England. Perhaps his actions failed to come to the attention of the proper authorities, or perhaps, given Wesley's age, as he was then in his eighties, they simply felt the problem would resolve itself soon enough. Whether or not this constituted Wesley's actually leaving the Church of England continues to be debated.

After Francis Asbury was "consecrated," he formed the Methodist Episcopal Church at a meeting in Baltimore, Maryland, in 1784 with other church leaders. The Methodist Church in America began to grow in earnest. The early church retained a fluid form. Much of the early development came at the hands of circuit riders. Circuit riders were both ordained ministers and laymen who traveled on horseback from one frontier community to another. They would preach, help establish churches, organize congregations, and build up the body of the church. Over time, structured systems and interconnections between far-flung communities began to be established.

The lay members, as well as members of the clergy, had to show a significant commitment to the church and the ideals upon which Methodism was founded. Most were expected to have had some form of personal conversion that grounded their understanding of religious experience. Additionally, they needed intellectual and oratorical skills for preaching, since preaching was considered such an essential part of Methodist spirituality, given the models set forth by George Whitefield and John Wesley. They were dedicated and hardworking, and if the church could not provide much in the way of monetary compensation, their enthusiastic zeal and satisfaction in the salvation of souls provided other means of fulfillment.

In addition to circuit riding and preaching, they began to participate in revivals and camp meetings. Given the emphasis on conversion and the experiential aspects of religion in Methodism, it is perhaps unsurprising that Methodist preachers would be in demand to preach at revivals and camp meetings.

Revivals and camp meetings centered on the experiential process of conversion, and many Protestant strains emphasized the importance of conversion as part of spiritual development. Through conversion, a person began first to inquire about the state of his or her soul. First came a sense of anxiety, a worry that the state of the individual's soul was not sufficient to garner salvation, a kind of existential angst. That led either to a sincere form of repentance, a willingness to reform one's life for God, or to a surrender of one's will to the will of the divine. With that renunciation and surrender came the moment of conversion, and a great influx of God's grace would bring the soul to peace and the certainty of God's love for the individual.

Revivals sought to encourage conversions en masse among those who attended. Preachers would focus first on the numerous failings of those attending, the myriad ways in which believers failed to serve God adequately. They painted portraits of how sinners would be punished in the great beyond, furthering the sense of anxiety that preceded conversion. They used specific hymns or songs that evoked the various stages of conversion and created powerful emotional waves across the audience. Their interaction with the believers gathered could be intense and challenging, wheedling, cajoling, and pleading, and almost guaranteed to produce a series of conversions on the spot. People would cry out, begin trembling all over, or swoon with religious devotion.

At the turn of the eighteenth century, camp meetings were added to revivals. On the western borders of North Carolina and Virginia and along the Ohio and Kentucky frontiers, people began to gather out in the woods for extended revivals. Numerous Protestant denominations participated, including not only the Methodists but the Presbyterians and Baptists. The meeting at Cane Ridge, Kentucky, in 1801 is arguably the best known of these meetings. Hundreds or thousands of individuals would gather at these meetings, which would last days or even a week. Numerous preachers would expound on the word of God, hymns would be sung, conversions would be celebrated, and all would leave with a sense of having had their faith renewed and their hope restored.

Many of the organizational patterns established by Wesley proved extremely helpful in the growth of the Methodist Church in America. General conferences were called quadrennially. In a general conference, representatives determined the major directions for the church to pursue. Annual conferences gave bishops the opportunity to meet with clergy, to perform ordinations, and to make clerical appointments to various congregations or towns. Classes at the local level could be sustained by lay leaders and might be visited from time to time by one of the circuit riders, who would provide them with preaching and further spiritual guidance. The overall demeanor of the Methodist congregation was set by adherence to the *Book of Discipline*, which outlined the life of the believer in good standing with the church.

Such structures proved very effective, and Methodist, United Brethren, and Evangelical churches continued to grow in the early years of the nineteenth century. By the 1830s, a movement began to encourage the development of Sunday schools in Protestant denominations, and many churches, including the Methodists, established regular school sessions. This may, in part, have contributed to their interest in education. For in the nineteenth century, the Methodists also began to establish a number of colleges and secondary schools. Today, we are familiar with the names of Emory University, Southern Methodist University (SMU), and Claremont, but many do not recognize the Methodist origins of these institutions.

Nor do most Americans realize how long and how deeply the Methodist Church has been involved with publication. The Methodists claim the first publishing house in America, in the form of the Methodist Book Concern, which was organized in 1789. The need for materials for the Sunday school movement contributed to their interests in publishing, as did the need for hymnals, copies of the Book of Discipline, and other materials for use in congregational settings.

Growth was not always without problems or difficulties, however. One of the gravest periods of stress for the growing Methodist Church came with the Civil War. The Methodists were extremely divided on the question of slavery. Certain groups were strongly aligned with the abolitionist movement, including the Wesleyan Methodists. Increasingly, in the first decades of the nineteenth century, Methodists in different parts of the country held distinctly different positions in regard to slavery. Certain groups, including the Wesleyan Methodists and the Free Methodists, were formed by those who participated openly in the abolitionist movement.

The Free Methodists also took part in the Underground Railroad. The Underground Railroad was a loosely organized collection of individuals and groups sympathetic to the plight of African American slaves and willing to help them escape from areas that allowed slavery. Participants helped runaway slaves find transportation, safe lodging, and secret routes and helped them in other ways to secure freedom. In addition to free blacks, Native Americans, and abolitionists, churches played an important part in sustaining the railroad. Among these church groups were the Congregationalists, the Quakers, the American Baptists, the Wesleyan Methodists, and the Free Methodists. The Wesleyan Methodists were founded in 1843 when a group of ministers and laymen decided to leave the Methodist Episcopal Church because of their divergent views on slavery, among other issues. Two years later, in Louisville, Kentucky, a much larger split occurred. Churches in slaveholding states broke away from the national church and established the Methodist Episcopal

Church, South. This division would remain in place until 1939. Even then, the reunification sparked another group of Southern members to splinter away from the church and form the Southern Methodist Church in 1940.

Nor was slavery the only way in which racial issues led to a splinter-ing of the Methodist Church. Richard Allen (1760–1831) was a freed slave who became a Methodist preacher. Converted to Methodism by a circuit rider, his owner was also converted and gave Allen the opportunity to pur-chase his own freedom. He did so and later became a "licensed exhorter," or lay preacher. Eventually, he came to be recognized for the power of his preaching and was even acknowledged by Francis Asbury. Allen was ap-pointed an assistant minister to a congregation in Philadelphia that was racially mixed. His work as a minister led him into an association with members of the Free African Society, a social support organization for African Americans. Many of the participants were Quaker or Episcopalian, but Allen was determined to remain faithful to his Methodist beliefs.

In 1794, Allen formed his own religious congregation, naming it the Bethel African Methodist Episcopal Church. Allen's decision to form his own congregation was prompted in part by the ongoing racism he experi-ence within the church. African Americans could not be buried in the same sections of cemeteries as other white church members. Some members ad-vocated that African Americans be limited to seating in a gallery that kept them separated from the larger church body. Allen's timing was good, as the African American population of Philadelphia was undergoing an increase at that time. His congregation steadily grew and, by 1813, had over twelve hundred members.

Following the founding of his congregation, Allen became increasingly disenchanted with the Methodist Church. He felt that white ministers failed to respect the independence of African American congregations and were not strident enough about abolishing slavery. In 1807, his congregation added the "African Supplement" to their articles of incorporation, and be-came the newly independant African Methodist Episcopal Church. Within ten years, they received formal, legal recognition of their status as an inde-pendent religious organization. In 1816, Allen met with representatives from other African American Methodist churches. Together, they formed the first African American denomination in the United States, the African Methodist Episcopal Church. This will be addressed in greater detail in chapter 13.

There would be other divergent streams that grew out of the Methodist church. In 1830, some five thousand members decided to split from the church because the denomination did not allow lay people to have full representation or permit congregations to elect their own district superintendents. They formed the Methodist Protestant Church, which remained a separate entity until 1939, when it joined with the Methodist Episcopal Church and the Methodist Episcopal Church, South, to become the Methodist Church.

Today, over forty denominations have descended from the teachings of John Wesley and his Methodist movement, standing as a testament to Wesley's influential role in the American religious landscape. In addition to the African Methodist Episcopal Church, the Free Methodists, and the Wesleyan Methodists mentioned above, Methodist influences can be found in the Church of the Nazarene. Methodism has also impacted the Pentecostals and the Holiness Movement, which arguably began in Methodist circles and will be addressed in greater detail in chapter 15. William Booth, the founder of the Salvation Army, was formerly a Methodist and incorporated some elements of Methodist thought into his organization. From the first humble schools and the Sunday school movement, today there are almost twenty universities and colleges named after John Wesley. Through their auspices and the thousands of Methodist congregations across the nation, Wesley continues to impact the American religious landscape.

5

JONATHAN EDWARDS, CONGREGATIONALISM, AND THE EVANGELICAL TRADITION

In chapter 2, we first met Jonathan Edwards and explored his role in the development of Calvinism in America. But Edwards is not associated only with Calvinism. He is also strongly associated with the religious denomination known as Congregationalism and the early stages of the evangelical tradition in America.

In chapter 2, we also learned how the congregations of the churches ruled social and political activity in New England towns. Accordingly, members of these churches came to be called Congregationalists. Many of these religious congregations sprang out of what were previously termed "Independents." In the aftermath of the Reformation, the Anglican Church in England elected to retain numerous practices associated with Roman Catholicism, including a sacramental structure and certain liturgical elements. Many of those who had withdrawn from the Roman Catholic Church resented the retention of these "Catholic" aspects in the Anglican Church. In search of greater personal freedom and more individual spiritual responsibility, they vowed never to be ruled by any "priest, prophet or king save Christ." Under the Church of England, where crown and church blend, these dissenters found themselves facing civil persecution—fines, imprisonment, and even execution. Many such believers thought immigration their best option in the face of such unjust treatment.

This decision to immigrate coincided with the development of Colonial America, and many of these congregations turned to the colonies for safe haven from their persecutors. On American soil, most Independents preferred to refer to themselves as Puritans; an overview of the Puritan story is provided in chapter 2.

One Congregationalist leader, John Cotton (1584–1652), who became a member of the Massachusetts Bay Colony in 1633, described his views of Congregationalism in a document he titled the "True Constitution of a Particular Visible Church." His work was widely read, both in America and back in England. Influenced by their reading of the work, five members of the Presbyterian Westminster Assembly signed a document that would later be described as the manifesto of Congregationalism. The viewpoint of the Independents was distilled by five men, Thomas Goodwin, Philip Nye, Jeremiah Burroughs, William Bridge, and Sidrach Simpson, collectively referred to as the "Five Dissenting Brethren." These five ministers and the few laymen who accompanied them adopted many of the articles of the Westminster Confession, which is considered by many to be the last great Reform document, clearly outlining the basics of Reformed thought and belief.

The Westminster Confession, which lays out the design for the government of the church in the Presbyterian tradition, is an articulate expression of Reformed faith and doctrine. But some felt it was not as clear on church polity, or governance, as it could be. It was subsequently revised at the Cambridge Synod in 1648. That revision came to be known as the Cambridge Platform and allowed for a bridging of the differences between Presbyterians and Congregationalists.

But Independents like the Five Dissenting Brethren still found themselves in disagreement with forms of church government outlined in the Westminster Confession. As a result, another meeting was called in 1658 in Savoy, which resulted in the drafting of the Savoy Declaration. In that document, those gathered modified the Westminster Confession to suit Congregational polity, or church governance. This document gives us a clear picture of the approach to the church known as Congregationalism, which became extremely influential in the life of Colonial America.

In the Congregationalist schema, the pastors, elders, teachers, and deacons of the church were chosen by the church itself. The call of vocation became a process of election within the church. Should a member of the church require censure, that censure would also come from the church itself. Should decisions need to be made with other congregations, the church would call a synod or council, but these meetings did not have the power to govern the individual churches or to censure the members of those churches directly. Congregationalist members were free to leave the congregation, should they find themselves dissatisfied, and could present themselves to other congregations to apply for membership. Congregationalist teaching remained heavily indebted to Calvinist doctrine but incorporated some more democratic innovations.

The early Congregationalist churches in the colonies were fortunate enough to have some very gifted members of the clergy in leadership positions. John Cotton's contribution in Massachusetts is noted above. Thomas Hooker (1586–1647) was a minister in Newtowne, Massachusetts, now known as Cambridge, home to Harvard University. Hooker was adamant in his support of democracy and became concerned that the Boston church had grown too elitist. As a result, he led a group of his followers to Hartford in 1636 to establish his own colony, Connecticut.

John Cotton's grandson, Cotton Mather (1663–1728), later became concerned that Congregationalists were in some forms too independent. He suggested that churches should join together in order to ensure that candidates for the ministry had adequate training and met minimal requirements; he also suggested that a form of collective government should have some judicial responsibility over the church at large. His recommendations were initially rejected; however, in 1705 and 1706, his plan for the training and examination of ministers was accepted.

By 1708, the Saybrook Platform was drafted. This document proposed that churches had an obligation to "consociation." Through consociation, one congregation could come to the aid of another in terms of monetary relief or support for ministry. It also proposed a penalty for congregations that failed to participate in consociation and for pastors who resisted support in handling disputes or adopting general procedures. This minimal structure would allow the Congregationalist Church to retain a defined identity and to weather the historical challenges that would soon face it as a tradition.

Perhaps the best-known figure associated with Puritan or Congregationalist thought is Jonathan Edwards (1703–1758). Edwards also grew up in the culture formed by the blue laws in Thomas Hooker's colony, Connecticut. Edwards grew up in a Puritan, evangelical household in East Windsor, Connecticut, where his father was a Congregationalist minister and his mother was the daughter of a Congregationalist minister. He was admitted to Yale at thirteen as a child prodigy. Edwards was introduced to the thought of John Locke and Isaac Newton and began to seek ways to synthesize their thought with his own orthodox Calvinism.

Edwards played a key role in the Great Awakening. His ability to produce deeply felt conversions among those to whom he preached began to spread rapidly. Supported by George Whitefield's preaching in his travels around the colonies, a highly emotional form of religious practice began to spread and be picked up by other pastors.

Some of the pastors, inspired by Whitefield's itinerant preaching, became missionaries and began missionary activity in the South. Presbyterian preachers from New York and New Jersey went to Virginia. Members of the Separate Baptists moved to North Carolina. Filled with missionary zeal and a style that emphasized the emotional dimensions of religious response, they came to be seen as evangelical, or members of the evangelical tradition. As time went on, a growing percentage of Southern Christians adopted this perspective.

The Great Awakening generated a certain amount of backlash. Many clergy thought the behavior witnessed at revivals and camp meetings was unbecoming, paid too little attention to doctrinal distinctions, and was too heavily based in the heart rather than the head. Some were opposed to the fact that people of different races mingled together to hear itinerant preachers or attend camp meetings and that social distinctions were not being carefully maintained in such gatherings. Evangelists and their followers in turn challenged the solemn nature of worship as most pastors presented it, voicing the opinion that, in many churches, worship had become sterile and dull.

Certain denominational divisions began to emerge out of this polarized landscape. Members of the Anglican and Quaker churches largely disapproved of the style of worship gaining popularity during the Great Awakening. But Baptists and Methodists, whose traditions emphasized the need for a conversion or spiritual awakening in full Christian development, tended to side with the more emotionalized style of preaching and worship. Congregationalists and Presbyterians were the largest denominational groups in America, but their members were divided on whether these highly charged forms of worship were appropriate.

By the nineteenth century, Congregationalist churches had become increasingly convinced of the need for greater missionary activity. In 1810, they formed the American Board of Commissioners for Foreign Missions. Sixteen years later, in 1826, the American Home Missionary Society would emerge, which focused on missionary work within the United States, often targeting Native American or African American communities. By 1846, that had evolved into the American Missionary Association.

By the 1870s, Congregationalist churches seem to have forgotten some of their early mistrust of cooperation on a larger scale. In 1871, the National Council of the Congregational Churches of the United States was founded. Each church still retained a great deal of autonomy in terms of determining its own style of worship and in questions of individual conduct. But Congregationalism had weathered the most pressing storms and was well established by that time. One of the greatest threats came early in the nineteenth century, when over one hundred churches left the larger body of Congregationalists to form the Unitarian Church. But the Congregationalists have endured, and, today, we know Congregationalists under the banner of the United Church of Christ (UCC). Congregationalists have also left another significant legacy to American culture. Congregationalists founded many of the most prestigious colleges in the country, including Harvard, Yale, Williams, Amherst, and Oberlin.

One figure strongly associated with the beginnings of the evangelical tradition, Charles G. Finney (1792–1875), served as president of Oberlin College. Finney was a convert to Congregationalism who began life in Puritan Connecticut in 1792. His parents moved to western New York when he was practically an infant, and Finney grew up close to the frontier. His parents managed to send him back to New England for schooling, and Finney learned Latin, Greek, and Hebrew and completed college. He turned to the study of law but increasingly became interested in preaching. While in Adams, New York, Finney also became interested in the study of scripture. For a period of two or three years, Finney was more and more attracted to the Christian religion but was still uncertain whether he truly believed. Neither of his parents had been practicing Christians, and he had few immediate role models or personal influences.

In the fall of 1821, Finney made up his mind that he must "make my peace with God." He spent several days in prayer but felt that his pride prevented him from making the type of commitment that real faith required. One evening, he found himself cast into a state of extreme agitation and anxiety, fearing he would soon die and be condemned to hell. The following morning, he had a profound vision of the atonement of Christ. The vision was so realistic that Finney came to a dead stop in the middle of a street while walking on earth.

He decided to forgo work and to walk to a deserted area outside of town to pray. In the midst of his prayer, he came to see that faith was not something that could be understood intellectually. Rather, it was an act of the will, an assent to the proposition God makes to each individual. He felt his "burden of sin" had been removed, and he had made the first, most critical step toward God. To his surprise, he found he had been praying for hours, and when he returned to town, it was almost noon.

That evening, he received a "baptism of the Holy Spirit." He had been to dinner with a friend and was helping to move books and furniture from one room to another. His friend departed, and when Finney turned to return to his rooms, his heart seemed to be "liquid." Finney felt that he had met Jesus Christ face to face, and breaking down in gratitude, wept at his feet. His "baptism of the Holy Spirit" came over him in waves, which he compared to the "breath of God," and Finney was a transformed man. Like most who have experienced profound conversion, he claimed his experience was ineffable, that he was not capable of describing it. Finney continued to experience wave after wave of the power of the Spirit, one minute feeling celebratory, the next, weeping.

In the aftermath of his baptism, Finney seemed to have a power to affect others in a profound spiritual fashion through his words. It was as if his words could cut through to other's souls. All of his companions, save one, followed in his wake and had conversions provoked by Finney. On a visit home to his parents, he converted them as well. Soon, he approached the minister of his church about entering the ministry. In 1824, Finney was formally licensed to preach.

Finney became an itinerant preacher of sorts. He traveled to the larger cities across America and in Great Britain, preaching from the heart. His sermons had powerful results, and entire congregations would fall on their knees or prostrate themselves on the ground. In one meeting in London, it is recorded that over fifteen hundred people were converted as a result of Finney's sermon. He had similar results in small communities in New York state, as well as in Boston, and Rochester. In one massive revival, held in 1858–1859, some estimate that as many as six hundred thousand people were "brought to Christ."

In 1833, Finney formally became a Congregationalist. Two years later, in 1835, he published his *Lectures on Revivals of Religion*. In that work, Finney compared the revival movement to farming and stressed that, with the right techniques, the harvest of souls could be as predictable as the harvest the farmer produces. But while Finney formally became Congregationalist, and Congregationalists are strongly associated with Calvinistic or Puritan thought, Finney disagreed with numerous theological elements of Puritanism. He rejected strict interpretations of limited atonement and bondage of the human will. Instead, he stressed the freedom of the will, the need to pursue personal holiness, and the possibility of perfection in society.

In 1845, Finney built the First Church in Oberlin, Ohio. At that time it was the largest church west of the Appalachians. Designed to house Finney's preaching, it could hold eighteen hundred people in the main sanctuary and another hundred and fifty in the choir loft. He remained as pastor of the church for thirty-seven years. The prominence of the church and his popularity as a preacher may have contributed to his being hired first as a professor in 1835 and then named president of Oberlin College in 1851. The school had been founded eighteen years earlier, in 1833, by a Presbyterian minister named John Shipherd.

As a community, Oberlin was strongly associated with the abolitionist movement. Several of the routes of the Underground Railroad met in Oberlin. Thousands of slaves were helped to freedom in Oberlin. The community overall was deeply opposed to slavery. Free African Americans in the town celebrated Independence Day on August 1, the day slavery ended in Jamaica. The progressive college admitted both women and African Americans and was an integrated and coeducational campus long before it was fashionable to be so. Many of Oberlin's students went South after graduation and participated directly in the Underground Railroad or served time in prison for helping escaped slaves. Charles G. Finney was the preacher's voice of Oberlin and remained in the position of president from 1851 to 1866.

The revivalism associated with Charles Finney, the dramatic itinerant preaching of George Whitefield, the emotional dimensions of John Wesley's Methodism, and the academic and theological credibility brought to religious affections by Jonathan Edwards all helped to shape the tradition we know as Evangelicalism. The term "evangelical" derives from the Greek word *evangelion*. It refers to "the good news" or the gospel. And at the foundation of the evangelical tradition is the need to spread the good news of the gospel through preaching and powerful religious services.

The steady growth of the Baptists and Methodists in America both reflected and contributed to the evangelical tradition. Protestantism had become the dominant religious perspective in the American religious landscape by the 1820s, and Finney and his fellow revivalists literally wanted to convert the entire country. Later decades in the nineteenth century would bring increasing numbers of Catholic immigrants and considerable hostility between Catholics and Protestants, as will be addressed in chapter 9. But in the early part of the nineteenth century, those streams that would later be identified as evangelical played dominant roles in shaping the American religious landscape.

These streams share certain religious similarities in terms of their priorities and their understanding. British historian David Bebbington describes four different characteristics of Evangelicalism.[1] The first, as noted above, is the emphasis on conversion, or "conversionism" as he terms it. The lives of believers need the power of God to transform them, and it is normative in most of these traditions for the believer to experience a profound encounter with God or with Christ in the form of a personal conversion. The second is a focus on activism. The gospel cannot simply be passively accepted or received but must be actively embraced and lived out in a purposeful way that involves personal effort. Under an Arminian interpretation of predestination, deep personal faith inspires devoted service. One could use free will for good purposes. The third, in Bebbington's view, is biblicism, a reliance on the Bible as a central source of insight and direction. The Bible holds an elevated and revered position in these denominational perspectives and is the foundation for preaching. Breaking open the Word is the central element of worship, and all other activities orbit around that process. The fourth and final characteristic is the tendency to emphasize the relationship between Christ's sacrifice and the sins of believers, which Bebbington terms "crucicentrism." The cross, as the sight of Christ's sacrifice, is central to one's understanding of and relationship to God.

The term "evangelical" is broadly applied today. If one groups together stylistically the numerous denominational groups associated with Evangelicalism one finds some pretty strange bedfellows. Of course, the denominations associated with the revivals come to mind, such as the Methodists and those also influenced by Arminianism, the Baptists, Moravians, and Mennonites, which are addressed in subsequent chapters. But one would also probably include the Dutch Reformed churches, and many would include the charismatic movement and Pentecostalism, which will be covered in greater detail in chapter 15. Groups that initially would seem to have little in common become grouped together under the broader category of Evangelicalism.

While Evangelicalism has also risen in other countries, such as Great Britain, as noted in Bebbington's studies, there is something characteristically American about the evangelical tradition. The greater emphasis on free will reflects the American belief in individualism and the ability of the individual to determine his or her own life story. Historically, the focus on activism reflected the energy of a young nation, busy carving out its place in the world and its conquest of the frontier. The idea that one could participate in one's own salvation sat more easily with American democratic institutions. The stern and arbitrary God of Augustine and Calvin may have been acceptable to people who lived their entire lives under the rule of a king or royal family. But democratic Americans wanted more freedom in their day-to-day lives and not to be beholden to aristocrats, whether human or divine.

It may be these factors that fueled the dramatic increases in Methodist and Baptist congregations, and their remarkable success in establishing themselves as significant religious traditions in certain parts of the country. These approaches may have been resisted in areas that had been settled for longer periods of time, where different denominations had already carved out a sense of belonging and achieved a certain level of public respect. But in the South and the Southwest, as one historian noted, evangelical Protestantism spread like wildfire. The Methodists and Moravians had long ago launched missionary efforts into Georgia. Baptists and others sent missionaries to the Southwest to Christianize the remaining Native American tribes. The work of Charles G. Finney brought evangelical Protestantism to a new prominence in the Midwest.

Staid Anglicans in the colonies were caught unprepared for the success and rapid increase of the evangelical tradition in the wake of the Great Awakening. Presbyterian Congregationalists were, perhaps, even more unprepared when streams of evangelical thought and practice began to transform their own tradition. The emphasis on the importance of religious experience, the spreading Arminian view of predestination that emphasized living a moral life, and the effectiveness of highly emotionalized forms of preaching in revivals had been duly observed by Congregationalist clergy. Some of them felt that their own strictly Calvinist position could use the infusion of new energy that seemed to come along with these perspectives. They founded what is termed "New Light" Calvinism.

The first division, called the New Light Schism, occurred among the Presbyterians in 1741. Scotch-Irish "Old Lights" maintained the importance of remaining theologically correct in terms of views on predestination and related matters. Calvinist doctrine, building on Augustine of Hippo (354–430 CE), maintained a dark view of human nature, that only God could determine who was one of the elect, those bound for salvation. The emphasis was on correct theological belief rather than on how one lived one's life or on visible signs of sanctity. The lack of emphasis on religious experience and living a religious life meant that some pastors had been found significantly lacking in those areas, indulging in drunkenness or in immoral behavior.

The New Lights wanted a looser interpretation of several doctrinal points, particularly predestination. Three men in particular helped to form the movement. The first was the president of Yale University, Timothy Dwight. The other two were Dwight's students, a theologian named Nathaniel Taylor and a Congregationalist minister named Lyman Beecher. They began to incorporate subtle elements of reform into their congregations and to move toward reform. They argued for modifications of theological thought in terms of the role of preaching. Taylor argued that preaching was the means by which one could spark and draw out the soul's own natural longing for a deepening relationship with God.

Two other New Lights, brothers William and Gilbert Tennent, argued from a slightly different angle. They emphasized the role of piety. Gilbert

Tennent drafted an argument entitled "The Danger of an Unconverted Ministry." Any genuine encounter with Christ, he argued, would result in a transformation, a conversion, which would play out in a life lived morally and that demonstrated personal holiness. They adopted the itinerant preaching style that had been so successfully utilized by Whitefield and others during the Great Awakening.

Old Light members considered such practices to be "enthusiasm." They adhered to more rationalistic perspectives on faith, emphasizing the correct intellectual understanding of theological doctrine. The church went into schism, and one group associated with the newer interpretations founded the College of New Jersey, which later came to be known as Princeton University. Its original mission was to educate ministers in the new perspective. The old guard held to their position but saw the attendance at their worship decline, while the congregations of the newer, younger pastors increased significantly.

The Congregationalists had a similar schism. George Whitefield's preaching left in its wake a new level of religious enthusiasm and fervor. Gilbert Tennent made an evangelical tour in 1740 and 1741. Other preachers took up similar practices, including James Davenport. It was all too much for the Old Light Charles Chauncey. He denounced the enthusiasts in no uncertain terms, defending the priority of adherence to logic over emotion, of reason over enthusiastic response, ideas that would ultimately lead to the development of Unitarianism. These divisions prompted Jonathan Edwards's articulate defense of revivalism.

Ultimately, the infusion of interpretive stances closer to evangelical positions seems to be what enabled the Presbyterians and Congregationalists to survive. In the wake of the condemnation of Edwards and others for "enthusiasm," Calvinism became more vibrant and, some would say, more balanced. It also caught some of the energy that surrounded the development of Evangelicalism and the fervor with which the newly converted pursued their spiritual lives.

Today, Evangelicalism is often associated with fundamentalism, although one isn't necessarily correct to conflate the two. What we know today as fundamentalism emerged out of a movement in the late nineteenth and early twentieth centuries. Fundamentalists take their name from a set of books called *The Fundamentals*, containing a series of essays written in opposition to liberal theological positions. American Protestants began to react negatively to numerous developments in theology and biblical studies as modernism began to be used in those areas in an effort to better understand the meaning of biblical texts. The movement started in 1878 at the Niagara Bible Conference. By 1910, with the publication of *The Fundamentals*, the General Assembly of the Presbyterian Church had determined five fundamental points that would characterize its perspective. These five points included belief in the inerrancy of scripture, the virgin birth and the divinity of Christ, the doctrine of substitutionary atonement, the bodily resurrection of Christ, and the bodily Second Coming of Christ.

From these "fundamentals," Christian fundamentalists adopted a literalistic approach to the interpretation of scripture. This often put them in direct opposition to widely spread scientific perspectives, such as Darwin's theory of evolution, and emphasized their separatist tendencies. One famous fundamentalist, William Jennings Bryan, is known for his role as prosecutor in the Scopes Monkey Trial, putting evolution on trial in the form of trying a teacher who had incorporated it into his curriculum.

Today, the term "fundamentalist" is used in a much less specific way. It is applied to every religion to describe people whose religious beliefs seem particularly traditional or tied to a literalist approach to reading scripture. There are fundamentalist Mormons and fundamentalist Muslims. There are fundamentalist Baptists and fundamentalist sects. But this is derivative from the earlier meaning, which referred specifically to a group of Christians who defined their faith in light of the five fundamentals.

Evangelicalism and fundamentalism have at times been fellow travelers in American religious history. But they have often been estranged, as well. One cannot assume that anyone who holds fundamentalist perspectives automatically believes in the evangelical aspects outlined by Bebbington— conversionism, activism, biblicism, and crucicentrism. Nor can one assume that a person who adopts an evangelical attitude necessarily adopts the five fundamentals that initially defined fundamentalism.

What one can be sure of is that the evangelical tradition that grew out of the Great Awakening, that was fueled by the work of Jonathan Edwards and the growth of the Methodist and Baptist religions in the nineteenth century, has left an indelible mark on the American religious landscape and will continue to exert its influence in the years ahead. The central elements in the Arminian view of predestination have become widely recognized and widely accepted. The stern God of strict Calvinism has been softened. The belief that human beings must cooperate with God by living their lives in a moral fashion is widely accepted, and the millions of dollars Americans spend on religiously based charities testify to their belief that free will can be put to good purpose. The evangelical tradition continues to be a major

voice in the development of American culture and a major factor in the beliefs that millions of Americans hold today.

NOTE

1. David Bebbington, *Evangelicalism in Modern Britain: A History from the 1730s to the 1980s* (Oxford: Routledge, 1989).

6

THE AMISH AND THE MENNONITES

No history of American religious experience would be complete without some attention to the Amish and the Mennonites. We first met the Mennonites in our chapter on German pietism, but now we will turn to a more detailed examination of their thought and practice and of their relationship to their religious relatives, the Amish.

In order to understand the core beliefs of the Mennonites, we must begin, once again, in Europe, long before Mennonite or Amish believers came to the shores of America. Both Mennonite and Amish belief systems emerged out of the Reformation and the volatile religious landscape that existed during the strident reforms of the period.

After the writings of Martin Luther ignited the great splintering of the Catholic Church known as the Reformation, the movement for reform divided into multiple streams. Some of those streams became mainstream Protestant denominations—John Calvin's reforms emerged in Presbyterianism and Congregationalism, Martin Luther's in Lutheranism, Henry VIII's in the Church of England and Anglicanism. But many smaller streams are less recognized. Among them is the stream formed by the Anabaptists.

The Anabaptists were a group of radical reformers who remained peripheral to the central current of the Reformation. The word literally means "rebaptizer," and many of the Anabaptists rebaptized Christians who converted to their belief systems. The Anabaptists found nothing in the gospel that mandated infant baptism. In fact, arguments for infant baptism did not emerge until the time of Augustine of Hippo. Controversy over the practice was widespread in the third and fourth centuries. The Anabaptists emphasized instead what they called a "believer's baptism." Baptism marked the beginning of one's adult acceptance of religious belief and should, therefore, be postponed until one came of an age that permitted such identification and commitment.

Like most of the other reformers, the Anabaptists emphasized the role of scripture over tradition. The Roman Catholic Church continued to dictate that revelation came from both scripture and tradition, but the reform movements gave primacy to scripture. One turned to biblical authority to settle questions of worship or polity. Knowledge of scripture and the ability to apply scriptural insights to everyday life were highly valued.

If the Anabaptists could agree with other reformers on the primacy of scripture, in other areas their beliefs stood in high contrast. Contrary to the Church of England, Anabaptists argued passionately for a strict division between church and state. The role of the church was to counter the world, and the church was to be a source of correction and a model for those outside of it. Thus, the church and the state should remain distinctly separate in the eyes of the Anabaptists.

This belief bled over into the idea of shunning as the preferred form of excommunication in Anabaptist groups. Since the secular world was innately corrupt and filled with sin, it was appropriate to relegate one whose sin could not be redeemed or transformed to that outside world. Heretics belonged outside the church, among the sinners, rather than in the pristine mold of the church itself. But while Anabaptists relegated heretics to the outside world and shunned them, they did not believe that treatment of the sinner should adopt the punitive stances common in their day. They opposed religious persecution, in part because they believed the state should play no part in regulating the life of faith. They opposed execution or imprisonment solely on the basis of religious belief and supported the freedom of conscience of the individual.

Finally, the Anabaptists collectively put great emphasis on how one lived one's life. A life of holiness should be demonstrated by a life of obedience, hard work, and appropriate charity. They strove for a kind of Christian perfection on earth, and their lives were carefully regulated by the religious community, with behaviors carefully enforced and high standards of asceticism and propriety.

In the Reformation, elements that would come to be identified with the Anabaptists emerged as early as the 1520s. A weaver and a Lutheran pastor led the organization of the Prophets of Zwickau, who challenged infant baptism. Their conflicts with civil authorities soon drove them from the town. The weaver, Nicholas Storch (d. 1525), subsequently traveled across Germany championing his cause. Eventually, he helped to lead the Peasant's War. The Lutheran pastor, Thomas Munzer, after leaving Zwickau, first went to Bohemia and later to Saxony. There, in Alstedt, he built up a body of believers and launched attacks on both Lutheran and Roman Catholic positions.

Munzer later traveled to the southern German city of Mulhausen and achieved dramatic success. He attracted an apostate monk, Henry Pfeifer (d. 1525), who became his partner in transforming the city. The angry and unsettled country people who had lost so much in the Peasant's War were quickly attracted to Munzer's beliefs, and the religious movement took on the air of a revolutionary group. A group of nobles recognized the threat, quickly launched an expeditionary force, and attacked the peasants at Frankenhausen in 1525. Munzer reconciled with the Catholic Church before being executed, while Pfeifer stalwartly refused the sacraments and was executed apostate.

In Switzerland, the Anabaptist movement developed in the city of one of the best-known reformers, Ulrich Zwingli (1484–1531). Anabaptists in Zurich defied the regulations Zwingli set forth for the city and, in doing so, breached both civil and religious law. As a result, many were martyred—beheaded, burned at the stake, or drowned. The defeat of the peasant forces in the Peasant's War, noted above, led to the dispersal of the remaining Anabaptists.

Ten years later, Munster, Germany, emerged as the new center of Anabaptist belief. In 1534, the city came to be run entirely by Anabaptists. They deemed it the "New Jerusalem" and instigated what can easily be called a reign of terror. Polygamy was legalized, and, soon, many of the leaders had multiple wives. John van Leyden pronounced himself the king of "New Sion" and promptly took twelve or sixteen wives, depending on whose account you read. He also eliminated private property, forced those who did not believe in Anabaptism to be baptized against their wills, and encouraged his citizenry of peasants, artisans, and shopkeepers to prepare for glorious victory on the battlefield. Francis of Waldeck, the bishop of the city, launched a military siege against the town to reestablish his authority. A year later, New Jerusalem fell, and the streets ran with blood. In the summer of 1535, the leaders of the Anabaptist movement in Munster were captured, imprisoned, and tortured. Their bodies were displayed in iron cages in front of St. Lambert's church.

Not all the Anabaptists met such a gruesome end, and not all espoused violence as a means to gain their ends. The capture of Munster seems to have resulted in another dispersal of the Anabaptists, some appearing shortly thereafter in England. A number of believers could also be found in the Netherlands, and it was from these areas that the Mennonites emerged. The Mennonites take their name from Menno Simons (c. 1496–1564).

Menno was born in Witmarsum, Friesland, the Netherlands, and trained for the priesthood. He was ordained a Roman Catholic priest at age twenty-eight and served for seven years in a parish in Pingjum. He was then transferred, and served from 1531 to 1536 in his native town of Witmarsum. As the events of the Reformation unfolded around him, Menno became slowly transformed. He was introduced to the writings of Martin Luther and slowly came to believe that Luther was right in placing the primary emphasis for the Christian believer on scripture.

When he began his service at Witmarsum, he heard of the execution of a man in Friesland for being rebaptized and was shocked by the violent act. It led him to deep reflection on baptism and when it should occur, whether at birth or only after a profound conversion and acceptance of God in one's life. He came to the conviction that it should occur after conversion.

These views brought Menno to leave the Roman Catholic Church in 1536, but he never adopted the extreme views associated with the Anabaptists at Munster. Instead, he took a more moderate course. Menno joined the Anabaptist movement by allying himself with peaceful group of Dutch Anabaptists. This was the Obbenite faction, so named for their founder, Obbe Philips, and shortly thereafter they convinced Menno to serve as their pastor.

Menno believed that Christians were called to a life of peace and service and not to military overthrow of existing structures. He did, however, sympathize somewhat with the Anabaptists in Munster and made some effort to help them. As a result, he was stigmatized, his life was imperiled, and he was forced to go into hiding. A year later, in 1537, he married and formally became an Anabaptist preacher. As a preacher, he undertook missionary activity in other parts of Holland and Germany. He served in the Netherlands from 1536 until 1543, then spent three years in the Rhineland, and fifteen years in the area of Denmark known as Holstein. Perhaps Menno's consistent traveling spared him a martyr's death, or perhaps it was the relative moderation of his views. He consistently supported peace and nonresistance, as well as continued to believe in the believer's baptism and separation of church and state. He died in Holstein in 1559.

Menno's congregations in Holland ultimately split into smaller groups, and their numbers slowly fell. Some of the Swiss Anabaptists had founded Mennonite communities in southern Germany, though, and several thousand had emigrated to Russia in search of religious freedom.

The Mennonites came to America in 1683, when a congregation was founded in Germantown, Pennsylvania. Once a beachhead had been established, word quickly spread to Mennonite communities in the Old Country of the promise of peace and prosperity in Pennsylvania. Soon, Mennonites from Germany, Holland, Switzerland, and Russia were crossing the Atlantic to join their brethren in America.

Today, twelve different branches of Mennonites are recognized in the United States, and believers are estimated at somewhere between fifty and sixty thousand in the United States and twenty thousand in Canada. Mennonite communities also remain in Holland, Germany, Russia, and Switzerland.

Many Americans today are more familiar with the Amish than with the Mennonites. The Amish have their origins in the Mennonites; they were also part of the Anabaptist movement in Europe, also emigrated to the United States, and also settled in Pennsylvania. In fact, the Amish are more correctly known as the Amish Mennonite, but most drop the Mennonite and refer to them simply as the Amish. The Amish emerged as a distinct stream in 1693 under the leadership of a man named Jakob Ammann (c. 1644–1708). The name Amish is based on Ammann's name, just as the name Mennonite reflects Menno Simon's name.

The organization of the Mennonites was congregational, and the church was governed by bishops, elders, and deacons. Ammann was an elder in the Mennonite church in Erlenbach, Switzerland. The split appears to have developed after some members of Ammann's church became lax in terms of enforcing the shunning of excommunicated members. Ammann became angry with certain elders over the disposition of a certain case. When they refused to accept his interpretation, he excommunicated two preachers and some of their associates.

Ammann was very strict about enforcing uniformity of dress among believers, about appearance in general, and about not participating in services held by the state church. He had excommunicated several members who failed to understand his strong opposition to attending state services; he had also had disputes regarding the use of tobacco.

Against this troubled background, the division took place in the summer of 1693. Recognizing that not all the ministers in his area shared his interpretations on issues related to shunning and the practice of biannual communion services, he set out on a tour of churches and held several meetings. Ammann decided that resistance against his teachings was primarily the work of a particular elder, Hans Reist, and decided to excommunicate him. He then continued to excommunicate five more men. Shortly thereafter, a group of Ammann's followers, the "Amish," held a meeting, which was considered the first Amish meeting.

Following Ammann's excommunications, division between the groups snowballed. Soon, Ammann had issued an ultimatum to all his congregants, demanding they support him in his views, or they would be excommunicated. Several attempts were made to reconcile Ammann to the larger Mennonite body, but neither side could overcome these differences in interpretation. On March 13, 1694, a group of Swiss ministers drafted a statement outlining their differences with Amman. Churches in the Palatinate fell in behind Swiss opposition. Although numerous attempts to reconcile continued over the next few years, positions became entrenched, and by 1698, the separation was irreconcilable.

In the eighteenth and early nineteenth centuries, Amish communities spread to other areas of Europe. Two groups developed in Switzerland, and several congregations in the Alsace region of France decided to follow Ammann's teachings. Some of their members immigrated into Bavaria and other parts of Germany. Two Amish congregations developed in Holland. But the establishment of these communities was accompanied by emigration to America, and some of the smaller Amish communities, such as one founded in Volhynia, Russia, disappeared when the majority of its members moved to American soil.

The first Amish arrived in America in the early eighteenth century. Like so many before them, they came to Pennsylvania in search of religious tolerance and rich farmland. Many of them settled in Lancaster County, as well as Berks and Chester counties. Settlements in these areas, in a sense, became springboards for further developments on American soil. In the nineteenth century, a settlement in Somerset County increased in size, mostly from immigration from abroad. The Somerset settlement soon had daughter colonies in Ohio and Indiana. Over time, between the establishment of new settlements by immigrants from Europe and of daughter colonies of existing settlements, the Amish came to be found in Pennsylvania, Ohio, New York, Indiana, Illinois, Iowa, Nebraska, Kansas, South Dakota, and Ontario, Canada.

Few religious groups have captured the American imagination as much as the Amish, and articles, movies, and books with Amish characters continue to crop up generation after generation. In part, this is because the Amish lifestyle is so visibly distinct from the lifestyles of most Americans. When they hear the term "Amish," most Americans think of what is actually called Old Order Amish, a term that only came into usage in America to distinguish groups of Amish Mennonites who resisted technological development and newer forms of social interaction. Their resistance to commonly accepted social changes has set them apart from the larger American population, who often see their lifestyle as quaint or antiquated.

Resistance to technology and disdain for the values of the secular world have allowed Old Order Amish to continue lifestyles long since left behind by the larger population. They have resisted complete assimilation into English-language culture. Instead, they often speak Pennsylvania Dutch, a form of low German also known as *Plautdietsch*, in their home environments. Church services are held in high German. Most learn English in school, even if it never becomes their primary language. Old Order Amish resist the use of the automobile, except in certain emergencies. They choose, instead, to travel by horse and buggy and to pursue a simple, rural life that allows this to suffice as their primary means of transportation.

Another concession to the Old Order is their manner of dressing. Their dress is simple. Men wear dark-colored suits, solid-colored shirts, and black suspenders, shoes, and socks. They wear black hats or straw hats with black hatbands. Once they marry, they stop trimming their beards, which grow distinctively long. Like Islamic woman who wear the veil, the Amish feel this way of dress demonstrates humility and the purity of their faith. Conformity in dress is a statement of religious orthodoxy and belief.

Women are similarly simple in their attire. They wear dresses made from solid-colored fabrics in subtle shades. The long sleeves and long skirts are broken only by white aprons and capes. Like the married men, they do not cut their hair and usually wear it in a bun. Married women wear a white prayer cap, and single women wear a black one. Neither women nor men adorn themselves with jewelry; nor do they use fancy buttons or attachments on their clothing. Simplicity and humility before God are the driving themes.

Other differences in the Old Order Amish center on their ways of worship and their ideas about education. Each settlement has "church districts," or congregations. Usually, these have around seventy-five members and may contain anywhere from fifteen to thirty families. Worship services are conducted in family homes for the most part, and no meetinghouses are constructed for that purpose. Services are scheduled on the fortnight, beginning in the early morning and finishing in the early afternoon, after which all present share the noon meal. When a group gets too large to meet comfortably in a private home, it is divided. The new district appoints its own bishop and a deacon. Lots are drawn to determine who will serve as preachers, and usually two to four serve each church district.

They retain a number of older forms of worship, including silent prayer before and after meals in their homes. They use a specific order of worship in the home churches, retain silent prayer and certain prayer books in public worship, and genuflect at the end of the benediction. They have also retained certain older burial practices, such as prompt burial without embalming, and certain courtship rituals, such as bundling, a practice where couples stay together prior to the marriage under controlled circumstances.

Given the Anabaptist emphasis on the separation of church and state, public school systems and regulations have long been problematic for the Amish. If Amish youth were required to attend public schools, as many states and school districts mandate, there is a stronger probability that they would come into greater contact with secular culture, be more influenced by secular values, and perhaps even elect to leave the Amish settlement. Therefore, the Amish have traditionally opposed higher education and chosen to educate their children only up to the eighth-grade level. After completing the eighth grade, children are expected to focus their energies on work in the home or on the farm until such time as they marry.

Several school districts found the consistent removal of Amish children from the schools after eighth grade to be contrary to local regulations. One case filed against the Amish went all the way to the Supreme Court. Since the Amish would not undertake their own defense because of their religious beliefs, they were represented by the National Committee for Amish Religious Freedom and an attorney named William B. Hall. In a landmark decision, *Wisconsin v. Yoder*, the Court ruled it unconstitutional to require the Amish to keep their children in school past eighth grade. The Court included protections under both religious freedom and parental rights in determining the case's constitutional legal dimensions before making the ruling.

Rather than seeking higher education, Amish adolescents learn practical skills that will be useful in their later life in the settlement. Young men learn animal husbandry, carpentry skills, farming techniques, and about the mechanical aspects of the simple tools employed. Young women learn household skills, cooking, and maintenance, as well as sewing and related skills.

Most Amish marry some time between the ages of sixteen and their early twenties. From age sixteen on, they are encouraged to be open to the possibility of marriage. Weddings generally take place in the late fall. An autumn communion service is held, and after that service, young couples apply for certification for membership in the community. Only registered members can be permitted to marry. The following week, the names of couples are announced to the community, and the fathers of the brides announce when and where the wedding will take place.

Remember, since the Amish do not practice infant baptism, young adults must be baptized before they can be considered for full membership in the congregation. They are usually admitted to the church between the ages of seventeen and twenty. Ministers give formal instruction to the youths, and baptism is usually held in the spring.

A few days after the names are "published," the couple is free to marry. Brides usually wear blue or purple dresses, and grooms wear black suits. Wedding dates are only set in November and early December. On reflection, the timing makes sense in a farming community where the first consideration must be given to gathering a successful harvest. Once the harvest is safely gathered, all community members can gather to celebrate the new alliance, to worship and feast together in honor of the couple. The couple will stay with the bride's family after the wedding, collecting the items needed to set up a household for themselves. Although individual practice may differ, they often build their own homes the following spring with the help of the community that welcomed them and helped them provision the home.

The Old Order Amish are more likely to have a strict interpretation of the practice of shunning, in keeping with Jakob Ammann's original scrupulosity over its practice, and to retain practices that are stricter and more formal. But not all Amish are Old Order. Some groups are more progressive, and some Mennonite groups practice few of the older customs and are well integrated into modern American life.

One contemporary believer, an Old Order Amish minister named Eli E. Gingerich, has summarized what he believes are the central components, the "essence" so to speak, of what it means to be Amish.[1]

First, Gingerich emphasizes that the Amish seek peace with God and accept the atonement of Christ's death on the cross for human sin. A renewal of heart and spirit means coming into compliance with the will of God and finding an adequate form of inner renewal. Second, the Amish believe that this peace with God should lead the believer to peace with every other living thing. That means not only with one's family members but with fellow believers. Behind this belief lies the Amish commitment to pacifism, which has been consistent throughout the centuries. Third, the Amish believe in a life of simplicity and mutual service. Many of what outsiders see as labor-saving conveniences the Amish see as a means of avoiding direct relationships to others in mutual service and interdependency. They seek to retain a tightly knit community and a life rich in human interaction, in part, by avoiding the use of such devices. Simplicity should guide the approach to mutual service and loving relationship. Finally, Gingerich reminds us that the Amish believe in separation from the world. The physical separation from the secular world, however, is simply the manifestation of the first of these components, the inner renewal that drives the relationship with God and with neighbor.

Gingerich supplements his four basic beliefs with three more, to give a fuller view of Amish belief and culture. Of these "supplemental" aspects, he reminds us that the primary Amish goal in training children is the inculcation of humility and cooperation, traits that will be invaluable in the closely knit communities in which most Amish spend their lives. These are closely tied to a sense of obedience and respect for authority, and children should be encouraged in these attitudes consistently, from a young age, in the different settings of home, church, and school. A second supplemental aspect is the relationship of the Amish as Christian to the Amish as representative of the Amish culture. The Amish culture should never take the believer too far from the Word as found in the Bible and the larger life of faith itself. It should not become an end in itself. Finally, the third supplemental aspect that Gingerich emphasizes is the role of fellowship in worship. As noted above, after worship services, the Amish gather for a shared lunchtime meal. At weddings, a celebratory feast is held for the congregation. These are not incidental but deliberate attempts to maintain a consistent feeling of mutuality and commonality in the Amish community and in the congregation. Fellowship is a celebration of the larger goals for the believing community. Additionally, since authority in the Amish tradition lies not only in church leadership but also within the believing community, fellowship is a time when that wisdom and authority can manifest its presence and help direct the community in larger issues.

This emphasis on fellowship and communal values may help to explain why Amish communities have been so relatively successful in terms of continuity, while many religious communities, such as the Shakers, have dwindled away. They also find expression outside of the Old Order, but different forms of expression. These beliefs among the Mennonites, for example, have traditionally played a large role in the development of mission work or volunteer service.

Today, the Mennonite Mission Network has ministries in more than fifty-five countries. The same network has also placed more than 170 mission workers in forty-six countries.

Mennonite missionaries have had a big influence on the African continent. The Africa Inter-Mennonite Mission was formed in 1912 by two small Mennonite groups. The leaders of the groups, Henry Egly and Joseph Stucky, had left the Old Order Amish to pursue a life that was more progressive and more oriented toward evangelism. With only thirty-five hundred people between the two groups, they seemed ill equipped to undertake a mission to a continent as vast as Africa. They determined that they would focus their work on the Congo, and on January 23, they formed the Congo Inland Mission for that purpose. Today, Mennonites in the Congo number almost two hundred thousand.

Mennonite mission work in Canada yielded similar results. Over 125,000 Canadians consider themselves Mennonite. But they did not limit their missionary efforts to these locales. The Mennonites have maintained missions and made converts in India, Indonesia, Ethiopia, and Brazil, as well as throughout Europe and North America.

Perhaps this missionary success is linked to the early wandering that the Anabaptists had to undertake to survive in the wake of the extreme forms of persecution they faced in the earliest days of their tradition. The scattering of believers that followed their expulsion from Zurich and the siege of Munster equipped them well for adjusting to life in new environments and among nonbelievers. As Anabaptists settled in Germany, Bavaria, Holland, and Russia, they developed precisely the skills that would help them to survive and prosper in missionary work. Their strong sense of identity, strong communal values, deep conviction in their faith, and early training in humility and obedience made for a strong missionary presence.

Today, there is greater diversity among those who belong to the Mennonite tradition. Among them, we count the Amish Mennonites, discussed at length above. But we also include the Mennonite Church, which is one of nearly twenty formally organized groups of Mennonites in North America. These groups have differences in terms of the lifestyles they choose to adapt and their precise religious practices, but all of them have roots in the Anabaptist movement. Another group is the Mennonite Brethren, whose congregations are now found in twenty nations throughout the world. Deeply involved in missionary work, they have large numbers of followers in India and the Congo. Another Mennonite group is the Brethren in Christ, which has 270 churches in the United States and Canada, and 1,100 churches in twenty-three nations worldwide. A final group associated with the Mennonite tradition is the Hutterites. Founders of the Hutterite Brethren originated out of the early Anabaptist congregations in Switzerland, Germany, and the area known as the Tyrol, which sits between southern Austria and northern Italy. Jacob Hutter became their leader in 1529 and developed the foundations of the Hutterian church. Hutter was later burned at the stake in Austria after refusing to recant his Hutterite beliefs. Many of the Hutterites emigrated to Russia after being given a promise of independent schools and exemption from the draft. But when the Russian government reneged on those promises, all of the Hutterites migrated to the United States. Many of the settled in South Dakota; some later migrated to Canada. Today, approximately one-quarter of all Hutterites worldwide live in the United States.

Diverse in the expression of their faith, fascinating in the lifestyles they have chosen to sustain, and devout in their belief systems, the Mennonites have left an indelible mark on the American religious landscape. Increasingly sophisticated in their interaction with the secular world, they have created cooperative ministries and aid organizations. They have also founded several colleges and seminaries, including Eastern Mennonite University, Goshen College, Hesston College, and Bluffton University. The American descendents of Menno Simon have thrived and prospered indeed.

NOTE

1. Gingerich as reported to Leonard Gross, "Background Dynamics of the Amish Movement," available at www.goshen.edu/facultypubs/GROSS.html (accessed February 19, 2005).

7

THE QUAKERS AND THE SHAKERS

The Quakers and the Shakers are two of the most distinct groups found in the American religious landscape. The Quakers originated in the seventeenth century, after founder George Fox (1624–1691) tried to lead Christians to a pure form of Christian practice and belief in keeping with the earliest days of the church. The Shakers, originally known as the Shaking Quakers, are a splinter group of the Quakers, founded by Mother Ann Lee (1736–1784) in 1772 after she received a vision telling her that the Christ Spirit was among us, the embodiment of the Second Coming of Christ. But fascinating as the story of Mother Ann Lee is, the story of the two groups must begin much earlier, with the early life of George Fox, whose spiritual style and beliefs have left such a lasting impression on the group he inadvertently founded, the Society of Friends, or Quakers.

Fox grew up in comfortable circumstances in Fenny Drayton in Leicestershire, England. His father was a weaver whose work was valued and well compensated. His parents were devout and followed the teachings of the Church of England, as did most of their friends and neighbors. As an adolescent, Fox was apprenticed to a shoemaker but showed little interest in learning a trade. He did demonstrate a certain seriousness in his nature and an interest in religion, which he pursued in an uncompromising fashion, doubtless reflecting his parents strict adherence to their faith.

At nineteen, Fox made friends with two men who were "professors" of religion. Traveling with them to a nearby fair, he was shocked when they proposed to drink toasts to one another's health. He returned home disillusioned, unhappy, and unable to sleep. In the course of the night, he heard a voice telling him to "be a stranger to all."

Fox's interpreted this in his characteristically uncompromising fashion. He picked up his Bible and walked out of his father's house without a penny, wandering the countryside in search of religious truth. The Church of England had little in its traditional practice to offer the budding prophet, so Fox was left alone to wander and reflect on the contents of the Bible and his own inner experience.

Left to his own devices, Fox developed a unique perspective on the spiritual life that became the foundation of Quaker belief. At the core of Fox's theology was the idea of the "inner light," a means by which the individual could communicate directly with God. Awareness of and obedience to the inner light meant one could listen directly to Christ's directives in one's life, receiving personal guidance and support. The most important thing a person could do, in the schema of George Fox, was to obey that voice and follow that light in every action of one's life.

From Fox's perspective, what most people associated with religion was only so many external trappings. The need to build churches, to train clergy, to dress in robes for ritual and sacrament fell away as unnecessary when one followed the directives of the inner light. There was no need to ordain clergy because every human being—man, woman, and child—had direct access to Christ through the inner light, or through being moved by the Spirit. In Fox's view, sacramental practices such as baptism and the Eucharist were largely allegorical and did not require any seal of ecclesiastical authority. This freewheeling view of sacramental life did become problematic in terms of securing the legality of marriages among the early Quakers.

Even if Fox's views were unorthodox compared to the dominant religions of the day, Fox himself must have been a man of considerable charisma, for he quickly gained an ever-increasing number of converts all over Britain. But his charisma did little to keep him out of prison. Fox was imprisoned on numerous occasions. On one occasion, with his usual disdain for the external structures of morality or justice, Fox suggested to a judge that he best "tremble at the word of the Lord." The judge responded by dubbing Fox a "quaker." The name stuck. From that time on, members of the Religious Society of Friends were known as Quakers.

When Fox was not in prison, he began to organize and structure his followers somewhat. Some of his believers did not fare well with only the inner light to guide them, and there were some incidents of libertine behavior or excess. Fox sought to correct this by developing an official discipline for the group. Others resisted any structuring of the society at all as contrary to complete reliance on the inner light. Some time around 1660, classifications of meetings emerged.

Meetings might be monthly, quarterly, or yearly. Smaller groups meeting monthly combined for larger quarterly meetings. Those groups meeting seperately on a quarterly basis joined one another for yearly meetings, again generating collective reports, in a system somewhat like that of Presbyterian synods. Distinct classifications of preparative, recognized, and notified meetings later appeared. Prior to Fox's death, basic guidelines had been established, which have been honored ever since by Quaker congregations.

Two established religious groups, the Calvinists of Presbyterianism and the clergy of the Church of England in particular, tried to dismantle the Society of Friends. Several of the Quaker's beliefs put them in opposition with dominant religions and ruling political powers. First, since they saw all external trappings of religion as empty forms, they refused to contribute financially to churches. That meant they refused to tithe or guarantee part of their income would be put at the disposal of the Church of England. The marriage of church and state in England meant this violated civil, as well as ecclesial, norms. Similarly, since the only true source of wisdom and justice was the inner light, Quakers often refused to takes oaths in court. Nor would they honor the presiding magistrate by removing their hats, as was the custom in recognizing those in positions of power.

Since Fox preached that all people—male, female, slave, or free—were of equal standing and value before God, the Quakers took a significant interest in the most vulnerable in society. They investigated the conditions in which prisoners were held and demanded better living conditions for those imprisoned. They did the same with those committed to mental asylums, investigating conditions, writing of those conditions, and lobbying for improvement in the care of the mentally ill. Perhaps best known is their opposition to slavery. At a time when slavery was almost universally accepted, the Quakers fought for its abolition. Finally, and least endearing in terms of their relationships to crown and legal authorities, Quakers were pacifists. This meant they refused to participate in combat, even during a time of war. At a time when military service was mandated, many Quakers ended up in prison for their noncompliance with military recruitment or participation.

Understandably, the Quakers were not welcome under the strict Puritan government of Oliver Cromwell. The Quakers began to experience considerable persecution on their native soil. Under the reign of Charles II, from 1660 to 1685, the numbers are startling, considering the relative size of the Quaker community. Records indicate that 198 Quakers were sent abroad as slaves, 338 died in prison, and 13,562 languished in jails.

Nor did the Quakers receive the warmest of welcomes in the United States. The Puritans of Massachusetts viewed them simply as a "cursed sect of heretics." Four Quakers, three men and a woman, where hanged on Boston Common. Others were deported or imprisoned. Some were identified as witches. For a time, the Quakers found freedom from persecution in the colony of Rhode Island, which mandated religious tolerance. But it was William Penn (1644–1718) who truly came to their aid.

As previously noted, Penn was the son of a military man, Adm. William Penn, who had provided valuable service to the British Crown. Brought up in the Church of England, the younger Penn was dissatisfied with the religious formation he received and was dismissed from Oxford for attending unauthorized prayer gatherings. He completed his education in France and, in his early twenties, encountered a Quaker named Thomas Loe, with whom he became friends. His friendship with Loe led him to become a Quaker. After writing some strident religious treatises, Penn was imprisoned in the Tower of London, but family connections secured his release.

In 1681, Penn convinced King Charles II to give him dominion over substantial lands in the English colonies west of the Delaware River. Penn, along with eleven other Quakers, bought proprietary rights to what is now eastern New Jersey. On that land, Penn launched his "Holy Experiment," creating a colony that practiced religious tolerance and putting into practice many of the central tenets of Quaker belief. The colony of Pennsylvania was created in 1682.

Back in England, the passage of the Act of Toleration in 1689 meant that Protestant dissenters could worship in public. It marked a transition toward greater tolerance for believers in religions outside of the mainstream. It helped the Quakers on some levels, but full tolerance was still a long time coming. The tenacity of the Quakers in holding onto their basic beliefs antagonized many political and religious leaders.

Over time, the Quakers in the United States came to be recognized as a group who valued and cultivated high moral standards and held clear and consistent beliefs, and they were increasingly well respected. In war times, they tended to provoke friction because of their refusal to serve in combat, but increasingly, on American soil, they were seen as just another denominational affiliation in an increasingly diverse religious landscape.

The Quakers continued their opposition to slavery on American soil and, so, became some of the earliest leaders of the abolitionist movement in America. One group of Friends in Germantown, Pennsylvania, publicly denounced slavery in what some consider the first religious support for abolitionism in American history.

Some of the most ardent supporters of abolition were a group of Quakers known as the Hicksite Quakers. The Hicksites were named for their founder, Elias Hicks (1748–1830), whose leadership resulted in a schism among the Quakers in 1827 and 1828. Hicks was a liberal Quaker preacher from Long Island who solidly supported the idea of the "Christ within" and began to diminish the importance of the virgin birth, the crucifixion, and the resurrection. Followers of Hicks challenged the necessity of having ministers or elders to lead them in religious practice, feeling that they could rely completely on the Christ within for guidance. More conservative, or orthodox, Quakers wanted to retain ministers and elders. After an encounter between representatives of the two groups outside of Mt. Pleasant, Ohio, the Quakers split into two groups, the Hicksites and the Orthodox.

The Hicksites are strongly associated with two progressive movements in the nineteenth century, abolitionism and the suffragette movement. In fact, suffragette leader Susan B. Anthony's family were Hicksite Quakers. Susan B. Anthony (1820–1906) came from a family with a long tradition of activism, so taking up an activist stance toward women's rights came naturally to her. She first became active in the temperance movement but was not allowed to speak because she was female. This, together with her friendship with Elizabeth Cady Stanton (1805–1902), moved her to join the women's rights movement. She became one of the most consistent voices in that movement, campaigning, lecturing, and traveling across the country. Later in her life, she also lent her support to the abolition of slavery.

Another Quaker who rose to leadership in the realms of both abolition and women's rights was Lucretia Mott (1793–1880). As early as 1818, Mott was serving as a Quaker minister. She and her husband became Hicksites after the schism in 1827. Mott and other Hicksites boycotted products that were produced by slave labor, including cotton and cane sugar. She also brought runaway slaves into her home. Some of the early women's rights societies first came together because antislavery groups would not allow women as members. When she attended the World's Anti-Slavery Convention in London in 1840, Mott found that groups there opposed women speaking in public. Stanton credits Mott with the idea of forming a women's rights convention, and Mott was one of the organizers of a convention later held in Rochester, New York.

Elias Hicks had taught his followers that no one needed to return a runaway slave to his or her owner as that would sanction the practice of slavery. In the eighteenth century, many progressive Quakers educated and freed slaves. Given that background, it is unsurprising that many of the Quakers played a part in the Underground Railroad, a loosely organized network of individuals and groups committed to aiding fugitive slaves as they fled to the North, to free states across the Ohio River or to Canada. Members would assist slaves by hiding them from bounty hunters or slave owners who tracked them following their escape. They also offered food and clothing, transportation, and other forms of assistance to slaves in flight. This was inherently dangerous work because legislation at the time considered slaves to be property and required individuals to assist in the return of property or face criminal prosecution. Participants in the Underground Railroad risked prison terms or worse.

Many Quakers were active in the railroad. One such couple was Levi and Catherine Coffin. A Quaker couple originally from North Carolina, the Coffins helped thousands of slaves to make their way to freedom. In fact, the Coffin house in Newport, Indiana, has been referred to as the Grand Central Station of the Underground Railroad, and slave owners, well aware of Coffin's success, referred to Levi Coffin as the president of the Underground Railroad. It is estimated that the Coffins assisted two thousand slaves in getting to freedom during the years they lived in Newport, and that not one of their charges failed to get to freedom. Eliza, one of the main characters in *Uncle Tom's Cabin*, was based on one of the slaves that the Coffins assisted. After leaving Newport, the Coffins relocated to Cincinnati, Ohio, one of the three main routes that slaves used to reach the North. In Cincinnati, the Coffins built a warehouse to supply free-labor stores and assisted another thirteen hundred slaves in the passage to freedom. In a literal biblical interpretation that would make George Fox proud, Levi Coffin said that he based his actions on Deuteronomy 23:15: "thou shalt not deliver unto his master the slave which is escaped from his master unto thee."

The liberal attitudes the Quakers espoused—women's rights, opposition to slavery, and pacifism—earned them considerable political and religious opposition in the nineteenth century. They passed through particularly difficult periods when the country was at war, in World War I and World War II. Some Quakers volunteered for medical and ambulance duty as a way of expressing their patriotism while honoring their pacifist beliefs. In World War I, the Quakers formed an organization, the American Friends Service Committee, to help believers who were conscientious objectors find ways to contribute to the war effort without violating their beliefs. The Quakers continue to find ways to practice these principals and to be a vibrant religious perspective today in the twenty-first century. They currently number around 300,000 worldwide, with 125,000 living in the United States, mostly in the Northeast and Midwest.

The Quaker belief also gave rise to one of the most unique religious traditions to ever grace the American heartland, the Shakers. The Shakers began as Quakers in Manchester, England. One Quaker preacher, James Wardley, had been impressed by the teachings of the millennial French prophets and began to incorporate similar perspectives into the Shakers' religious practice and belief. In the 1740s, they began to commune with the spirits of the dead and sometimes demonstrated passionate shaking in their services. They soon began to be called the Shaking Quakers.

Ann Lee (1736–1784), who is generally recognized as the foundress of the Shakers, joined the Shaking Quakers in 1758. Lee was the illiterate daughter of a blacksmith and had been sent to work in a textile mill as a young woman. She married, in 1762, a blacksmith named Abraham Stanley, but the marriage was not a happy one. Lee lost four children in a row, all of whom died as infants. Small wonder that she later became convinced that celibacy was essential for progress in the spiritual life.

In the 1770s, a wave of persecution hit the Shaking Quakers, and Lee was imprisoned. During her time in prison, she had a vision. She became convinced that sexual activity prevented the furtherance of Christ's work here on earth and that celibacy was the best way to help manifest the kingdom of God on earth. A few years later, Lee had another vision and convinced several of her followers, as well as her husband and brother, to accompany her to America. They settled outside of Albany, New York, in 1774.

Mother Ann, as her followers began to call her, became convinced that she represented the second half of God's dual nature. The first half of God had come to earth in the form of Christ, a male. The second half, correspondingly, must be female, and Mother Ann believed she was that embodiment. The new millennium had begun with her birth, and she was called to lead the community into full spiritual growth, just as Christ had done for the early Christians.

Lee's unorthodox beliefs about the Second Coming were difficult, if not impossible, for most Quakers to accept. Over time, the Shaking Quakers came to be known simply as the Shakers, and a deep split emerged between the Shakers and their Quaker origins. Additionally, their beliefs about the Second Coming offended many conservative Christians and brought varying waves of persecution down onto the early Shakers.

In the late 1770s and early 1780s, a religious revival swept across New England. This revival, known as the New Light Stir, brought an increasing tolerance for millennial groups, and that tolerance permitted the Shakers to begin recruiting members in earnest. In 1780, Joseph Meachum and his followers joined the Shakers.

Meachum would become Ann Lee's successor as leader of the Shakers, and under his competent leadership, the Shakers would grow and spread through New York, New England, Ohio, Kentucky, and Indiana. After hearing about Ann Lee's claims about the Second Coming, Meachum sent an associate to determine if there might be any truth to her claims. The friend returned convinced. Meachum spent a day with Lee in May 1780 and emerged convinced as well. After Lee's death, in 1784, Meachum assumed leadership of the Shakers. He became convinced that the Shakers needed to have both male and female leadership, and that he should establish a female leader with authority equal to his own. He selected a woman named Lucy Wright from Massachusetts. In 1792, he established the United Society of Believers, Shakers, in New Lebanon, New York. He and Wright were confirmed in the two top roles of leadership for the society.

Traditionally, outsiders have had some difficulty in learning about the Shakers' beliefs. Many misinterpretations of their beliefs, especially about the Second Coming of Christ, abound. The Shakers do not believe that Christ has already come, as prophesized in the Book of Revelation. Instead, the Shakers believe that the Christ Spirit has come among us, is living in and among believers, and that it continues to inform believers. In other words, from a Shaker perspective, the millennium is not a distant event at some point in the future. The millennium is occurring now for anyone who has truly opened his or her heart to being transformed by Christ. As more and more individuals converted to Shakerism, the Christ Spirit is seen to spread, and the transformation of the world spreads with it. The role of the Shakers is to foster the spread of this spirit.

One lives out the Christ Spirit by adopting what has been called the "three C's" of the Shaker belief system. Those three C's stand for confession, celibacy, and community life. The first step toward the embrace of a millennial life is to free oneself from sin. This involves confession of all of one's sins to an elder. In the process of doing so, one is regenerated, or reborn. Then, one must adopt a life of celibacy. Since the Shakers are trying to create the millennium here on earth, they base their decision to live celibately on instructions from Christ in the New Testament. "For in the resurrection they neither marry nor are given in marriage but are like angels in heaven" (Matt. 22:30). Having confessed his or her sin, the Shaker believer experiences a moral resurrection. As one who is resurrected, one is like the angels in heaven and does not marry. The third dimension of Shaker belief is living within the community. The community has similarly been cleansed of sinful ways and reflects a new creation. Based on their reading of accounts of the early Christians, the Shakers shared everything and worshipped God collectively. In a sense, they recreated the unity lost in the Fall, the unity experienced between God and God's creatures before human sin interfered. The Shaker community is one that reflects God's love for his creation.

In the early years of the nineteenth century, the Shakers were still spreading the joyful news of their new interpretation of the millennium. One of their foundational theological texts appeared, *The Testimony of Christ's Second Appearing,* written by John Meacham, David Darrow, and Benjamin S. Youngs. The text describes how the Christ Spirit has operated in the past and serves as a public testimony of Shaker belief. It also addresses another core Shaker belief, the way in which light and understanding grow with ongoing revelation. Each person's coming into awareness of faith and of the role of the Christ Spirit helps to spread the light and to increase the level of revelation for humanity as a whole.

This light and understanding is reached through personal spiritual experience. Just as George Fox proposed what was essentially a mystical understanding for the early Quakers, the Shakers believe that individual religious experience is the font and source of the religious stream. In this perspective, religious experience is primary. Later, one can write down and reflect on religious experience, but such writings must never take primacy over the experience itself. It is the actual relationship with God, and not the communication of the same, that is at the core of Shaker belief.

Some Shakers have described themselves as monastic, and, in many ways, the Shaker system has a great deal in common with Roman Catholic monastic orders. Both have a dynamic view of the human relationship to God, and both see the correct route for the true believer to be to enter wholeheartedly into the development of that relationship. Both practice communal forms of ownership and believe that community can play a vital role in the spiritual development of the individual. Both separate themselves from the economic and political structures of the larger world in order to pursue their vision.

Like most communities that emerged from the Reformation, however, the Shakers have a more Protestant understanding of the role of scripture. Because of the premium placed on religious experience and the personal relationship with God, the Shakers did not adopt fundamentalist or literalist approaches to biblical interpretation. Rather, they saw the Bible as a form of past revelation and emphasized the value of certain books, such as the Book of Revelation.

Like the Methodists and the Mennonites, the Shakers followed an Arminian interpretation of the role of grace in salvation. This semi-Pelagian stance does not rely entirely on God's grace for one's route to salvation but assumes that the person must work with God and that predestination is conditioned. Many of the Western Shakers were Presbyterian prior to their conversion and, so, brought harsh memories of the strict Double Predestination asserted by John Calvin. They sought a more affirming view of human nature, one that was more positive in its basic assumptions about the nature of the person.

The growth of the Shakers came on the coattails of the revivalist movement on the American frontiers. Shaker emphasis on conversion and conviction brought familiar elements to those who had attended revivals and were swayed by religious enthusiasm. They also found the Shaker emphasis on a developed personal relationship with God attractive.

Initially, the Shakers were known for their unorthodox styles of worship, for the fevered shaking that sometimes occurred in their worship sessions. Many elements of their worship services were derived from their Quaker origins. The Shakers, too, would sit and wait for the Spirit to move within one of those present. But the Shakers would often respond with a form of violent trembling, begin spinning, or move into dance. They practiced ring dances and marches. Sometimes, under the influence of the Spirit, they would speak in tongues, prophesize, or enter into a spiritual trance and have profound visions. Many of these dramatic responses would be familiar to those who had attended large camp meetings or revivals on the frontier.

But the Shaker philosophy differed from many of the surrounding Protestant belief systems in their emphasis on communal living. Shaker communities developed rapidly in the first decades of the nineteenth century. By the 1830s, nineteen communities had been started in eight states.

Shaker communities were built according to standards that reflected the central tenets of their faith. Architecturally, there was an emphasis on simplicity and functionality. Mother Ann told them, "Put your hands to work and hearts to God." One worked in the eye of God, and, so, Shaker constructions were well made and well designed. The Shakers have arguably become more famous for their furniture and architectural designs than they ever were for their religious vision. A number of the Shaker communities have been preserved as historic landmarks, and, today, visitors can still see their elegant housing and functional furniture and the clean lines of their crafts. The interested traveler can visit nine of the communities that are open to the public. Only one remains active, the community at Sabbathday Lake, Maine.

Since the Shakers saw themselves as creating heaven on earth and sought to redefine the relationship between the sexes based on celibacy and equality, some of their houses are built in two parts, mirror images of one another, and designed for the men to inhabit one side and the women to inhabit the other. They became known for their sense of the practical and for their sense of beautiful design. Shaker furniture has remained popular in terms of design right up to contemporary times, and a number of Shaker products developed as the number of communities grew and began producing. The farms attached to their communities were generally well run and provided additional sources of revenue. They strove for self-sufficiency, as that would minimize contact with the tainted outside world. They became self-contained communities, manufacturing goods to meet many, if not all, of their basic needs.

By the mid-1800s, the Shakers had grown to an estimated five thousand members, scattered across their nineteen communities. They weathered the Civil War well, since as pacifists, they contributed food and medical aid to both sides of the conflict. After the Civil War, membership in the communities began to fall. From a high of over six thousand, membership had dropped to twenty-four hundred by 1874. By the 1890s, there were only about a thousand Shakers left. By the 1980s, only a few members remained. There have been numerous debates about why the Shakers had such a precipitous decline. Some lay the blame on their practice of celibacy. But other monastic traditions, such as the Benedictines and the Trappists follow a rule of celibacy, and yet their traditions continue. More likely, the hard work required to sustain the communities and the strenuous spiritual lifestyle expected of those who joined just became less and less appealing to most Americans, who favored material comfort and more forgiving forms of religious practice.

While the Shakers evolved out of the Quaker tradition, it is important to remember that they made substantive changes in their religious vision in the process. There are numerous differences between the Quakers and the Shakers. The first and most obvious difference between the two groups is the Shaker demand for celibacy. The Quakers as a group are more family oriented, and many Quaker families have demonstrated generations of activism in areas related to Quaker beliefs.

Another set of differences involves the interaction of the two groups with the larger world. The Shakers were isolationist. They withdrew into their beautifully designed communities and worked toward self-sufficiency so that they could have as little contact with the outside world as possible. The Quakers have a deeply interior dimension to their religious belief, but they have been actively and ardently involved in the outside world, pursuing social-justice issues, equal rights, and humane treatment of those in prisons and mental institutions.

The Quakers, by and large, never accepted Mother Lee's teaching about the Second Coming and did not accord her the spiritual authority that the Shakers did. Instead, the Quakers remained committed to the spiritual authority they found in the inner light and in the light of scripture.

The Shakers did continue a number of practices that originated with the Quakers—these included emphasis on simplicity, acceptance of a true work ethic, and belief in financial responsibility—but pursued them with their own vision and in the light of their own tradition as it emerged. Many of the elements that infused the Shaker tradition are today given voice in Pentecostalism or evangelical Protestantism.

Both groups, the Quakers and the Shakers, have contributed great riches to the American religious landscape. Both took moral stances that later became much more widely accepted and established in American culture. They have contributed to the end of slavery, to improvement in women's status, to care for those in institutional settings, and to education, and they have offered an introspective alternative to those religious traditions that focus more on the external trappings of religious practice than on the internal call of the divine in the heart of the individual believer.

8

BACON, SWEDENBORG, AND TRANSCENDENTALISM

The American movement known as transcendentalism was to have an enduring impact on the American social landscape, ultimately impacting the environmental movement and the civil rights movement, as well as American religion and philosophy. To understand the streams of ideas that came together in the confluence known as transcendentalism, one must begin centuries earlier and an ocean away, in England of the sixteenth century.

Francis Bacon (1561–1626) is considered by many to be the father of empiricism, a scientific method that emphasizes observation. Using an inductive method, Bacon came to believe that scientific knowledge could be best developed through controlled experiments and systematic forms of observation. Bacon began to notice how much superstition impacted the human behavior of his day and the ways in which people would focus only on incidents that supported their existing systems of belief. He came to believe that through more careful attention to sensory input and personal experience, we can develop more reliable systems of knowledge to inform our actions, thus freeing us from the influence of superstition.

In the aftermath of the Reformation, under Elizabeth I and England's determined efforts to consolidate the position of the Church of England, most English scientists were already familiar with empiricism. They knew the work of Occam. As the scientific revolution began to build steam, thinkers like Bacon, John Locke, and David Hume developed and expanded the scope of the empirical method, creating a body of knowledge that would be used both to support and to undermine the power and influence of the church.

One of the effects of the scientific method was a change in the way we interact with nature. Bacon felt that the knowledge most desperately needed by mankind could be found through empirical observation of the natural world. Science, from his perspective, would enable the human enterprise to take control of the natural world, and we would no longer be left to nature's caprice.

This was a profoundly optimistic view of nature and of human capacity. Adopting the empirical methods of Bacon, with emphasis on rationalism and observation, adherents began to believe that through controlled application of the scientific method, the secrets of nature could be explained and, once explained, could be put into the service of mankind. A second, subtler shift occurred with the adoption of Baconian perspectives. This was the idea that the world consisted of nothing that couldn't be measured, observed, and investigated by the scientific method. Thus, the adherents of naturalism, as this approach came to be called, found themselves in direct opposition to those who believed that a greater power transcended the material world, those who believed in supernaturalism.

Four beliefs characterized naturalism as it emerged in its early phases. The first was the idea of a hierarchy of being, where humans occupied a realm between supernatural beings, such as angels, and lower beings, such as animals. The second belief was that since the most valuable forms of knowledge could be secured from careful study of the natural world, there was no reason to allow the limitations of theological perspectives, doctrine, or dogma to interfere with this process. The process of intellectual advancement was no longer beholden to the church or conducted under the control of the church. The third belief had to do with the replacement of "unscientific" perspectives, whether based in emotion, superstition, or religious thought, with "real" knowledge and values determined by the application of empiricist methods to the natural world. Finally, naturalism reflected an optimistic view of the human condition and science's potential role. It was easy to believe in science as an exclusively good force, until we saw the effects of technology run amuck—environmental contamination, global warming, and the nuclear-arms race. In its early stages, however, one of the central tenets of those who believed in the preeminence of science was that the use of science would benefit not only the world but humanity in its relationship to that world.

Naturalism would come to serve as a foundation for much of the thought of the transcendentalist movement. Several of the beliefs that characterized naturalism can be found in structural positions associated with the transcendentalists. The naturalistic dismissal of the role of the church, for example, finds a parallel in the transcendentalists' refusal to organize themselves along the lines of a traditional religious organization. The transcendentalists never built churches, or trained clergy, or gathered a congregation to adhere to a specific set of beliefs. Instead, as a loosely formed group, they explored philosophical, religious, and literary thought and honored the rights of each individual to determine what religious perspectives were best.

While the transcendentalists did not view themselves as rigorous scientists, eternally wedded to the scientific method, they did see themselves as progressive in their thought and their beliefs. Given their interest in religion and the impact of religious belief on human motivation and behavior, they were perhaps considerably friendlier toward religion at large than their scientific brethren, but they shared with them a sense of intellectual superiority that sustained them in their nonconformist attitudes toward established religion.

Finally, the transcendentalists shared a kind of optimism. They believed that the study of nature, the contemplation of nature, could provide profound insights into the most important aspects of the human condition and could stir up interior consciousness. Deep forms of spiritual truth could come out of intentional engagement with nature.

The transcendentalists owe their perspectives on nature, in part, to the thought of Swedish mystic and theologian Emanuel Swedenborg (1688–1771). Swedenborg was an extraordinary figure, who transcended any divide between science and religion. Swedenborg's father was a professor of theology and dean at Uppsala University, a man considered somewhat pompous but very good at storytelling. His mother was an heiress whose family had been very successful in mining. Swedenborg grew up in a prosperous household, observing his father's spiritual healing and listening to his father's popular sermons. Initially, Swedenborg turned not to ministry, like his father, but to science. He studied mathematics, philosophy, and the natural sciences, absorbing the Cartesian worldview that informed these disciplines.

Swedenborg's intellect was voracious, and he soon went beyond ordinary scientific study. He expanded his interests to metallurgy, astronomy, chemistry, and optics. He studied the human nervous system and anatomy, anticipating numerous developments in the understanding of the brain and the circulatory system. He learned numerous languages—Greek, Latin, and Hebrew, along with modern languages. Over time, he came to serve on the Swedish Board of Mines and to experiment in the development of microscopes and telescopes. He became interested in crystallography and magnetism and the movement of the solar system.

When he was fifty-five, Swedenborg's life took a dramatic turn. Living in Holland from 1743 to 1745, he began to undergo what he termed a "vastation." His moods began to shift radically; he had visions and reported his body being flung around a room by unseen forces. He experienced a tremendous shuddering, heard the sound of thunder, and suddenly became aware that "something holy was upon me."

The experience marked a turning point in Swedenborg's life, and he turned to religious writing in an attempt to document his experiences and share them with others. Swedenborg felt that he was called to explain the meaning of scripture to others, that he now had the ability to travel between worlds, to go to heaven and hell and report on his experiences to those limited to this worldly realm.

Swedenborg also had an interesting exchange with John Wesley, the founder of Methodism. Wesley knew of Swedenborg's writings and had once referred to Swedenborg as an "entertaining madman." Sometime thereafter, a letter from Swedenborg was delivered to Wesley. In the letter, Swedenborg said that the spirit world told him that Wesley desired a meeting with him. Wesley was astonished by the letter, as he had secretly desired to meet with Swedenborg but had not told a soul of his wish to do so. Wesley offered to meet with Swedenborg when he returned from a six-month journey he was about to undertake. Swedenborg responded that he would die on the twenty-ninth day of the following month and that, therefore, a meeting six months later would come too late. Wesley gave a great deal of thought to the exchange with Swedenborg, and while he ultimately decided that some of Swedenborg's views were heretical, he was obviously intrigued by the intensity of Swedenborg's belief and the inexplicable aspects of his spiritual knowledge.

The aspect of Swedenborg's thought that had the most impact on the transcendentalists was his idea of what are called correspondences. Swedenborg's "Doctrine of Correspondences" stated that God allowed sickness and suffering for human beings. But God's divine providence also provided the means of healing in the natural world. If one could identify the corresponding plant, mineral, or animal, one could treat the illness successfully. Swedenborg's ideas later had a significant influence on Samuel Hahnemann, the founder of homeopathy, and the spread of homeopathy in America closely followed the spread of Swedenborgian teachings and communities.

Carried further, Swedenborg's idea of correspondences suggests that every life event has a potential meaning. Our spiritual work is to master the symbolism of life, to learn how events in our own lives correspond to spiritual meaning. Part of the process of doing so means coming to awareness of the spiritual correspondences between human life and nature. Similarly,

Swedenborg believed there were correspondences that governed our relationship to scripture.

From Swedenborg's perspective, certain books of the Bible had greater spiritual power than others; they had a kind of "spiritual sense." The obvious, or natural, meaning of the passage or phrasing in these particular books could be correlated to deeper spiritual truths. In other words, they "corresponded" to them. Not all books of the Bible had these correspondences. The existence of these correspondences had been explained to Swedenborg in his meetings with angels and even Christ himself, and, therefore, Swedenborg was the only one who truly knew the nature and extent of these correspondences in scripture.

Like Wesley, the Lutheran Church in Sweden eventually decided that such views meant Swedenborg was heretical, and he was forced to leave the country. But Swedenborg had developed a vision of transforming spiritual consciousness throughout the world. A prolific writer, he devoted over thirty volumes to the description of what his "New Jerusalem" would look like. As a result of his writings, Swedenborgian communities sprang up, and a new denomination emerged—the Church of the New Jerusalem. Swedenborg's writings were widely read in America in the nineteenth century and, as a result, came to the attention of the transcendentalists.

Eugene Taylor cites the first contact between the transcendentalists and Swedenborg as the delivery of a homily at the commencement of Harvard University in 1821.[1] Sampson Reed, who was preparing for ministry in a Swedenborgian church delivered a talk entitled "An Oration on Genius." Ralph Waldo Emerson (1803–1882) graduated from Harvard the same year and was entranced by Sampson's talk. In fact, he managed to get a copy of the homily and considered it a "treasure." When Reed later developed his Swedenborgian ideas into a book, *The Growth of the Mind* (1826), Emerson used that book as a model for his own first book, *Nature* (1836). More importantly, the ideas that Reed put forth became deeply imbedded in Emerson's own philosophical outlook and, thereby, became foundational for the transcendentalist movement.

The main effect of Reed's writing on Emerson was that Emerson began to understand the Swedenborgian conception of correspondences. Since Swedenborg maintained that elements of the natural world had correspondences to the soul, one could reach a level of divine consciousness by immersing oneself in nature. Nature came alive with the promise of spiritual enrichment. Because one could work out one's own relationship to God with just nature and interior reflection, there was no need to rely on organized churches or to study dogma or doctrine. Transcendentalism was extremely individualistic, minimizing the communal dimensions of religious practice.

Emerson soon gathered a coterie of like-minded souls around him, and a group of them decided to meet at the home of George Ripley. Meetings of the group came to be known as the Transcendentalist Club, and it attracted an elite group of talented thinkers in diverse disciplines. Among the member were Bronson Alcott, Margaret Fuller, and William Ellery Channing. One of those attracted to the group was Henry James Sr. (1811–1882), the father of philosopher and psychologist William James and novelist Henry James.

Henry James Sr. had his own encounter with Swedenborgianism. While living in England on a country estate, he had some sort of psychological and emotional collapse, followed by an experience of complete desolation. When he told a friend, one Mrs. Chichester, about the experience, she was quick to describe it by the term Swedenborg had used, as a "vastation." James became intrigued by the work of Swedenborg and began devouring his many volumes. Henry James Jr. would later remember his father packing his Swedenborg books for their many travels around Europe.

Henry James Sr. seems to have formed an ambivalent attachment to the teachings of Swedenborg. He later wrote a book entitled *The Secret of Swedenborg*. While he championed the thought of Swedenborg, he was not convinced that it warranted being institutionalized in a formal church structure, and he accused Swedenborgians, who favored a church structure, of being Pharisees. James's distrust of organized religion was completely in keeping with the transcendentalist movement and was something he could share with Ralph Waldo Emerson.

After James and Emerson met, they became fast friends. James and his family were living in New York City in those years, and Emerson soon became a frequent visitor to their home. Having just lost a son of his own, Waldo, in 1842, Emerson offered a blessing to William James when he was an infant and came to serve as William's godfather. His visits to the James household were so frequent that one room in the house was simply called "Mr. Emerson's Room."

Emerson was at the heart of the transcendentalist movement. Arguably, he and Henry David Thoreau became its most influential members, casting long shadows on the American religious landscape. Emerson came to be known as a lecturer, an essayist, a philosopher, and a writer, and his opinions were much sought after in his time. Younger writers and thinkers would make pilgrimages to his home in Concord, Massachusetts, hoping to soak up some of the wisdom espoused by the elder statesman of American thought.

Emerson was born to a family of eight in 1803. His father was a Unitarian minister and served at First Church in Boston. The Unitarians had emerged as a separate group from the Calvinists. Originally called the Liberal Christians, the Unitarians came to substantially different doctrinal positions than the Congregationalists from whom they split off. The Unitarians objected to two main tenets of Calvinist doctrine. First, Calvinists, following Augustine, believed that only God could select those who would gain salvation, the elect, as they were called. Calvinists expected those participating in their congregations to demonstrate why they believed they were members of the elect. The Unitarians, or Liberal Christians, had doubts about this view of predestination and had also been exposed to the more Arminian views of the Methodists.

The Liberal Christians also had doubts about the development of doctrines on the Trinity. They adopted the view of Arius, whose work sparked the Council of Nicaea in 325 CE. Arius believed Christ was of a different substance from God the Father. Adopting Arian views, the Unitarians believed Christ was human, but the human being who achieved the closest relationship to God.

As a result of these differing views, the Unitarians split from the Congregationalist churches that had housed them and began to establish their own congregations. William Ellery Channing (1780–1842), who dropped by the Transcendentalist Club, was a popular Unitarian preacher. He was also known at the "apostle of Unitarianism." He founded the Berry St. Conference of Ministers, which evolved into the American Unitarian Association, and was widely known for his interest in abolition, his pacifism, and his views on education.

Like Channing, Emerson's father had convinced his congregation to follow him into Unitarianism, and he became the minister of First Church in Boston. But Emerson's father died when Emerson was eight. Intellectually, Emerson was greatly influenced by his aunt, Mary Moody Emerson, who introduced him to neoplatonism and Hindu scriptures.

After graduating from Harvard in 1821, Emerson became a pastor, like his father, in the Unitarian Church. But he never really took to life as a minister. By 1832, he resigned as pastor and never returned to that role. He became a lecturer, bought a house in Concord, Massachusetts, and turned his attention to full-time study and writing. In 1836, he published his first book, *Nature,* the one he modeled after Reed's book. The first meeting of the Transcendentalist Club followed in September 1836, and the ideas for which he was known began to be widely disseminated.

In 1838, Emerson was asked back to Harvard to speak to students in the Divinity School. He urged the students to come to a firsthand knowledge of God and to resist conformity to a stale and lifeless religion. His speech sparked a controversy, and Emerson was banished from Harvard's campus for thirty years.

Emerson never directly responded to the controversy, but the flap did enhance his reputation, and he soon had more requests for lectures and talks. He would travel by train, crossing the country to give lectures, and soon became widely known. By the 1840s, he began opposing slavery publicly and, later, he became one of the most articulate voices in the argument for emancipation of the slaves. He also supported increased educational opportunities for women and supported that perspective when he made Margaret Fuller the editor of the transcendentalist journal, the *Dial.* He is probably best remembered for an essay he published in 1841, entitled "Self-Reliance," in which he stated, "To be great is to be misunderstood." Emerson died the same year as his old friend, Henry James, in 1882.

Another close friend of Emerson's was the other person most commonly associated with the transcendentalist movement, Henry David Thoreau (1817–1862). Thoreau was born in Concord, Massachusetts, the third of four children, to a pencil manufacturer and his wife. The family moved to Boston for two years, from 1821 to 1823, but then returned to Concord. At sixteen, Thoreau returned to the Boston area to study at Harvard. He took courses in Latin and Greek, history, philosophy, and several modern languages and made himself familiar with the extensive holdings of the library. By 1837, at twenty, Thoreau graduated.

His first employment was a teaching position in Concord. However, the administration of the school mandated physical punishment of students. Thoreau refused to comply and was fired from the job after two weeks. More importantly for the rest of us, Thoreau began to keep a journal in that year, for it was through his journals that many would come to know this admirable, complex thinker. It was also during this period that Thoreau began to develop associations with some of the prominent Unitarians in the area, including Channing and Emerson. Thoreau was impressed by Emerson's transcendentalist views, and Emerson was enough impressed by the young Thoreau to provide him a letter of recommendation for another teaching position.

Unable to secure a position, Thoreau decided to open a school in Concord with his brother. The brothers implemented a curriculum that reflected Thoreau's own values, with no corporal punishment and with time spent in nature.

Thoreau seemed to drift for some time, living for a while in Emerson's house, doing odd jobs, becoming interested in a couple of ill-starred romances. In 1842, his brother John developed lockjaw, or tetanus, and died in Thoreau's arms. Thoreau decided against continuing the school alone. To get away from the powerful associations with the death of his brother, Thoreau took a job as a tutor to the children of Emerson's brother and relocated to New York.

A year later, he returned to Concord and penned what would become the manuscript for his first book. Writing about a canoe trip taken with his brother several years earlier, he wrote *A Week on the Concord and Merrimack Rivers* (1849). The book combined the account of the trip with Thoreau's reflections on history, philosophy, and one's relationship to nature, as well as his poetic musings.

Thoreau was eager to spend more time immersed in nature and, so, proposed that he build a house on Flint's Pond, just outside of Lincoln, near Concord. The board of selectmen denied him permission, and Thoreau returned to Emerson with his disappointment. Emerson suggested another alternative. He had recently bought some property that had a pond on it, Walden Pond, and suggested that Thoreau build there.

Thoreau took Emerson up on the offer, building a small house, and lived simply and deliberately. He lived in close contact with the animals and vegetation in the area and wrote a volume concerning his reflections on nature, his relationship to the natural world, and the way one's relationship with nature reflects one's self-knowledge and interior consciousness. These musings became one of his best-known works, *Walden: or, Life in the Woods* (1854). Thoreau remained at Walden Pond for two years.

It was during his time at Walden Pond that a famous exchange with Emerson took place. The U.S. government had undertaken a war with Mexico, and the local poll tax was used to finance the war. In addition, portions of the taxes were used for the enforcement of slavery laws, which Thoreau opposed. Thoreau refused to pay his poll tax for several years, and, eventually, the town constable was sent to arrest him. The constable himself offered to pay Thoreau's tax, but Thoreau also refused that offer and, so, spent a night in jail. In the apocryphal story, Emerson came to visit Thoreau in jail. "What are you doing in there?" he asked. Thoreau replied by asking Emerson if he supported the war with Mexico. "No," came the response. "Then what are you doing out there?" he asked Emerson.

The night in jail became the basis for one of Thoreau's most famous essays, "Civil Disobedience" (1849). Thoreau's time in jail gave him time to think about the ways in which governments coerce us. Thoreau's "Civil Disobedience" came out of a lecture delivered at the Concord Lyceum, which was a progressive center for education. Since Concord was known as a stronghold of abolitionist thought, the question of slavery loomed large in local consciousness. Thoreau ruffled the waters by taking the position that citizens were moral participants in oppression when they failed to confront it. It stripped away moral neutrality from those who were not actual participants in slavery or other forms of oppression, echoing his comment to Emerson from his jail cell.

Thoreau's indictment of the passive acceptance of injustice or oppression at the hand of the government has been heard around the world and through the centuries since. Russian novelist Leo Tolstoy commented on it. Mahatma Gandhi, who led the people of India to independence from the British colonial system, credited its influence. Civil rights leader Martin Luther King Jr. incorporated Thoreau's stance into his own, and while King's famous "Letter from Birmingham Jail" (1963) does not cite Thoreau explicitly, its composition mimics many of the elements of Thoreau's prophetic voice from jail. Like Thoreau, King encouraged civil disobedience in the face of government oppression and injustice.

In the 1850s, Thoreau became more outspoken about slavery. In 1854, he gave a speech titled "Slavery in Massachusetts," and later that same year, he gave another titled "The Last Days of John Brown." In these speeches it became clear that Thoreau felt armed force was an acceptable response if required to end the dramatic injustices of slavery. He defended John Brown's attack at Harper's Ferry. But, in the 1850s, Thoreau also developed tuberculosis. He continued to work, writing and lecturing between bouts of illness and weakness, while his condition deteriorated. In 1862, Thoreau died, at the relatively young age of forty-four. Although he never actually made a living on his writing, Thoreau left a lasting legacy in naturalism, civil rights, political thought, and philosophy.

Thoreau was not the only transcendentalist to become well known for his naturalism. Another naturalist often associated with the transcendentalist movement was considered by some to be the "father" of American environmentalism—John Muir (1838–1914). Muir was born in Scotland but immigrated to the United States when he was eleven. His father was a deeply religious shopkeeper, but the family settled on a farm in Fountain Lake, Wisconsin. Muir had a tough childhood, being beaten regularly by his father and working long and hard on the farm. Still, he managed to teach himself math, geometry, literature, and philosophy and demonstrated a life-long curiosity that would later characterize his work in nature. At twenty-two, he left home and began studies at the University of Wisconsin, Madison. He never received a degree and studied only those areas he deemed valuable.

In the years after his college studies, Muir began to wander. He traveled to Canada in 1864 to avoid serving in the military. After the war, he returned the United States. Temporarily blinded in a factory accident, when his sight returned, he walked from the Midwest to Florida, then by boat traveled to Cuba, hoping to get to South America. He settled for New York and then sailed to California via the Panama Canal. He made it to San Francisco but chose to get back to the natural world and entered the Yosemite Valley. He had finally come home.

Muir's relationship to nature has many of the same elements as Thoreau's. He lived simply. He hiked and spent a great deal of time in the wilderness, carrying only a cloak or blanket and simple food. He came to know the intricate system of hills and valleys in Yosemite intimately. The Yosemite Valley would become his life's work.

In 1869, Muir spent a summer as a shepherd at Tuolomne Meadows in the High Sierras and wrote a book about his experiences, *A Record of My First Summer in the Sierras* (1911). The experience encouraged him to undertake a closer study of the Sierras, looking at geological formation and the impact of glaciers. He theorized that the unusual formations of Yosemite were caused by the movement of glaciers. His theory was later accepted, which brought him to widespread public notice.

Muir didn't refer to himself as a transcendentalist, but he had a great regard for the writings of Ralph Waldo Emerson. He had first encountered Emerson's works in college and had deeply immersed himself in Emerson's writing during his travels in the Sierras. Photographs of Emerson and Thoreau adorned the mantle of his fireplace. In 1871, Emerson came to visit Muir in Yosemite. Thirty-five years younger than Emerson, Muir encouraged the elder statesman of transcendentalism to camp out under the stars with him and celebrate the beauty of the created world. But other members of the party, concerned for Emerson's health and rest, prevented Muir from carrying out the plan. As an alternative, he took Emerson to see the sequoias, telling Emerson "You yourself are a sequoia."

Following their meeting, the two exchanged letters and books. The next year, Asa Gray, a professor of botany at Harvard visited Muir and made the first ascent of Mt. Ritter. In 1873, Muir made a solo climb of Mt. Whitney, the first ascent of the eastern route. A couple of years later, Muir began to write and lobby for the protection of many of the beautiful areas he had come to know so well. He guided the U.S. Geodetic Survey through Nevada and Utah. He led the fight for the preservation of Yosemite Valley and played a key role in preserving the Grand Canyon and the Petrified Forest. He campaigned for the establishment of Sequoia National Park and Kings Canyon. He was one of the cofounders of the Sierra Club and became the group's first president. Many consider him the father of the American system of national parks.

Thus, the transcendentalist movement, with its deep roots in Baconian naturalism and the correspondences of Emanuel Swedenborg, travels through philosophy, political science, literature, and religion and comes back to the celebration of the natural world in the work of Muir. Diverse in its expression, singular in its celebration of the individual, and amorphous in the many streams of influence that came out of it, transcendentalism remains a vibrant force in the civil rights movement, environmentalism, and contemporary thought. The unique and profound relationship of the American people with the beauty of their created land has been sustained by men like Thoreau, who celebrated the interior transformation that accompanied his immersion in nature, and Muir, who protected and preserved some of the most remarkable landscapes in the world. By doing so, contemporary transcendentalists and naturalists can continue to wander, to reflect, and to write of their deep and abiding connection to the natural world.

NOTE

1. Eugene Taylor, *Shadow Culture: Psychology and Spirituality in America* (Washington, DC: Counterpoint, 1999), 61–62. I am indebted to Taylor's treatment of transcendentalism throughout this chapter.

9

CATHOLIC–ANTI-CATHOLIC

Few groups threatened the American sense of Protestant identity as much as the Roman Catholics, and, so, it is unsurprising to find some of the most strenuous persecution of a religious group on American soil in the anti-Catholic movement of the nineteenth century. The American mistrust of and resistance to Roman Catholicism started much earlier than the nineteenth century. In fact, the origins of anti-Catholic prejudice can be traced back to the period immediately following the Reformation. From the earliest days of the Reformation, Martin Luther had made a particular point of denigrating the Roman Catholic pope, calling him, among other things, a "whore of the devil." Luther cooperated with a group of scholars in Magdeburg to create a propagandist history of the Roman Catholic Church to be used against the church. Its primary goal was to discredit Catholicism. Over subsequent centuries, numerous imitations of this Magdeburg history would be written, fueling an attitude that came to be designated as No-Popery.

In England, where the fledgling Church of England felt particularly threatened by the Roman Catholic Church, the spirit of No-Popery became institutionalized in numerous laws. Catholics could not become lawyers or teachers or participate in universities. When a group of Catholic activists attempted to blow up the houses of Parliament in what came to be known as the Gunpowder Plot, anti-Catholic sentiment accelerated in England. The English dimension of "New England" meant that many of the early settlers in the colonies brought anti-Catholic sentiments along with them when they settled in America.

The most influential centers of the No-Popery movement in America were Massachusetts and Maryland. The charter granted to Sir George Calvert, Lord Baltimore, for the colony of Maryland should have supported a tolerant view toward Catholicism. Calvert himself was Catholic. But few Catholics followed Calvert to Maryland, and the majority of the population was staunchly Protestant. Maryland Protestants ended up banishing Calvert from his own province and made it clear that Catholics would not be permitted to hold office in Maryland.

Massachusetts' intolerant attitudes toward Catholicism grew out of its Puritan heritage. Seventeenth-century laws stated that priests entering the colony should be banished. A second offense meant they could be executed. They went so far as to forbid the entry of Irish into the colony because they brought with them their Catholic faith. By 1700, the only place where a Catholic enjoyed full liberty was Rhode Island. And it was only after Thomas Jefferson's presidency, with the separation of church and state, that anti-Catholic sentiment began to lose some of its power.

If government structures moved toward greater tolerance between members of different religions and denominations, one group did not. These were the authors of an ongoing stream of anti-Catholic propaganda that painted a dark and sinister portrait of the Roman Catholic Church. Convents were filled with the graves of dead babies. Priests were seducers, and Jesuits were the worst form of priest, casuists all and eager to deceive. The pope was a direct threat to American democratic structures, and all Catholics would hold their primary loyalty to the pope and not to the American government. Many publications, newspapers and magazines, were openly anti-Catholic in both their editorial views and reporting. The numbers were relatively small, and most of the vehemence toward Catholics was restrained to verbal attack, but a mistrust and hatred of all things Catholic was kept at a low boil in the back of the American consciousness.

In the 1820s, this simmering distrust erupted into the radical response of nativism. The biggest single trigger was the dramatic increase in foreign immigration during that period. In the 1820s, wave after wave of Roman Catholic immigrants began to arrive on American soil. Several factors fueled the rising tide of immigrants. Peace was achieved after years of Napoleonic wars, and it was safer to travel. The Industrial Revolution brought more and more mechanization into the workplace. As a result, wages fell in countries like England. Ireland's ongoing political and economic strife meant many were eager to seek a better life.

Since the English had been defeated by the Americans in the War of 1812, they were not eager to send immigrants to the country, potentially making it stronger still. Instead, they directed those emigrating to Canada. But few of those who arrived on Canada's shores elected to remain there. Many times they simply walked across the borders to American soil.

The Irish lumber industry became a key player in the rise of immigration to America. On an annual basis, lumber vessels offered cheap transportation to Canada. Once they arrived in Canada, those transported were allowed to earn a modest stake by loading the vessel for the return voyage. They would load lumber onto the ships, collect their modest wages, and begin an overland journey to America.

Many of these figures who arrived in American cities were ill equipped for adaptation to the American way of life. They were impoverished and often needy and swamped the fragile social infrastructures of cities. Many "native" Americans saw them as an unwelcome and unnecessary drain on available resources and a burden to American taxpayers.

Americans were also suspicious of the newcomers for other reasons. Some thought they had been sent deliberately to America so that their home nations could avoid the expense of supporting them. Some English port cities openly shipped their poor to America. Since many of the Irish and German immigrants were clearly Roman Catholic, some began to believe that a dark and sinister Catholic plot lay behind the immigration, that it was a means by which the Roman Catholic Church could seize control of America and her peoples. These fears were furthered by the dramatic increase of Roman Catholic infrastructure during this period, as the Catholic Church struggled to meet the spiritual needs of the thousands who had come to America.

Awareness of the growing numbers of Catholics and the growing Catholic Church was increased by the celebration of the Papal Jubilee of Leo XII in 1827. In addition, the first Provincial Council of Catholicity in America was held in Baltimore, Maryland, in 1829. The sight of so many members of the Catholic hierarchy, with all the attendant pomp and circumstance, was intimidating to many Americans.

In the 1820s, another controversy in Philadelphia also elevated concern. Questions arose as to who should hold the rights to church property. Some felt that the laymen who served on the councils and contributed toward the purchase or development of the property should do so. Henry Conwell, as bishop of the local diocese, tried to force the laymen to give over the property rights by withdrawing privileges from the pastor at the cathedral, William Hogan. Upon their refusal, Hogan was excommunicated, and the pope issued a brief against the laymen involved. Although, eventually, the church won the property rights they sought, the press coverage of the case was far from flattering, reinforcing misconceptions about the church and furthering the image of the church as an enemy to democracy and American values. Many newspapers printed editorials that supported the laymen and decried the manner in which the church had seized the property. Petitions were circulated, and some Protestants lobbied for laws that would require lay trustees to have ownership of church property. The three elements together, the Papal Jubilee, the Baltimore Provincial Congress, and the Hogan controversy, kept less-than-flattering perceptions of Roman Catholicism circulating in the American press and in public response to these events. When combined with successive waves of Catholic immigrants, it made for an explosive situation.

The first spark came in the form of the founding of the Anti-Masonic Party. Those scandalized by the secret society of the Masons were eager to hear more about that other secretive organization that held such sway over its followers, the popish church. As revivalism began to spread in America, at the hands of preachers like Charles G. Finney, Protestant perspectives gathered new believers and reinvigorated those who already believed. Americans became eager to protect their Protestantism and increasingly willing to resist Catholicism.

By 1830, the scene was set for the emergence of nativism. Initially, it was a small group of clergymen who decided to unify their efforts against Catholicism. They established an anti-Catholic newspaper, *The Protestant*, in New York. Articles addressed the "unholy dominion" of the papacy, and the "Mystical Babylon" it represented. Other Christians resisted the aggressive nature of the reporting in the *Protestant,* fearing it would only make Catholics seem like martyrs and, thereby, strengthen the church. Some objected to the perspective as un-Christian and contrary to Christian values. The *Protestant* only intensified its attacks, but it lost moderate support, and the owners sold the periodical. It was later transformed into a monthly, its tone softened, and it became extremely popular. Similar anti-Catholic viewpoints could be found in such newspapers as *Priestcraft Unmasked* and *Priestcraft Exposed*.

This successful torrent of propaganda led to the formation of the earliest nativist societies. Organizations such as the New York Protestant Association came into being. Debates were organized—some with Roman Catholic representatives presenting their perspective, some without. The latter was usually preferred in Protestant circles. The content of attacks on Catholicism subtly shifted over time. They may have begun with theological critique and exchange, but they deteriorated into stark criticism and misrepresentation of Catholic morals. Catholic religious orders became dens of vice, thoroughly corrupt, and eager to attract and corrupt others.

This sentiment came to a head in Charlestown, Massachusetts, where a mob of lower-class men took it upon themselves to burn down the Ursuline convent. There were earlier precedents. In 1829, the homes of Irish

Catholics in Boston had come under attack. Much of the attention focused on the Ursuline convent in Charlestown came after a rival Protestant school had been founded for the young women of the area. When Roman Catholics continued to send their daughters to the Ursulines to be educated, resentment against the school grew.

Tempers were fueled by the stories of young women who had "escaped" the convent, one of whom was mentally unstable and ultimately returned. Rumor had it that she had been forced back into the convent. Eventually, the town selectmen demanded the opportunity to visit the convent and interview the woman in question to determine whether she was being held against her own will. On August 11, about forty or fifty men broke into the convent and set it alight. The following night, the mob returned and burned fences, trees, and whatever was left. Only the presence of armed troops prevented them from burning a nearby Catholic church. In the aftermath of the burning, no remorse was shown. So deep was the antipathy toward Catholicism that the participants felt that no wrong had been done. When the local bishop tried to reestablish the sisters in Boston, handbills began to circulate, and they began to fear that they would once again be attacked. When those responsible for the attack were tried, they were acquitted, and the state was not required to reimburse the Ursulines for their losses. Ultimately, in the court of public opinion, the act had been sanctioned as appropriate.

Nativism was not limited to the Boston area but spread steadily. In 1835, in a book published under the title *Six Months in a Convent*, Rebecca Reed told of her trials during convent life and her daring escape. Shortly after its publication, the mother superior of the convent wrote to rebuke the author. That spurred a response to the mother superior from an anonymous author, who did not limit the reply to the mother superior but was highly critical of all of Catholicism throughout the United States.

These various publications helped to develop a larger reading audience for the periodic volleys in the battle over anti-Catholicism. New anti-Catholic newspapers followed, including the *Downfall of Babylon, or the Triumph over Popery, American Protestant Vindicator* and *Defender of Civil and Religious Liberty against the Inroads of Popery*. They were so successful that they were soon imitated in other parts of the country. Bardstown, Kentucky, saw the founding of the *Western Protestant*, and Baltimore had a new journal, the *Literary and Religious Magazine*. As the newspapers and journals spread, so, too, did anti-Catholic societies.

Many of the new societies were not content with denouncing Catholic principles and morals but actively engaged in saving souls from the perils posed by Catholicism. A whole new missionary drive was directed toward Catholics among groups such as the Society for the Diffusion of Light on the Subject of Romanism, the Society for the Diffusion of Christian Knowledge, and the American Society to Promote the Principles of the Protestant Reformation.

Arguably, the most important volley in the war against Catholicism came in the form of Maria Monk's *Awful Disclosures of the Hotel Dieu Nunnery of Montreal,* published in 1836. Monk was reportedly a Protestant convert to Catholicism who decided to become a nun. After taking her vows, according to her report, she was required to have sexual relationships with the priests because of her vow of obedience. Children were regularly born from such relationships, then were baptized and promptly strangled. In the basement of the convent was a hole where the bodies of such babies were disposed of. Supposedly, when Monk found herself pregnant at the hands of one of the priests, she could not bear the thought of her child's strangulation and, so, decided to escape. Afterward, she penned the book.

Maria Monk's mother told a very different version of her life. According to Monk's mother, her daughter had never been in the Hotel Dieu convent. Instead, she had been a wild and uncontrollable young woman, who was confined to the care of the Magdalene sisters. The Magdalene sisters made a specialty of housing fallen women, or young women whose behavior was incorrigible. A lover, and most likely the real father of her child, helped Monk to escape from the Magdalenes. The man was later identified as Rev. William K. Hoyt, who was active in a nativist society. After he took Monk to New York, he saw the opportunity for a publishing coup. Later, legal proceedings disclosed that it was actually Hoyt who wrote most of book.

The publication of the book proved extremely controversial. Roman Catholic supporters of the convent published accounts of the plot to manufacture the book. Legal proceedings developed, and affidavits were filed. Protestants demanded an examination of the interior of the convent to see if the reports of where bodies were to be found were true. When two uninvolved Protestant pastors made the inspection and failed to find any evidence of the charges in the book, they were accused of being secret Jesuits. Another woman emerged who proclaimed herself a fugitive from the Hotel Dieu convent and proclaimed that everything Monk had written was true. That woman's tales were quickly exposed as untrue, but not before they sparked another investigation of the convent. When that investigation once again found nothing, the investigator was accused of being employed by the Jesuits.

Monk continued her charges against the Catholic Church. After disappearing from the public eye, she emerged again with reports of having been kidnapped by Catholic priests in an attempt to prevent her from speaking out. In 1837, she published *Further Disclosures by Maria Monk, Concerning the Hotel Dieu Nunnery of Montreal; also Her Visit to Nuns' Island, and Disclosures Concerning That Secret Retreat.* According to Monk, Nun's Island was where all the pregnant nuns went to bear their illegitimate children.

Monk had little to show for her efforts. Her financial backers ended up with most of the profits generated by her publications and her sensationalistic lectures. Several lawsuits disclosed massive corruption among those who surrounded her. In 1838, she gave birth to her second illegitimate child. The *American Protestant Vindicator* promptly reported that the pregnancy had been perpetrated by the Jesuits to destroy her reputation. Monk eventually married, then divorced when her husband could not afford her spending patterns. In 1849, she was arrested as a pickpocket. Shortly thereafter, Maria Monk died in prison.

If Maria Monk's life could not be considered a success, certainly her books were. They continued to be published in reprints and remained popular through the Civil War. She made it clear that there was a market, an American hunger for books that defamed Catholicism and preyed on the prurient interest of American readers in the sexual lives of the Catholic religious. To some extent, American readers continue to relish such portrayals.

The regular volleys from the anti-Catholic press also began to color the American attitude toward immigration, and areas that had high rates of immigration became the battleground between nativists and immigrating Catholics. The Mississippi Valley was increasingly being settled, and Protestants became alarmed by the increasing numbers of Catholics immigrating to the area. Protestant journals linked the increase to a plot that was being fomented by the Society of Jesus, or the Jesuits. The Jesuit order had been reestablished in 1814, following a forty-one-year suppression. Protestant journals asserted that the order had only been restored on the condition that members of the order play a key role in the conquest of America by Catholic forces. Jesuits were portrayed as spies and advance agents, who came before the great flood of Catholics that would follow. They were not always easy to spot, since often they traveled in disguise, intent on Roman domination. Two missionary societies, the Association for the Propagation of the Faith and the Leopold Association, were singled out as key players in the popish plot.

Protestant opposition to immigration was galvanized by two issues. First, they resented the political power that immigrants were able to garner once they began to participate in elections. Second, they resented the poverty of so many of the immigrants and the demands it placed on American taxpayers. In 1838, the Native American Association asked Congress to repeal immigration laws and asked for a longer waiting period before immigrants received the right to vote. The appeal was ultimately unsuccessful but demonstrated the level of hostility toward the largely Catholic immigrant population of the period.

In the 1840s, organized Protestant resistance strengthened. The Protestant Reformation Society in New York hosted lectures and provided speakers to church and other groups. The speakers were notoriously anti-Catholic, portraying convents as brothels and celibacy as a form of tyranny. Money collected from the lectures and speeches was used to finance publications, and the tracts that were produced rehashed the same points and were distributed for free in Protestant churches and among other groups.

Presbyterian stronghold Princeton University even formed an organization named the Committee on the Romish Church, Public Morals and Infidelity to distribute information on the dangers of popery to students at the school and to the local townspeople. In 1841, the American Protestant Union was formed in New York as a "national defense society" against the popish invasion. In Philadelphia, the Protestant Beneficial Association was founded. It allowed only Protestants as members.

Since readers had begun to evidence some skepticism toward the more outrageous claims, like those of Maria Monk, Protestant organizations began to develop more sophisticated arguments against Catholicism. One journal in Baltimore, the *Literary and Religious Magazine,* focused on theological arguments geared toward pastors. New journals sprouted up across the country. In Baltimore, the *Pilot and Transcript* noted the dangers Catholics posed in the political scene, while the *Saturday Visitor* reported on the general problem. Jackson, Tennessee, had the *Jackson Protestant;* New Orleans, Louisiana, the *New Orleans Protestant;* Albany, New York, the *Reformation Defended against the Errors of the Times;* Cincinnati, Ohio, the *American Protestant;* and Philadelphia, Pennsylvania, the *Protestant Banner.*

By the mid-1840s, many members of Protestant churches envisioned themselves as participants in a new reformation. They saw the pastors that led the anti-Catholic movement as Martin Luthers or John Calvins. The nativists decided that it was time their viewpoint was reflected on the national political scene. Two factors drove the politicization of the No-Popery movement. The first was simply the widespread hatred of Catholicism that emerged out of the inherited mistrust of English settlers and was ripened by the ongoing stream of anti-Catholic publications. The second was the nativist fear of the immigrant. The immigrant was portrayed as the potential agent of the downfall of beloved social, economic, and political structures in America. These fears were heightened by the increasing number of immigrants arriving on American shores—in 1842, one hundred thousand immigrants arrived; by 1847, twice as many came. From their perspective, these huge numbers of impoverished, poorly educated immigrants were obviously susceptible to immoral behavior and disrespect for American laws, values, and principles.

In New York, Boston, Baltimore, Philadelphia, and Detroit, fights broke out between nativist gangs and Catholics, and in some cases, troops had to be brought in to quell the fighting. Such violence was laid at the feet of the immigrants, not the nativists. Since many of the immigrants became staunch Democrats, the political dimensions of the increasing numbers of immigrants soon became apparent. The American Republicans decided to incorporate nativist proposals into their campaign. They vowed to change naturalization laws to extend the time before immigrants got voting rights and to centralize jurisdictional power over immigration issues in federal courts. By 1844, the U.S. Senate was ready to consider extending the time before voting rights were established. The debate that surrounded the discussion of this change became the focal point of nativist resistance to Catholic immigrants. A similar change was proposed in the House of Representatives.

In 1844, one of the worst series of riots broke out in the city of brotherly love, Philadelphia. The city had come a long way from the days when William Penn founded Pennsylvania as a refuge for persecuted religious groups. The riots were set off when Bishop Francis Patrick Kenrick wrote to the school board to complain that Catholic students were being required to read Protestant Bibles and to perform Protestant religious exercises in public schools. The school board decided to allow parents to select what version of the Bible their children would read.

The American Protestant Association quickly publicized the incident as representative of the unacceptable interference of "foreign prelates" with American values. Increasing friction was evident in the city, and that tension exploded when a group of Irish laborers threatened members of the American Republicans for announcing a meeting in the third ward. On Monday, May 6, a notice invited "Native Americans" to meet at a specific location to vent their indignation. Several thousand men complied, and a mob gathered. When shots were fired, the crowd deteriorated into chaos, and several members of the group were killed in the fighting that followed.

The following day, two Irishmen were captured by a Protestant mob that wanted to kill them. While calmer citizens of the city pled for peace, the mob headed for Irish neighborhoods, shouting and destroying property, until meeting with armed resistance from the Irish. The third day, mobs gathered in Kensington and began setting fire to Irish homes. They set torch to St. Michael's Catholic Church and St. Augustine's Church. The violence had reached its high point, and events began to wind down after the night of fire.

The events in Philadelphia evoked a storm of criticism from other parts of the country. All seemed calm until Independence Day. Another fight broke out between American Republicans and Irish workers. Riots continued through July 7 before dissipating. After the riots stopped and the dead were buried, certain groups objected strenuously to the treatment of the Catholics of Philadelphia. The Quakers were particularly outspoken. But of the two grand juries called, both attributed the violence to the Catholics. St. Augustine's Church was eventually restored with public funds, but St. Michael's never was because it lay outside of the official boundaries of the city. The citizens of the city of brotherly love did not seem to recognize that they had committed any wrongdoing in the Philadelphia riots. Nor did they show remorse. To the contrary, the cries for blood spread to New York. On May 9, nativists were urged to meet in Central Park to confront Catholic rioters. Archbishop John Hughes had over a thousand armed men stationed around each church. They were instructed not to break the peace but to defend church property. Just before the meeting was scheduled to begin, notices were posted around the city announcing it had been postponed, and what would have resulted in certain violence was avoided.

In the period between 1845 and 1850, nativism began to decline. National attention turned to the Mexican war and the question of slavery, and those elements seemed more threatening than the Catholic immigrants. Nativist groups retrenched, formed closer relationships with Protestant churches, and anticipated renewed support for their cause. By the early 1850s, tensions about the slavery issue and the divisions that would ultimately fuel the Civil War began to take precedence in the minds of many Americans. Nativism might have ground to a halt had not the American Roman Catholic hierarchy played into the hands of such groups.

Formed in Europe, the attitudes of many members of the hierarchy and clergy assumed a close connection between government and the Roman Catholic Church. The American situation was far more tenuous—the number of Catholics was lower, they had no government support, and the few resources available were taxed by the constant need to develop new churches, schools, and dioceses. Insensitive spokesmen like Archbishop John Hughes of New York talked of the decline of Protestantism, playing directly into American fears.

These fears culminated in the rise of the Know-Nothing Party, which emerged out of nowhere in 1854 and promptly died in 1856. The group was most likely founded in 1849 by Charles B. Allen of New York and was originally known as the Order of the Star-Spangled Banner. In 1852, Allen turned the organization over to James W. Barker, a merchant. Barker quickly expanded the organization. The following year, branches were formed in New Jersey, Maryland, Connecticut, Massachusetts, and Ohio. Ultimately, the Order of the Star-Spangled Banner became the groundswell that was the Know-Nothing Party and, soon, began to rack up political victories. By 1856, the party was confident it could get one of its candidates into the White House. But the passage of the Kansas-Nebraska Act in 1854 refocused national attention on the divisions that would lead to the Civil War and drained the political wind from the Know Nothings' sails. A series of incidents demonstrating the incompetence of states in which the Know Nothings had achieved positions of political leadership further undermined confidence in the party. But, ultimately, it was the question of slavery, which brought much deeper divisions to the American landscape, divisions that would only be settled by civil war, that destroyed the Know Nothings.

It must be said that while the Roman Catholic hierarchy struggled on, trying to defend itself against various manifestations of the nativist and anti-Catholic movements, it was also immersed in building the foundations of the Roman Catholic infrastructure. With the rise of the Second Empire, the French embraced Catholicism with fervor, and a kind of second honeymoon prevailed. Soon, France had a surplus of vocations to the priesthood, and it was to French soil that many of the early American bishops turned for manpower to build the American church. At the same time, onerous economic and political situations in Ireland meant that many Irish priests were eager to try their luck elsewhere, and American bishops regularly made recruitment trips to Irish seminaries.

One of the cornerstones for church development was Mt. Saint Mary's outside of Baltimore. Founded in 1808 by the Sulpicians, who specialize in training men for the priesthood, the seminary produced a generation of leaders in the early church. Among the early graduates were John Hughes, who became archbishop of New York; William Quarter, first bishop of Chicago; John McCloskey, a subsequent archbishop of New York; and Cardinal William Henry Elder, who became archbishop of Cincinnati, Ohio. Other graduates included William George McCloskey, president of the American College, Rome, and, later, bishop of Louisville; Francis S. Chatard, president of the American College, Rome, and, later, bishop of Vincennes;

Michael Augustine Corrigan, yet another archbishop of New York; Richard N. Whelan, first bishop of Wheeling; Francis X. Gartland, first bishop of Savannah; and Francis P. McFarland, third bishop of Hartford.

Religious orders also made huge contributions to building up the infrastructure of American Catholicism, particularly in the field of education. The Jesuits began establishing schools across the nation. The Christian Brothers, the Benedictines, the Salesians, and the Marianists also made strong contributions to Catholic education in America. The Sisters of Charity, Sisters of Loretto, Sisters of Mercy, and other nursing sisters made foundational contributions to American health care and continue to show strong associations with hospitals.

By the end of the nineteenth century, the American Catholic Church was well established, and most Americans had accepted the presence of Catholics in America. Some prejudice remains to this day, particularly in areas with low numbers of Roman Catholics, such as the southeastern sections of the United States. But Catholics, understanding the pain of persecution in their own past, have helped to integrate other new groups into the increasingly diverse landscape of the American religious experience. With the increase in Hispanic populations throughout America, the American Catholic Church promises to play an even larger role in the years ahead.

10

AMERICAN JUDAISM

Like Roman Catholic history in America, American Jewish history has been marked by waves of immigration corresponding to changes in countries across the Atlantic. The earliest Jewish immigration to the Americas came as a result of Spanish monarchs Ferdinand and Isabella's order to expel the Jews in 1492. Some estimate that as many as 120,000 to 150,000 Jews left Spain after the publication of the edict. Hoping to avoid the inquisitors of the Holy Inquisition, many of those who did flee found refuge in the Netherlands. The Flemish had close ties to Spain under Charles V, and many economic and mercantile connections between the two nations remained active. Because of this, Jewish immigration became linked to Dutch colonization. One group of Jewish settlers crossed the Atlantic to settle in Recife, Brazil, but that colony was quickly captured by the Portuguese. Fleeing the Portuguese, two dozen settlers sailed north to the Dutch colony of New Amsterdam in 1654, marking the beginning of Jewish history in the United States.

Those who had endured the expulsion from Spain, the Iberian Peninsula, or the Middle East, are often referred to as Sephardic Jews, and they are one of two groups commonly addressed in discussions of Judaism in America. The other group is known as the Ashkenazim, or Ashkenazic Jews. These Jews emigrated from Germany and were sometimes considered "German" rather than "Jewish" by the Sephardic Jews already established on the U.S. mainland.

The American story begins, by and large, with the Sephardic Jews. By the time of the American Revolution, over two thousand Jews lived in North America. They tended to settle in large urban areas that had substantial economic and mercantile development. They favored port cities, like

New York, but settled in area as diverse as Savannah, Georgia, Charleston, South Carolina, Philadelphia, Pennsylvania, and Newport, Rhode Island.

With the success of the American Revolution, a nation emerged in which religious freedom was not only tolerated but enshrined in governmental structure, and America became much more attractive to Jewish settlers. Anti-Semitism was still widespread, but, overall, the American Jewish population had an increased sense of security in the aftermath of the Revolutionary War.

For some Jews, life in American meant a certain level of accommodation to the American ways of life, and some began to think that not all of the Jewish customs and practices that had been brought over from Europe were necessary or pertinent to their new environment. In 1825, one progressive group of young Jews in Charleston became concerned with the many threats to Judaism. There was the threat of losing members to the missionary activity of many Christian denominations. The Unitarian movement appealed to some young Jewish intellectuals, with its attendant freedoms and the diminished role of organized religion. Some began to feel that if Judaism was to survive in the United States, it would have to do a better job of adjusting to the American scene, and that meant introducing certain modifications, or reforms. This group of Jews in Charleston suggested giving sermons in English, proposed abandoning the use of Spanish language in rituals, and argued for more decorum in religious practice. Eventually, they formed a society, the Reformed Society of Israelites for Promoting True Principles of Judaism According to Its Purity and Spirit. Many historians consider this movement as the first Reform congregation in America.

When the petitions of the Reformed Society of Israelites were rejected, the group decided to leave its previous congregation and establish its own. Ultimately, the new congregation did not succeed, and the members drifted back to the older congregation, but they did establish the need for reform in the American context. Significantly, if they were not successful themselves, their actions established a precedent for later movements that reflected many of the same elements. The question of reform would become a central issue for Jewish Americans over the course of the nineteenth century. Whether and to what degree to reform became the basis for important distinctions among Jewish people in America.

The face of American Judaism was about to change regardless of one's position on reform, however. For fifty years, from 1820 to 1870, waves of German immigration brought hundreds of thousands of Ashkenazim from Germany and central Europe. The earliest of these settlers, eager for religious community, joined existing Sephardic synagogues. But as their numbers increased, fueled by persecution, political unrest, and poverty in European nations, the Ashkenazim began to chafe at the cultural assumptions that came with Sephardic practice. They began establishing their own German-language synagogues and associations, and distinct streams of American practice developed.

At the same time, the concentration of Jews in Atlantic port cities began to break down. Jews, along with other Americans, began moving inland, to the frontier, and to the West. Accommodating quickly to diverse conditions, they began to establish business networks, developing banking and retail companies, relaying goods to hungry customers far from established retail centers.

In the first decades of the nineteenth century, many of the synagogues were managed by lay leadership. This is reflected in the confidence, agency, and active engagement of the Reformed Society of Israelites. But as the number of immigrants continued to increase, styles of leadership began to shift. The 1840s saw an increase in the number of synagogues headed by immigrant rabbis. These immigrant rabbis were a diverse group. Some were solidly conservative, eager to maintain as many of the practices of the Old Country as possible. Others were more progressive and embraced the ideal of German Jewish reform that had begun to emerge among American populations.

This reform, in part, reflected Jewish interaction with Protestant congregational models. Jews became familiar with many of the elements that regularly characterized Protestant churches and began to adapt them to their own congregations. Isaac Leeser (1806–1868) is considered by many to be the architect of American Jewish life. Based in Philadelphia, he became intrigued by Protestant educational approaches. He adapted Sunday schools, hospitals, and the religious press to the Jewish context. It was Leeser who founded the first Hebrew publication on American soil, the *Occident and American Jewish Advocate,* in 1843 and who also founded the first Jewish publication society. His interests in education expanded and deepened, and he began to address Jewish education at all ages. In addition to publishing textbooks for Jewish children, he established the first Jewish college, Maimonides, in Philadelphia, then went on to develop the nation's first rabbinical college.

The exceptionally gifted Leeser served not only as an educator but as a liturgist and translator. Leeser was a traditionalist hazan-minister. He reflected a tradition in which someone who was not ordained might effectively serve as a rabbi. In the interest of improving liturgy, Leeser translated both Sephardic and Ashkenazic prayer books. His translation of the Bible into English was used in Jewish synagogues for five decades. And his collected sermons fill ten volumes. Leeser's communal vision and eagerness to unify the diverse voices of American Judaism cast a long shadow.

Another giant in American Reform Judaism was Isaac Mayer Wise (1819–1900). Born in Steingrub, Bohemia, he studied at a rabbinical school in Jekinau, at the University of Prague, and at the University of Vienna. Coming to the United States in his late twenties, he assumed the leadership of an Orthodox synagogue in Albany, New York, in 1846. After divisive exchanges on the observation of the Sabbath, Wise left with a group of followers to establish a new congregation. In the same year, 1850, he was called to head up the Congregation Bene Jeshurun in Cincinnati, Ohio. Once settled, Wise turned to publication. He edited two publications, one in English, the *American Israelite,* and one in German, *Die Deborah*, and used them as platforms to broadcast his own ideas about the reform of American Judaism. He also wrote a prayer book, *Minhag America*, and promoted it as a liturgical basis for all American congregations.

Some of Wise's greatest contributions were organizational. In 1873, he became the founder of the Union of American Hebrew Congregations. He hoped the organization could unify both Reform and Orthodox congregations under one mantle. He also founded the Hebrew Union College in Cincinnati, hoping that both Orthodox and Reform congregations would make use of the college to train rabbis. As first president of the college, he continued his work toward unification.

His attempts at unification were not successful. In 1883, Conservative Jewish leaders pulled away from the college and established the Jewish Theological Seminary of America, which continues to serve as an important source of training for American Conservative Judaism. Wise began to realize that his work at unification would never meet with full success and, so, turned his own time and energy to becoming a spokesman for the Reform movement.

Gathering a group of rabbis in Pittsburgh, Pennsylvania, in 1883, Wise and his colleagues developed what is called the Pittsburgh Platform, which is recognized as the statement that clearly defines classical Reform Judaism. The rabbis argued for viewing Judaism as religion and not a nationality, for diminishing ethnic identification in Judaism, and for developing a more rational faith that could comfortably dialog with the discoveries of science.

Six years later, Wise would play a critical role in the organization of the Central Conference of American Rabbis. Holding an initial meeting in Detroit, Michigan, in July 1889, Wise recommended the formation of an association that could unify rabbis across the nation and provide a venue for them to offer one another support and encouragement.

Wise's organizational brilliance is clear. His decision to formulate a triadic structure, consisting of a congregational group, a seminary, and an organization of rabbis, was duplicated by both his rival factions, the Orthodox and the Conservative movements. Wise never allowed his success to slow him down, working up until his death in 1900 and leaving a legacy that spanned theoretical, practical, and organizational arenas.

Not everyone agreed with Wise's views, and the Pittsburgh Platform brought about clear divisions in American Judaism. The Orthodox resisted many of the reforms Wise endorsed. Rather than accommodate American culture and practices, they felt a better way to insure the survival of Jewish identity was to reinforce elements from the longstanding traditions of Judaism.

The numbers of the Orthodox increased dramatically in the last decades of the nineteenth century when pogroms, virulent anti-Jewish attacks, increased in Russia and the Austro-Hungarian Empire. As persecution on the other side of the Atlantic increased, so did the waves of immigrants that poured into the United States. One estimate holds that between 1870 and 1914, two million Jews immigrated to the United States.

In many ways, these waves of immigrants were different from earlier waves. Many were country folk, with less education and less urban sophistication, than some of the earlier immigrants. Most spoke Yiddish and were eager to form Yiddish-speaking communities in their new country. Once in America, they were largely working-class people, who, over several generations, would improve their standing through hard work and education.

Immigrants in these waves were not prepared to adopt the significant changes proposed by the Reform movement and, so, generally embraced the Orthodox movement. Living displaced lives, recovering from the threat of persecution, they sought familiarity and security in longstanding traditions, and their numbers soon swelled the Orthodox movement's adherents.

However, the relationship between established Ashkenazim and this later wave of Eastern European Jews was not an easy one. More established German Jews were proud of their adaptation to American ways of life, of their education and relative economic success. Some of them felt that the low levels of education and the lack of sophistication among the newest wave of immigrants would increase anti-Semitism. These divisions can be seen in New York City, where the Jewish community became divided. Even today, there remains a separation between Eastern European and German Jews in New York, and each has its own set of congregations, cultural institutions, and community practices.

Not all historians accept the idea of three distinct waves of Jewish immigration in America—the Sephardic wave, the German wave, and the Eastern European wave. Today's scholars have come to realize that historical patterns were far more complex. They have pointed out how frequently these groups actually overlap, rather than succeed, one another. Some Eastern European Jews came to the American colonies before the Revolutionary War. While many talk of a predominantly German wave of immigration in the mid-nineteenth century, the majority of those immigrants were actually Polish. To further complicate the historical project, not all Jewish groups are equally represented in scholarship and in published accounts, further distorting the lens through which we view the development of American Judaism.

The history of Judaism in America also confounds usual theories about immigration and accommodation to American culture. With most ethnic groups in the United States, distinct stages of assimilation can be tied to specific generations after immigration. Members of the first generation remain distinct outsiders. Their foreign customs and ways, their language preferences and accented English, and their values formed in the Old Country set them apart from mainstream American culture. The second generation is often eager to assimilate. Often the first generation of native English speakers, they are eager to be as American as possible and to distance themselves from their ethnic parents. The third generation often loses its ethnic identity entirely, as distinct values and cultural patterns are lost in the swirl of the larger American culture.

American Jews did not follow this pattern. There are parallels in the first and second generations with the typical pattern of ethnic assimilation. But the third generation broke the mold. Instead of disappearing into American culture, third-generation Jews began to "reassert" their Jewish identity, to celebrate the Jewish cultural experience and seek ways to sustain that identity.

Scholars attribute this difference to various sources. As Jews from different ethnic or national backgrounds intermarried, there emerged a nondistinct form of American Judaism. Jews adapted more quickly than many immigrant groups to the American educational system and took advantage of the opportunities that presented themselves. Accordingly, they soon rose to higher economic classes and experienced greater economic security and greater security in their own social standing. Finally, Jews were able to draw parallels between their own religious identity and practice and that of the dominant Protestant culture. After all, many of the reforms in Jewish practice had been based on exposure to Protestant religious life. Jews felt less shame about their own identity and less willing to get rid of patterns that seemed consistent with those of the larger population.

Another aspect distances American Jewish history from the history of other ethnic or religious groups. That has to do with how recently large waves of Jewish immigration occurred. While many ethnic groups, such as the Irish, experienced their greatest influx during the early or mid-nineteenth century, Jewish immigration did not reach its peak until after the turn of the twentieth century. The largest wave came between 1900 and 1924, when Eastern European Jews arrived in unprecedented numbers. Some estimate the total to be as high as 1.75 million.

This wave of immigration once again restructured Jewish community life in America. Many of the immigrants were concentrated in cities on the East Coast. They brought their own cultural flavor to Judaism, to its rituals and practices, and to Jewish political views. If only by sheer numbers alone, they raised the profile of Jews in America, as well as the level of achievement associated with the Jewish people.

World War I had a unifying effect on American Jews. Many members of the Jewish community still had family members in, or close ties to, Europe. They became increasingly concerned about the impact of fighting on their homelands. They also formed organizations to assist those affected by the war. This meant that Jews from very different backgrounds and social levels came together, collaborating in the effort to help war victims. Groups that would otherwise be focused on distinguishing themselves from one another now had a common cause and common goals. They raised millions of dollars for relief efforts and demonstrated an increased recognition of the potential impact political and international affairs could have on the international Jewish community.

But enemies abroad were not the only challenges they faced. The rapid increase in population between 1900 and 1924 did not come without cost. The early part of the twentieth century was also the period associated with the most virulent anti-Semitism in American history. Just as anti-Catholicism grew and flourished in the years when Catholic immigration was at its highest, a similar pattern emerged in response to high levels of Jewish immigration.

After the end of World War I, when the common enemy had been defeated, many Americans began to fabricate enemies at home, and Jews were often placed at the top of the list. The highest levels of anti-Semitism in America came between the two world wars. During that period, anti-Semitism was practiced openly and without apology. Jews were openly discriminated against in the job market. Private schools often rejected Jewish applicants, and Ivy

League colleges routinely rejected applicants with Jewish surnames. The economic hardships brought about by the Great Depression left people frightened and anxious about their own financial viability, and the Jewish population served as a perfect scapegoat for the projection of fear and anger.

Part of the rise of postwar anti-Semitism resulted from a document known as "The Protocols of the Learned Elders of Zion." The document itself was a hoax, created as disinformation by the secret police of the Russian czar. The creators of the document hoped that the outrage it provoked would direct the attention of the Russian people away from the czarist government and encourage them to blame Jews for Russia's problems. Even today, the document surfaces among anti-Semites, but its views no longer reflect the American mainstream and are increasingly associated with extremist groups.

The protocols themselves assert that an international Jewish conspiracy strives for global conquest, manipulating the economy, driving liberal causes, and transforming the curriculum in schools. In a sense, this could be considered the "original" conspiracy theory, and while long ago proven a hoax, the document continues to surface in neo-Nazi, patriot, or militia movements.

The protocols were brought to the United States by an expatriate Russian named Boris Brasol. Once here, the document came to the attention of Henry Ford, the founder of the Ford Motor Company. Ford was a vocal anti-Semite in the early part of the twentieth century. He came to believe that many of the world's problems originated with the Jewish people and launched a personal campaign utilizing his considerable economic power. A newspaper he owned, the *Dearborn Independent,* regularly ran articles on the role the Jews played in the Russian Revolution and World War I. The Jewish faith, it was suggested, would undermine the American Christian way of life. Many of these articles were published in an anthology titled *The International Jew: The World's Foremost Problem.* Ultimately, that volume was reproduced in over a dozen languages and is thought to have had significant influence in Germany as Hitler began his rise to power. Throughout the 1930s, Ford seemed unrepentant about his distrust and fear of the Jewish people. He funded business ventures in Nazi Germany and accepted an award from Hitler. Eventually, Ford retracted his views, and subsequent generations of his family did their best to transform such attitudes within the company he bequeathed to them. But in many ways, Ford's extremity reflects the extreme response of the American people to the sharp increase in the number of Jewish immigrants.

Anti-Semitism in America hit its highest levels in the period between the world wars. It was fueled, in part, by the impact of the Great Depression and the eagerness of the American public to find someone to shoulder the blame for their bleak economic conditions. The prevalence of anti-Semitism among the American public may have contributed to America's reluctance to get involved in World War II, long after reports of the Holocaust began to reach American shores. Like the adherents of many other traditions, American Jews had to negotiate a process of integration into American culture that was at times difficult and even dangerous. The cost of maintaining America's self-image as a white, Protestant nation was most often paid by those on the margins of the mainline religious traditions.

But a focus on the tragic dimension of American Jewish life in the twentieth century can cause us to lose sight of the positive dimensions of the American Jewish experience and the many contributions that Jews have made to American life and culture. American Jews made an inestimable contribution to the establishment and growth of American commerce, as immigrants often brought with them considerable skill in commerce, retail sales, or banking. Similarly, it is impossible to estimate the multiple contributions American Jews have made in terms of intellectual work. The value that Jews have traditionally placed on education and scholarship has resulted in generation after generation of Jewish scholars. One area in which Jewish contributions have been consistently underestimated is the development of media, and especially that most American of dream towns, Hollywood. In the early days of cinema and television, it was often Jewish investors or businessmen who pioneered the high-risk movie industry. Whether in the California film industry, in music, or on the Broadway stage in New York, American Jews have made a disproportionate contribution to American entertainment.

Today, the American Jewish landscape reflects four major movements and a number of much smaller groups. Conservative Judaism remains one of the largest of these groups. Estimated at 45 percent of the Jewish population, Conservatives consider Jewish law (*halakhah*) binding and emphasize the obligations one has in observing Jewish law: one is expected to observe all of the commandments, keep the Sabbath, and keep kosher. Conservatives see Jewish law as something that will naturally evolve as our ability to understand the law grows and strengthens. Therefore, they feel free to change some interpretations of Jewish law. They allow women to be ordained as rabbis, and their members are allowed to use motorized transportation to drive to services on the Sabbath.

Reform Judaism, whose origins were addressed earlier in this chapter, also makes up about 45 percent of the Jewish population. Rather than define themselves by assiduously maintaining Jewish law, Reform Jews seek to develop the moral autonomy of the individual believer. They encourage an intellectual engagement with the core of the belief and the cultivation of a well-thought-out, personal moral stance. They are considered the most politically liberal and most lenient in terms of religious practice. They have arguably absorbed more from Protestant denominations in terms of the way religious life is carried out and may seem the most familiar to non-Jewish individuals in terms of structure and organization. They are most likely associated with liberal social causes. Reform temples are likely to use less Hebrew in their worship services and are less likely to insist that members keep kosher.

Orthodox Judaism, which comprises less than 10 percent of the population, takes a much more conservative view of Jewish law. Orthodox Jews reject any idea of evolution in the understanding of the Torah, the first five books of the Jewish bible. They view the Torah as a divine gift from God to the Jewish people through Moses, and other Jewish groups can see their interpretation as somewhat rigid. The Orthodox maintain strict divisions between male and female roles in practice and liturgy. Women and men are often physically separated during services, and women are not ordained as rabbis. Orthodox Jews can be recognized by their more conservative forms of dress and their insistence on following specific rules with regard to hair and the color of clothing, and they are considered the most conservative of the larger Jewish groups in America.

One of the more extreme groups among the Orthodox is the Hasidic movement. Hasidic Judaism derives its name from the Hebrew term *Chasidut*, which mean "pious," and from the word *chesed*, which means "loving kindness." The movement originated in Eastern Europe in the eighteenth century and spread to many nations, including the United States. When Eastern European Jews experienced harsh persecution, many turned to the Talmud. The Hasidim, sometimes called the Ba'al Shem Tov, felt that Jewish believers had become too intellectualized and abstract and insisted on a recovery of deep spirituality and the joy that accompanies it. Initially resisted by many Jewish leaders, Hasidic Jews have earned a grudging respect over time.

Finally, the smallest of the major groups is called Reconstructionist Judaism. At less than 5 percent of the population, the group's numbers are small but its influence is disproportionately large given the scope of its members' intellectual contributions. They see Jewish life as continually evolving and are considered by many the most liberal of the major Jewish groups in America today. Reconstructionist Judaism does not champion the Jews as the chosen people or see Jewish law as ultimately binding.

The existence of these groups in the American Jewish landscape, as of the Sephardim and Ashkenazim before them, remind us of the diversity inherent in this faith. While those who are not Jewish tend to view Jewish thought, religious practice, or belief as monochromatic, the truth is that many differences can be found within Judaism.

The year 2004 marked the 350th anniversary of Judaism in America. It was in the summer of 1654 that the group of refugees expelled from Recife, Brazil, landed in New York, then called New Amsterdam. Recognizing the material goods that the group had lost on their expulsion from Brazil, the Dutch West India Company ordered Gov. Peter Stuyvesant to allow the Jewish settlers to remain in New Amsterdam, provided "the poor among them shall not become a burden to the company or to the community, but be supported by their own nation." Although that initial decision affected only two dozen Jews in New Amsterdam, it set the stage for three and a half centuries of Jewish life in North America.

Scholars like Jonathan Sarna used the 350th anniversary as an opportunity to celebrate the significant contributions that the Jewish community has made to American life, to teach the larger American public more about Jewish life and history, and to encourage new scholarship. A new generation of Jewish scholars promises to transform our understanding of Jewish life in America. This generation of scholars, in Sarna's view, highlights the diversity of the American Jewish experience rather than emphasizing the similarities between different groups. They explore the relationships Jews have with others in numerous different settings. This group also focuses its work not on the centuries of immigration and the immigrant experience but on the years between World War II and the 1960s. By focusing and framing Jewish experience after the Holocaust, this generation of scholars is free to examine the fundamental impact the Holocaust had on Jewish identity, the role of Jewish liberalism, and the political and religious divisions that have emerged since that time.[1]

The impact of the Holocaust, in which over six million Jews died at the hands of the Nazis, on contemporary Jewish identity cannot be understated. And the Jewish identity that emerges in the aftermath of the Holocaust and the establishment of Israel in 1947 looks very different from that portrayed by earlier generations of scholars.

Today's American Jewish communities face the ongoing challenge of not only mourning and commemorating this tremendous loss and honoring the dignity of those who died, but of not allowing their own identities to be eclipsed by the enormity of the event.

The integration of the Holocaust into Jewish American life and identity brings a new urgency to issues of anti-Semitism, religious freedom, relationship to tradition, and the meaning of being Jewish in contemporary society. It also demands recognition from other American religious traditions and a new set of relationships that must be negotiated as American Jews carve out their own unique place of belonging in American history and in contemporary American life. It further challenges our fundamental assumptions about the benevolence of our God and the limits of human destructiveness in our relationship to other religious traditions. As a result, the American religious landscape, as well as the American Jewish community, has been forever transformed.

NOTE

1. Jonathan D. Sarna, "The Chronicle Review—American Jewish History: A Chance to Reflect," *The Chronicle of Higher Education* (October 1, 2004), at http://chronicle.com/temp/reprint.php?id=xpjywqwy119zmje1ke5nswxrq2qonjk (accessed April 24, 2005).

11

ANGLICAN TO EPISCOPAL

Like so many religious traditions that make up American religious history, the Episcopal Church of America had its roots in the Anglican tradition, the Church of England. The Church of England came into being under the leadership of King Henry VIII of England. In the tumultuous climate of the sixteenth century, the Roman Catholic Church's dominion over European religion was shattered. Believers followed Reformers and rulers into new religious traditions in the aftermath of the Reformation. Much of Germany and several Scandinavian nations became Lutheran, Calvinism dominated the Netherlands, and England followed Henry VIII into the Church of England. Frustrated by his inability to produce an heir with his wife and his thwarted attempts to have his marriage annulled, the brilliant, articulate, and rebellious Henry VIII mandated an autonomous church for England. He established the king of England as the titular head, while maintaining many of the traditions associated with Roman Catholic practice. He also entrusted the education of his two youngest children, Edward and Elizabeth, to Protestant tutors.

When Edward assumed the throne for his brief rule, Thomas Cranmer, the archbishop of Canterbury, solidified Anglican doctrine and worship. He introduced the Forty-Two Articles as a confession of faith to the church and issued two editions of the book that guides worship in the Church of England, the Book of Common Prayer. He also established Anglican worship in English, not Latin. Later, when Edward's half-sister Elizabeth assumed the throne, she saw the church as a "middle way" between Roman Catholicism and Calvinistic Protestantism. Elizabeth's church would recognize the first four ecumenical councils, utilize the Book of Common Prayer as a guide to worship, combine Protestant and Catholic interpretations, and leave room for a wide range of views under the umbrella of the church. Cranmer's Forty-Two Articles were replaced with the Thirty-Nine Articles, and a book of homilies was issued. This revision of the Anglican vision came to be known as the Elizabethan Settlement, or the Reformation Settlement, and is viewed by many scholars as the real beginning of the Church of England.

The Anglican Church was among the earliest denominations to come to America. While Roman Catholicism dominated in the Spanish colonies of the Southwest and California, the Church of England came ashore with the earliest settlers to the colonies on the eastern seaboard. Anglican clergy were holding worship services in America in the sixteenth century. When Jamestown, Virginia, was settled in 1607, the Church of England came officially to American soil. In the colony of Virginia, the Anglican faith flourished in its early days, and, by the 1780s, over a hundred parishes had been established there.

Early parishes were substantially different from what we think of today when we use the word "parish." They consisted not of one church but of three or four. In addition, most parishes had a church farm attached, which was called a "glebe." The glebe could be farmed to provide food for the rector and his family, could be leased out for farming by someone else, or could provide land for the future construction of additional buildings or schools.

Anglican parishes were administered by what was known as a "vestry," composed of twelve laymen. The management of the churches by the vestry system centralized the decision-making power in the hands of a few, mostly wealthy, men. Strong ties were often forged between local families and landowners, and those participating developed a vested interest in the well-being of the church and its property. While efficient in some aspects, in terms of providing consistent local management for example, there were drawbacks to the vestry system. One is that they sometimes marginalized the clergy. Members of the vestry remained in leadership roles for years on end, while many of the clergy were hired for one-year contracts. But perhaps the greatest disadvantage was the associations many people made. Since the vestry was made up of primarily wealthy men, church government was conflated with the needs of the financial aristocracy in the area. With the rise of anti-English sentiment, in the days prior to the Revolutionary War, the church was associated with the English aristocracy in particular, which made its political situation more difficult.

By the middle of the eighteenth century, more and more diverse Protestants were settling in the area. When Virginia was an English colony, most settlers belonged to the Church of England, but that was quickly changing. Baptists and Presbyterians arrived, followed by the Methodists, and began to woo converts away from the Anglican Church. This, combined with increasing sentiment against the Anglican Church because of its affiliation with the English crown, weakened it. After the Revolutionary War, Presbyterians and Baptists urged the commonwealth to confiscate properties belonging to the Anglican Church. Its having once been the "official" religion of the area gave it an unfair advantage in terms of land and buildings, they argued. No one religion should be so favored. In 1802, the general assembly passed what came to be known as the Glebe Act.

Under the Glebe Act, any church built prior to 1777 could be seized by the county on the death or resignation of the parish's rector. The county was then free to sell the property and use the proceeds for the public's benefit. In an effort to retain its property, the Episcopal Church fought the Glebe Act, but the court of appeals that ultimately heard the challenge was evenly divided, and under Virginia law, a tie supported the earlier ruling. The Glebe Act was disastrous for the Anglican Church in Virginia. Out of some two hundred and fifty churches in the state, fewer than thirty-five are still Episcopal churches. Demoralized, their property seized and their churches plundered, the Episcopal Church in Virginia fell into dramatic decline.

The growth of the Anglican Church, however, was not limited to Virginia. As early as 1700, a hundred Anglican churches could be found in New England. The early eighteenth century marked a rich period of growth in the establishment of Anglican churches in Rhode Island, New Hampshire, Massachusetts, and Connecticut. Churches were also established in the middle colonies. King's College, which is now known as Columbia University, was chartered in 1754 with requirements for an Anglican president and chapel services. Churches were erected in New York—Staten Island and lower Broadway—as well. New York congregations served as foundations for further growth in New Jersey and the Hudson Valley. William Penn's "holy experiment" in Pennsylvania also attracted some Anglican settlers. The oldest Anglican church was Christ Church in Philadelphia, Pennsylvania, founded in 1695.

Another significant area of Anglican growth was the land around the Chesapeake Bay. Since Maryland had been an English colony, under an Anglican monarch, the Roman Catholic Church was forced to recognize and make way for the Church of England. By the 1760s, there were over forty parishes in Maryland. Development in those areas spilled over into North and South Carolina and, ultimately, Georgia as well.

Georgia is unique in the history of Anglicanism in America. Chartered by James Oglethorpe as an alternative to debtors prison for impoverished English, it was only nominally Anglican. Georgia had few Anglican pastors, and those who were there often ran into significant resistance, as seen in the experiences of John Wesley in Georgia, discussed in chapter 4. The Anglicans were dramatically outnumbered by those who practiced other faith traditions or none at all, and there was no established social infrastructure to support the development of churches.

Wesley and other missionaries came to America under the auspices of the Society for the Propagation of the Gospel in Foreign Parts (SPG). In the eighteenth century, the society recruited and sent out more than three hundred missionaries to the American colonies. The society targeted primarily English-speaking lands but also funded some evangelization among the Welsh, Dutch, Germans, and Native Americans. Thomas Jefferson once described the missionaries of the SPG as "Anglican Jesuits."[1] Many of the SPG missionaries were more successful than Wesley, who encountered considerable opposition to his theological interpretations and ministerial practices and returned to England in 1737.

The Great Awakening, associated with the impact of Wesley, Jonathan Edwards, and passionate fellow preacher George Whitefield, had relatively little impact on the Anglican Church. The staid Anglican churches objected to the emotionalism associated with religious revivals and saw them as yet another threat to membership. Accordingly, they rarely allowed preachers associated with revivals or camp meetings to preach to their congregations. Those Anglicans who did find the emotionality of the revivals appealing tended to leave the Anglican Church rather than transform it from within. Many of these members found themselves attracted to the new Methodist tradition or to the Baptists.

Those who remained in the Anglican Church faced a public relations crisis during the Revolutionary War. The use of the title "Church of England" placed them in political alliance with the English crown. Thus, it was in pre-Revolutionary America that the term "Episcopal" first came into usage. The title first used was "Protestant Episcopal," noted as early as 1780 in Maryland. By using the term, church members hoped to clarify that they were not Roman Catholic but that they retained an episcopal form of church government. In 1789, at the General Convention, the church adopted "A General Constitution of the Protestant Episcopal Church in the United States of America." But American Episcopalians continued to use the name Anglican, especially when they referred to their relationship to the Church of England.

Another problem arose after the American Revolution when the bishops of England would no longer ordain American candidates for the priesthood. Yet, the American church had no bishops who could perform ordinations. Ten Connecticut clergymen gathered to remedy the situation. They elected a former SPG missionary to be their first bishop, Samuel Seabury.

Seabury was eventually consecrated by three Scottish bishops since the English bishops refused to consecrate him, and after his return, he began ordaining Episcopal clergy for America in 1785. He also began organizing the Episcopal Church in America. The General Convention in the same year allowed the nascent church to develop an American Book of Common Prayer, address the consecration of future bishops, and write a constitution, as noted above. The Episcopal Church still utilizes the operational features developed in the General Convention in 1789. Clergy are organized into three groups—bishops, presbyters (also called priests), and deacons. Much of the organizational structure that came out of the early Episcopal Church was the work of William White, whom many consider the father of the Episcopal Church. White served for forty years as presiding bishop and authored many of the early pastoral letters from the House of Bishops.

Several men served as shepherds to the Episcopal Church in its growth in the early nineteenth century. One, John Henry Hobart, was the bishop of New York. Hobart was a strong believer in evangelization and the New York church expanded significantly under his leadership. Alexander Viets Griswold, bishop of the Eastern Diocese, and William Meade were also strongly evangelical and emphasized the growth of the church. But perhaps the most notable evangelical of the early leadership in the church was Jackson Kemper. Kemper participated in the Domestic and Foreign Missionary Society, which supervised western and northern expansion of the church.

Individual churches were encouraged to support missionary activity but few could afford to support work far from home. Growth was slow, and, so, the General Convention in 1821 formed the Domestic and Foreign Missionary Society. But participation in this group was voluntary, and it did not produce the hoped-for result. Thus, the Episcopal Church pursued a new model in 1835. First, the church decided that individual churches should not be responsible for the support of mission work; rather, this should be the responsibility of the entire church. Second, the General Convention decided to send missionary bishops into areas without any established church whatsoever.

Kemper was the first missionary sent to the West under the new plan. These early Episcopal bishops were given responsibility for huge amounts of territory, more than any one man could realistically oversee. Kemper's territory included what are now the states of Indiana, Wisconsin, Minnesota, Iowa, Missouri, Kansas, and Nebraska. As historian David Holmes reports,

> The missionary district of Joseph C. Talbot (consecrated in 1860 as missionary bishop of the Northwest) covered one million square miles; Talbot described himself as "the bishop of all outdoors." Salt Lake City was the seat of Bishop Daniel S. Tuttle (consecrated 1867), but he carried the title of "Bishop of Montana, with Jurisdiction in Idaho and Utah."[2]

Like the Roman Catholic bishops who helped to build up the Roman Catholic infrastructure in the American West and Southwest, these missionary bishops had their work cut out for them. They were expected to model themselves after the New Testament apostles and spend their time traveling, preaching, exhorting, organizing congregations, supporting the establishment of new churches, and expanding existing churches. They were also expected to do so with very little financial support and with few fellow workers in the vineyards of the Lord.

But if Episcopalian missionary bishops were short on financial support and fellow clergy, other factors worked in their favor. Their resistance to the highly emotionalized forms of worship that blossomed after the Great Awakening made them appealing to those who preferred a more sedate approach to worship. Their willingness to allow the consumption of alcohol and dancing meant that those frightened off by Baptist restrictions might make a home with them. The elements they shared with Roman Catholicism—including the episcopal structure and emphasis on the sacraments—meant Catholics felt relatively at home with the Episcopalians.

Upon entering an area, the missionary might look for those with nominal or past association with the church. Then, they would encourage the formation of an "association." Associations oversaw the acquisition of land, the construction of church buildings, and the establishment of regular worship in rural areas. Periodic visits by the bishop could be used to spur membership and provide a social diversion in towns lacking many social amenities.

The Episcopal Church also undertook missions to Native American populations. The SPG underwrote missionary work among the Iroquois, with particular attention to the Mohawk. Bishop Hobart of New York established a mission to the Oneidas, and James L. Breck focused energy on the Chippewa in Minnesota.

Minnesota's bishop Henry Whipple played an important part in disseminating information about the ill treatment of Native Americans in the nineteenth century. Following the massacre of Gen. George Armstrong Custer's troops, Whipple headed up a government commission that investigated the event. He also lent his name to a volume that documented the disastrous policies and the suffering of the Native Americans, Helen Hunt Jackson's *A Century of Dishonor* (1881).

The Episcopal Church also undertook considerable missionary activity in South Dakota. William Hobart Hare, the grandson of Bishop Hobart of New York, was considered the "Apostle to the Sioux." He brought over seven thousand Native Americans into the church, and, by the time of his death, it is estimated that membership in the region included as many as twenty thousand Native Americans.

The last great missionary effort directed toward Native Americans was in Alaska at the turn of the twentieth century. Peter Trimble Rowe, first bishop of Alaska, covered the vast territory and established schools, missions, churches, and hospitals. He was assisted by Hudson Stuck, his archdeacon, who also weathered difficult travel, extreme temperatures, and great distances to further the work of the Alaska mission.

While seeking to expand its membership through missionary bishops and active missionary work with Native Americans, the Episcopal Church faced other threats to its membership. One of the best known of these was the Oxford movement, begun in England in 1833 by three Anglican priests. Edward Bouverie Pusey (1800–1882) was a religious scholar and translator of St. Augustine's *Confessions*. John Keble (1792–1866) was a priest, poet, and church reformer. John Henry Newman (1801–1890) was a philosopher, educator, and leader of the Tractarian movement, who ultimately converted to Roman Catholicism. The Tractarian movement gets its name from a collection of essays entitled *The Tracts for the Times*. The movement recommended that three teachings be considered essential for Christian belief.

The first of these was the apostolic succession, the idea that the ability to ordain is garnered from the unbroken line of bishops going back to the earliest days of the church. This is a belief shared by the Roman Catholic, Eastern Orthodox, and Anglican churches. Only clergy thus ordained hold full power in God's eyes. Second, the Tractarians emphasized the regeneration that accompanied baptism. Baptism provides a critical form of spiritual rebirth. Third, the movement emphasized the Real Presence in the Eucharist. Communion is not simply a symbolic meal, as believed in some other traditions, but Christ's body and blood are in some way truly present in the Eucharist.

Because these beliefs were associated more with what is sometimes termed "high" church (involving forms of worship that emphasize the use of sacraments, candles, and ritual that stands in continuity with Catholic tradition), they came to be known as "ritualism." Because they emphasized the connections between the Anglican Church and the Roman Catholic Church, Anglicanism was sometimes referred to as "Anglo-Catholicism."

The movement encouraged believers to stress the continuity with older practices of the faith, prior to the establishment of the Church of England, and, so, many of the architectural and other features of Roman Catholic churches came to be found in Anglican churches, including stained-glass windows, altar styles, and altar ornaments. Similarly, many other Catholic traditions were emphasized in Anglican practice. These included the Eucharist, saint days, confession, and prayers for the dead. Anglo-Catholicism also restored the use of religious orders. So, today, we will see Benedictines who are either Roman Catholic or Anglican, for example.

Anglo-Catholicism made its presence known in the United States in the 1840s. Beginning in Wisconsin, it soon found champions in New York and Massachusetts. Soon, Anglican churches were distinguishing themselves from one another in their manner of worship and the extent to which they had adopted some of the high-church elements associated with Anglo-Catholicism. Other Anglican churches emphasized the Protestant aspects of their own history and resisted the integration of Catholic elements into church practice and belief. Throughout the 1860s and 1870s, the role of Anglo-Catholicism in the American Episcopal Church was hotly debated.

Nor were the issues related to Anglo-Catholicism settled in those decades. For subsequent decades, the debates polarized the American Episcopal Church. Those who saw themselves as more inclined to Protestant beliefs and Evangelicalism resented and resisted practices that seemed, to them, Roman Catholic. They emphasized instead that the Episcopal Church was seen as another Protestant denomination in what was primarily a Protestant nation. Anglo-Catholicism challenged the core of such beliefs, provoking a significant revision of Episcopalian identity.

But the church was able to remain cohesive and did not simply drive those with dissenting beliefs out of the congregation, as might have been done in earlier periods. It retained its unique position between the Protestant and Roman Catholic streams and increased its ability to attract new members from those whose previous practice was Roman Catholic or Eastern Orthodox. It also expanded the riches from which Anglican liturgy could draw, with greater emphasis on "smells and bells," on the tactile and visual elements of worship, vestments, and church architecture.

If the Tractarian movement and its ritualism emphasized the Episcopal Church's shared spiritual heritage with the Roman Catholic Church, the Episcopal approach to education also shared many elements with the Roman Catholics. Perhaps no church other than the Roman Catholic demonstrated a greater commitment to the development of primary and secondary education on American soil. Even the earliest Anglican churches usually had schools attached, even if only in the form of regular lessons from the parson. By the early nineteenth century, numerous Episcopal boarding schools had been established. Mimicking the exclusive boarding schools of the upper classes in England, the Episcopal boarding schools targeted the children of the upper and upper-middle classes.

In the early days, the schools were primarily concerned with the formation of the students, almost always boys, as practicing Christians. It was the school's job to produce young men with proper manners, a sense of what was socially appropriate, a certain level of discipline, and a clear moral stance. As the Episcopal boarding schools gained in popularity and status, many of them became breeding grounds for candidates for the Ivy League schools. One of the most prestigious, Groton, produced two presidents, a presidential candidate, several tycoons, and a secretary of state. By the 1930s, most of the schools had established curricula designed to prepare students for college. Episcopal boarding schools for girls developed later and were usually headed up by a woman known as the headmistress. The women in leadership positions, although excluded from ordination, strove to achieve a certain kind of spiritual formation in their charges, encouraging poise and self-confidence and a commitment to social awareness.

The Episcopal Church's commitment to education has never really played out in the world of higher education. As a denomination, it ranks among the last in terms of supporting and developing church-related colleges. There are notable exceptions, however, that prove the rule. The Episcopal College of William and Mary was chartered in 1693. It opened in Williamsburg, Virginia, in 1697. Columbia University in New York was originally founded as King's College by the Episcopalians in 1754. Similarly, the University of Pennsylvania began as the College of Philadelphia with strong Episcopal support in 1755. St. John's College, which now has campuses in Annapolis, Maryland, and Santa Fe, New Mexico, began as an Episcopal College.[3] In the first half of the nineteenth century, the Episcopalians chartered or opened some forty-odd colleges, mostly in the Northeast.

Those preparing for ordination in the Episcopal Church usually attended one of the Episcopal churches that supported a faculty in theology, such as the College of William and Mary. Under the Anglican Church, it was necessary for those seeking ordination to travel to England to complete their studies and sit for examinations. After the Revolutionary War, in the period of flux when the English began to refuse to ordain American candidates, many of those preparing worked privately with a rector, studying and assisting in the day-to-day management of the parish until they were deemed ready for the full responsibilities of the deaconate and priesthood.

It was only at the General Convention in 1817 that the church recognized the need for a theological seminary for the Episcopal Church. They founded the General Theological Seminary in New York. A series of other seminaries developed in its wake, as local churches demanded seminaries that were closer to home and theological orientations that better matched the local perspective in terms of liberalism or conservatism, ritualism or Evangelicalism. In the Episcopal tradition, bishops determine where their candidates for ordination should receive their seminary training. Given the possibility of consistent support from specific bishops, seminaries have developed across the country in such diverse areas as Tennessee, Connecticut, Minnesota, Illinois, Ohio, Pennsylvania, Texas, and California.

The early twentieth century brought significant organizational change to the Episcopal Church. In 1919, the church decided to develop a National Council to work for the goals of the denomination between meetings of the General Council. The National Council was made up of twenty-four elected bishops, priests, and lay people. The 1919 General Convention also called for a new wave of effort in fund-raising and pledged to do a better job of identifying and providing for the financial needs of member churches. Many of the patterns adopted in the reorganization were based on models observed in business, as the church sought to improve efficiency in its operations and increase its revenue stream and accountability.

The Episcopalians did not prove themselves to be socially progressive, but neither were they among the most conservative Christians around. Congress gave women the right to vote in 1919, and Episcopalian women sought greater participation in the church. The same General Convention noted above, however, in 1919, voted down women's right to vote in the church assemblies and voted against their being represented on the Board of Missions.

Like the Roman Catholic Church, the Episcopal Church had excluded women from the deaconate and the priesthood. Women, however, were encouraged to participate in "appropriate" activities, such as volunteer work, sewing circles, and Sunday school. When the popularity of the Oxford movement spread, it brought with it a push for women's "sisterhoods." Not all members of the church supported the idea. Many thought it was too much like the women's orders in the Roman Catholic tradition. Instead, at least one of the sisterhoods, the Sisterhood of the Holy Communion, was patterned after a German Lutheran community. Other sisterhoods deliberately patterned themselves after Roman Catholic women's orders and incorporated daily prayer, habits, communal life, and the traditional vows of poverty, chastity, and obedience.

Through participation in the sisterhoods, Episcopal women were able to contribute to many of the institutions that the church supported, including orphanages, schools, and hospitals. But life within the sisterhoods appealed to few women, and the church decided it needed to redefine the means by which women could contribute to the church. In 1889, the General Convention authorized women to take the office of deaconess. Candidates must be single or widowed, they determined, and must complete two years of training for the deaconate. They would receive salaries and would not be required to live in community. Many of the deacons committed themselves to education, health care, or missionary work.

Episcopal deaconesses, however, did not hold the same position as male deacons. Male deacons were ordained by the bishops. Deaconesses had a true vocation, they had received a "call" from God, but could not celebrate the Eucharist, preach, or lead worship services. And, as noted above, deaconesses could not marry. They were expected to resign from the position should they choose to marry.

The deaconesses, however, laid important groundwork for the Episcopal Church's later decision to ordain women. This is one of the major distinctions between Episcopal and Roman Catholic or Eastern Orthodox practice. By the early 1970s, the Episcopal Church began to rethink the role of women in the priesthood, and by the mid 1970s, a majority of bishops actually favored women's ordination. In the summer of 1974, three Episcopal bishops ordained eleven women to the priesthood. The governing bodies of the church had never approved such a move, and the three bishops in question were not active—one had previously resigned and two were retired—so they could not be reprimanded through the standard channels. An emergency session of the House of Bishops was called to declare the ordinations invalid formally.

Two years later, in 1976, the General Convention approved the ordination of women to the priesthood, although a clause in the ruling allowed those bishops who could not ordain them in clear conscience to decline. The ordination of women is not fully accepted even today, but, slowly, the number of ordained women has grown in the Episcopal Church, and by the 1990s, over a thousand women had been ordained in the American Episcopal Church. In

1988, the Diocese of Massachusetts presented Barbara C. Harris as a suffragan bishop. A storm of controversy followed, but in February 1989, she was consecrated as the first female bishop in a church with an episcopal structure.

The Episcopal Church remains divided on the question of women's ordination, and many of the more conservative congregations still resist it, including many of those who identify most strongly with the Anglo-Catholic tradition and emphasize ties between the Roman Catholic and Episcopal traditions. But more and more Episcopalians are accepting women in the priesthood and their presence in roles of authority in parish life.

From its solid presence in American colonial life, through the tumult and reorganization brought by the Revolutionary War, the Episcopal Church continues to contribute to American religion. Its missionary activity, commitment to education, and extraordinary impact on generations of American leadership all emphasize its solid position in mainline denominations, regardless of the relative number of its members. The shadow cast by King Henry VIII lingers in a church that retains many ties to its Roman Catholic heritage but carves out a unique spirituality and religious presence in the ever-shifting dynamics of the American religious landscape.

NOTES

1. Cited in David L. Holmes, *A Brief History of the Episcopal Church* (Harrisburg, PA: Trinity Press International, 1993), 45.
2. Holmes, *Brief History*, 65.
3. See discussion of same in Holmes, *Brief History*, 139.

12

LUTHERANS, GERMANS,
AND SCANDINAVIANS

To understand the growth and development of the Lutheran Church in America, one must begin with the world of Europe in the sixteenth century, delving into the history of those European nations that embraced the teachings of Martin Luther in the aftermath of the Reformation.

Martin Luther (1483–1546) was a critical figure in the tumultuous events of the sixteenth century. Many consider him the key figure in spurring on the revolution in religion known as the Reformation. Luther nailed his Ninety-Five Theses to the door of the Wittenberg Castle church door on October 31, 1517. Martin Luther, who was an Augustinian monk, objected to Roman Catholic practices that were widely accepted in his day. In the theses, he particularly objected to what was called the sale of indulgences. Indulgences were a means whereby one could, in effect, "purchase" forgiveness for sins by making a monetary donation. Specific indulgences were issued to raise money for papal projects or when church-related expenses demanded new sources of revenue. Luther declared the practice corrupt and emphasized that God's forgiveness could only be found through one's personal relationship with God. No amount of good works or financial payment could be substituted for personal devotion, piety, and trust in the grace of God.

Within three years of nailing his Ninety-Five Theses to the church door, Luther had clearly developed his own ideas about justification and established his own perspective on how salvation was achieved. Luther was not opposed to good works. Rather, he thought it critical that one see good works as secondary. When one loved and believed in God, one would naturally be inclined toward good works, but that sprang from the depths of

133

one's personal relationship with God. The believer stands before his or her beloved God and basks in the light of God's grace. Only after the love of God and the acceptance of God, through the freedom found in that relationship, can one proceed to works. One must resist the temptation to allow works to enslave the believer as a substitute for a radical reliance on grace. The relationship to God, through grace, becomes the compass point for the Lutheran believer.

This is also connected to the Lutheran views on sin. Following Augustine, Original Sin is acknowledged. But Luther goes further. In light of Original Sin, the acts of anyone who is not justified before God cannot be fully pleasing to God, even if performed with good intention or for the benefit of others. Justification comes when God grants the human being the righteousness of Christ. That can only come through faith and the belief that Christ has reconciled one to God. Good works spring out of such justified faith, but works do not in themselves secure salvation. That has already come through justification. Rather, good works are simply a response to the fulfillment found in the relationship with God and the promise to love and serve God that flows out of justification.

Given that Luther was educated and trained in the Augustinian order, his theology retained many elements of Augustinian thought. In fact, in spite of his towering reputation as a reformer, there is relatively little variance in his thought from orthodox Roman Catholic positions when compared to other Protestant traditions. Lutheranism is even considered by some to be "orthodox Protestantism"; in agreement with the Roman Catholic and Greek Orthodox churches, it endorses the central authority of scripture and the three oldest creeds, the Apostles' Creed, the Nicene Creek, and the Athanasian Creed.

These creeds are combined with six other statements of faith, or "confessions," to become what is known as the Book of Concord. This central text of Lutheran doctrine was published in 1580 at the command of Elector Augustus of Saxony. The other six statements of faith include the Augsberg Confession (1530), the Apology of the Augsberg Confession (1531), Luther's Large Catechism (1529), Luther's Catechism for Children (1529), the Articles of Smalkald (1537), and the Form of Concord (1577).

The Augsberg Confession, which was presented at diet, is considered core to the accepted creed of the Lutheran Church. It was drafted not by Luther himself but by his friend and follower Philipp Melanchthon (1497–1560), a professor at Wittenberg. As John Fletcher did for John Wesley, Melanchthon gave practical shape and depth to the substantial theology of Luther.

Lutheran faith could be characterized as, first of all, biblical, which flows from the endorsement of the central authority of scripture. It is also confessional. The confessional documents that make up the Book of Concord, noted above, are derived from scripture but guide the believer in the application of scripture to the challenges of daily life. Finally, the Lutheran tradition is also liturgical and sacramental, with an emphasis on liturgical celebration of worship that more resembles Roman Catholic, Episcopal, or Orthodox liturgy than the austere worship services of some Protestant denominations. Also, like the Roman Catholics, the Lutherans practice closed communion. Only those who have expressed their commitment to the Lutheran confession are permitted to take communion in Lutheran liturgy.

Luther's Ninety-Five Theses and subsequent writings set off a series of virulent reforms throughout Europe. His work spread rapidly and had a great influence on other reformers, including John Calvin, as discussed in chapter 2. But the tradition he personally founded, which came to be known at Lutheranism, first took root in his own native Germany. After writing his Ninety-Five Theses, Luther translated the New Testament into German. That, along with his other works, quickly became available through the auspices of the printing press, which enabled the dissemination of his thought widely in a relatively short time. Soon, thousands of Germans were focusing their attention on the role of God's grace in their lives, falling away from Roman Catholic interpretations and declaring themselves Lutherans.

The formal structure of the belief system was first established with the Augsberg Confession in 1530, which clearly delineated differences between Lutheran and Roman Catholic positions. Northern Germany came into the Lutheran flock when Lutheran state churches were established by alliances between reigning princes. Soon after, Lutheranism quickly spread to Scandinavia.

From the fourteenth century, the Scandinavian nations, Sweden, Norway, and Denmark, were united under the rule of the king of Denmark. Danish king Frederick I decided to adopt Lutheranism in 1526 and, by 1529, had proclaimed Lutheranism the only true religion in the lands under his rule. The Lutheran Church in Denmark was organized somewhat similarly to the Church of England, in that the king reigned at the head of both church and state, with bishops below him in the hierarchy. Subsequently, the state church seized the dioceses of the Catholic Church and established Lutheran bishops in their place. Hostility toward the Catholic faith grew, and by 1546, Catholics were denied basic civil rights and priests were being driven out of Denmark. The practice of Lutheranism continued to spread, and by the 1550s, Lutheranism was forcibly imposed on Iceland.

Norway followed Denmark into the Lutheran faith under Frederick I. Sweden, however, rejected Danish rule in 1521. Gustavus Vasa, who led the cause to liberate Sweden from Danish rule, was declared king and seemed predisposed to accept Lutheranism as an alternative to the Roman Catholic tradition. But the Swedish transition to Lutheranism was not to be so smooth. Under a subsequent king, fighting broke out between Lutherans and Calvinists. That was followed by the rule of two Catholic kings, John II (1568–1592) and Sigismund (1592–1604). By the 1680s, the pendulum had swung back to Lutheranism, and Swedish law required all citizens to participate in the state church.

Some of the earliest European settlers in America were Lutheran. According to some records, the first Lutheran worship service in America was held by Rasmus Jensen by the Hudson Bay in 1619. As early as the 1620s, Lutherans had emigrated to America and established small towns and settlements in the northeastern United States. Lutheran communities developed in New York, New Jersey, and along the Hudson River valley. One group of Swedish Lutherans arrived in America in 1637. By 1638, they had constructed a Lutheran church in Wilmington, Delaware. In 1664, after New Amsterdam, now known as New York, was captured by the English, Lutherans were free to practice their faith there.

German Lutherans arrived in Pennsylvania in 1693 and promptly established Germantown, an area that has since been absorbed by the city of Philadelphia. Subsequent waves of German immigrants would leave their homelands in Alsace and the Palatinate to establish themselves along the Hudson River valley. Communities of Lutherans developed up and down the Atlantic seaboard, in New Jersey, Virginia, and the Carolinas. One group, from Salzburg, even founded a community in Georgia in 1734. By the middle of the eighteenth century, some thirty thousand German Lutherans considered eastern Pennsylvania their home.

As the Lutheran community in and around Philadelphia continued to grow in the 1740s, it became clear that American Lutherans would need greater ecclesial organization. Rev. Henry Melchior Muhlenberg (1711–1789) had been educated in Halle, a center of German pietism. He was sent from Halle to provide instruction and guidance to German Lutherans living in Pennsylvania. After his arrival in America, he began to organize the Synod of Pennsylvania.

Muhlenberg's son, Rev. Frederick Muhlenberg, would organize the second American synod in 1773 in New York. Soon, theological and political differences emerged between the two groups. New York Lutherans began to make changes to the liturgy and catechism, changes that the Pennsylvania Lutherans resisted. One of the most controversial of these changes was the introduction of the English language into worship services. Divisiveness over this and other issues began to split up congregations. Some Lutherans recognized the possibility of losing any sense of unity between various branches and, so, proposed a union that all Lutheran synods could join. The General Synod of Lutheran Churches was organized in 1820. The unification proved only temporary, however. The Pennsylvania Synod later withdrew from the General Synod, only to rejoin it again in 1853.

Like Muhlenberg's son, Samuel Simon Schmucker (1799–1873) was part of the second generation of Lutherans in America. Schmucker attended and graduated from Princeton Seminary, run by the Presbyterians. Perhaps because of his education in a Presbyterian seminary, Schmucker became convinced that American Lutherans should balance out their European heritage with characteristics adopted from other Protestant groups in the United States.

Schmucker became a central figure at the Gettysburg Lutheran seminary. He saw religious indifference and rationalism as looming threats to the practice of Lutheranism in America. A strict adherence to the Augsburg Confession and Luther's Small Catechism could preserve the faith, however. But he also favored the incorporation of practices not traditionally associated with Lutheran practice in America. Revivalism was one, which could bring new energy into worship. Schmucker authored a book entitled *A Fraternal Appeal to the American Churches* in 1838 and supported the burgeoning, interdenominational Sunday school movement. He even became a founder of the American Interdenominational Evangelical Alliance in 1846. But when's Schmucker's idea of progressive Lutheranism led him to suggest modifying the Augsburg Confession, he began to lose the support of many more-traditional Lutherans. In 1855, modification of the confession was proposed anonymously, and divisions between the more Europeanized and more Americanized Lutherans were inflamed.

Other trends were disturbing to more traditional Lutherans as well. Some of the differences, including those that surrounded the use of the English language, were generational. First-generation immigrants were often most comfortable with worship services performed in the same manner and language as those in their homeland. They believed it best to recruit clergy who had been trained in Europe and to continue many of the faith practices that had sustained them prior to their immigration. Second- and third-generation Lutherans often did not speak the language of their parents or grandparents and were impatient with such deference, believing the church should do a better job of adapting to its new home. They began to demand theological training, hymnals, and catechisms in English, further fueling the tensions between traditionalists and progressives.

The views of progressives like Schmucker held a prominent place until the middle of the nineteenth century. After that time, the demographic makeup of Lutherans in America was changed by dramatic increases in the number of immigrants.

Some of the growing evangelical influences in the Lutheran Church began on the other side of the Atlantic. Disturbed that as a member of a Reformed group, he could not take communion with his Lutheran wife, King Frederick William III of Prussia had combined Lutheran and Reformed traditions into a single state church. He named it the Evangelical Church of the Prussian Union. While theologians like Friedrich Schleiermacher argued for the validity of such a union, some Lutherans rejected the joining of their church in this ecumenical fashion and, feeling the sting of religious persecution, became determined to emigrate in search of greater religious freedom. They settled in Missouri and became the seminal members of what would eventually become the Lutheran Church, Missouri Synod (LCMS).

The Missouri Synod was founded by Rev. Carl Ferdinand Wilhelm Walther (1811–1887). Walther, a native of Saxony schooled in the Old Country, immigrated to America in 1838. He came to be called by his opponents "the Lutheran pope of the West." One group of Saxon immigrants, settling in Perry County, Missouri, just south of St. Louis, joined with Walther in organizing numerous churches into a synod. Walther was inexhaustible in his efforts for Lutheranism. He started a publishing house, began a newspaper, initiated a Lutheran theological journal, and dedicated his energy to bringing together divergent synods.

Walther became president of the German Evangelical Lutheran Synod of Missouri, which later became the LCMS. In addition to forming the synod, he helped fellow believers recognize the growing need for theological training in their area and in their particular theological perspective. Ultimately, LCMS established two seminaries, Concordia Seminary in St. Louis and Concordia Theological Seminary in Ft. Wayne, Indiana. Support for Walther's traditional views grew, in part, out of the traditional perspectives of other recent immigrants, who rejected adaptations to the American environment made by other Lutheran synods, including adopting Methodist preaching styles that minimized the role of confessional documents such as the Augsburg Confession.

Walther supported the perspective held by Charles Porterfield Krauth (1823–1883). Krauth, in his book *The Conservative Reformation and Its Theology*, argued for the importance of Old Word teachings in Lutheran practice in the New World. Krauth argued for a profound respect for and adherence to the Augsburg Confession, which he considered the "germ of our being" for Lutherans. Walther followed Krauth's devotion to the confessional documents and required his ministers to state that they saw no contradiction between the confessional documents and scripture.

By the early 1840s, another Lutheran synod had formed in Buffalo, New York. Leaders of the Missouri and Buffalo synods initially hoped to merge their two groups, but differences in doctrinal interpretation soon blocked that possibility. Nor did the Missouri Synod remain stable in its own right. Some of its members began to question its theological positions, particularly its position on congregationalism. Unable to resolve these differences, they separated and formed the Iowa Synod in 1854.

More challenges emerged in the years surrounding the Civil War. Prior to the war, the General Synod represented two-thirds of the Lutheran population in the United States. But in 1863, five southern synods withdrew to organize the General Synod of the Confederate States. After the war, these synods elected not to rejoin the General Synod but reformed their existing organization and renamed it the United Synod in the South. Other fractures emerged along the dividing lines between liberal and conservative. Thirteen synods withdrew from the General Synod to form the General Council. Yet another group of synods organized in 1872. The fourth synodical organization, the Synodical Conference, grew strong in Missouri and the West. Each of these synodical groups represents itself as the "true" source of the Lutheran tradition in America. But the Lutheran landscape is far from uniform or cohesive and remains somewhat fragmented and fractured. American Lutherans remain a divided lot. Some divisions stretch across nationalistic lines, with Germans, Swedes, Norwegians, Danes, and others represented within the elastic Lutheran structure. Other divisions, as noted above, follow more Americanized "revivalist" or European "confessional" lines. As other Protestant traditions began to split between evangelicals, who pursued a modern Americanized faith, and fundamentalists, who resisted new interpretations of doctrine or dogma, the Lutherans, too, experienced unrest along those lines.

Prevailing interpretations were also challenged as the number of Lutherans continued to increase in the second half of the nineteenth century. As immigration from Scandinavia and Germany increased, the number of practicing Lutherans also increased. In the years between 1840 and 1875, a total of fifty-eight new synods were organized. By the latter part of the century, the elements were in place for the development of specific churches, such as the American Lutheran Church and the Lutheran Church in America.

The last four decades of the nineteenth century saw a dramatic upsurge in immigration from the Scandinavian nations, Norway, Sweden, and Denmark. Events in the late 1860s dramatically increased the number of immigrants from Scandinavian countries. In the middle of the nineteenth century, there were few established shipping companies that plied the route between Europe and America. By the 1880s, over twenty different companies were competing for passengers on trans-Atlantic crossings. This led to significant competition between the companies, and in an effort to build their sales, some companies turned to the relatively untapped market of the Scandinavian nations. As early as the 1860s, shipping companies actively sought out Scandinavians for emigration.

In addition, the emigration of one member of a family often led to the subsequent emigration of other family members. Once established in America, Scandinavian immigrants were often able to afford to send tickets to family members who remained behind. Communities grew along family lines, as close-knit immigrant families grew one by one.

Scandinavians adapted well to the American landscape. They were used to a hard life, given the short growing season and harsh winters of their native lands. They brought good skills with them, including experience in farming and logging. Using forestry skills to clear the land, they turned to farming, inspired by the amount of land and its availability in the broad expanses of the Midwest, after leaving nations that had only small areas of land suitable for farming. In the last two decades of the nineteenth century, increasing numbers of young adults immigrated and settled in Midwestern cities. The impact of these waves of immigration was substantial. In 1850, in Wisconsin, for example, less than one-third of the population was born in another country. Of that third, 34 percent was German, and only 8 percent of the population claimed Scandinavian heritage. By 1890, three-quarters of the population had been born outside of the United States. Germans had grown to over one-third of the total population of the state, and Scandinavians to over 10 percent.

The impact of German and Scandinavian Lutheran immigration was heaviest in the Midwest, made up of the states of Illinois, Wisconsin, Minnesota, Iowa, Nebraska, North Dakota, and South Dakota. In Wisconsin, in the period between 1850 and 1900, the heaviest immigration was Norwegian. Most were poor farmers or farmhands, eager to own land and to settle in or near communities with other Norwegian families. After arriving and securing land to work, the immigrants would grow high-value crops and sink their incomes back into payments for the land or the machinery to work that land. They adapted well to American farming techniques and recognized that the larger amounts of land under cultivation would require the use of more machinery and other adaptations of their traditional farming techniques. Cooperative farming or business ventures were often made with other Norwegian immigrants on the basis of trust, usually with an individual one knew well or whose family one knew and trusted.

Germans also immigrated to the Midwest in large numbers. German immigrants tended to be more diverse than Scandinavian immigrants. Approximately one-third were Catholic, and some were Jewish, but the overwhelming majority was Lutheran. They came from a wide variety of socioeconomic levels in Germany and pursued both urban and rural lifestyles in the United States. German immigration was so steady in the Midwest that Milwaukee, Wisconsin, came to be known as the "German Athens," and by 1850, 40 percent of its population was originally from Germany. German-language newspapers, schools, and social clubs flourished.

German and Scandinavian immigrants had a number of things in common. They had both made the transition from Old World to the New. They had strong community ties grounded in and sustained by language and religious belief, with the majority being Lutheran. Both groups tended toward the traditional and resisted being too quickly acculturated into the world of the "Yankee." While more of the German immigrants settled in cities, large numbers of both Germans and Scandinavians pursued farming in the rich, fertile soil of the Midwest.

For the most part, they also shared the indelible imprint of the Lutheran faith on their daily lives. Lutheran teachings emphasized respect for God, church, and government. They were generally good citizens who valued what America had to offer. In both Scandinavian and German settlements, the clergy played an important role in the community. Once called to a church, the Lutheran pastor had a relatively high level of autonomy and could pursue local needs without bureaucratic clearance or obstruction.

In Norwegian communities in particular, the church was the heart of the community. Families consistently attended services—few dared not to. The church provided valuable social contact. Only through church attendance and participation could one keep up with marriages, births, and deaths in the area. In rural areas, families might remain isolated throughout the week, and church became a high point, even if attendance required traveling a significant distance.

This sense of value ascribed to church may help to explain why the Lutherans have always embraced missionary work, although not with the fervor of some of their more evangelical Protestant brethren. Adopting the Augustinian framework of the two cities, the City of Man and the City of God, Martin Luther held what was called the Two Kingdoms Doctrine. God's mission could be carried out in both kingdoms, and mission could play a critical part in doing so.

The earliest Lutheran missionaries attended the University of Halle, a stronghold of German pietism. Frederick IV of Denmark sent a group to the East Indies as early as 1705, and over fifty missionaries followed in their footsteps. The Danes also launched a mission to Greenland in 1721. Throughout the nineteenth century, Lutheran missionary societies were founded and continued to grow. One was founded in Leipzig, Germany, another in Berlin, and several in Scandinavia. But overall, those nations that sustained Lutheran state churches were occupied with the work of sustaining those large complex, systems. Missionary work, instead, grew out of areas that had once been mission areas themselves, like the rural areas of the United States.

The United States, in its drive westward to develop coast to coast, understood the value and importance of missionary work. As early as the 1840s, the Pennsylvania Ministerium was recruiting missionaries in Germany. Frederick Wynekem became a traveling missionary and broadcast an appeal for Lutheran missionaries to work beside him in the spiritual fields of America. One who responded to that call was Adam Ernst. Ernst received his ministerial training in Germany, then traveled to America. After further training on American soil, he served as pastor for a group of Lutherans in Eden, New York, and later went on to pursue mission work in Canada.

The LCMS, noted above, also supported numerous missionary efforts in the U.S. and Canada. One example is Carl Diehlmann, an LCMS pastor in New York, who agreed to serve in Fisherville, Ontario, after Ernst. Ernst withdrew for health reasons but later returned to missionary work in Canada. Ernst regained his health and went on to publish a Lutheran magazine with a group of LCMS pastors. By the 1870s, the

LCMS was establishing missionary schools and providing teachers to staff them.

Some of the synods in the western part of the United States were founded and supported in their critical early days by missionary activity. The California Synod, founded in 1891, was supported by the Board of Home Missions and the Women's Home and Foreign Missionary Society. Members of the women's society provided financial support for so many missionaries in the California Synod that some referred to it as the "Women's Synod."

Lutherans also supported missionary work among Native Americans. Lutheran missionary N. L. Nielsen worked among the Cherokee in the late nineteenth century. The United Danish Evangelical Lutherans established a mission among the Cherokee in 1892, taking over work begun by the Moravians fifty years earlier. Thirty years later, the Norwegian Evangelical Lutheran Church supported the work of a woman missionary, Helen C. Frost, to the Eskimos in Alaska. Working in Teller, Igloo, Shishmaref, and Sitka, Frost served as a combination nurse, teacher, and welfare worker for decades.

Missionary activity was extended to the Hawaiian Islands as well. German settlers brought Lutheranism to Hawaii, and by 1883, the Lihue Lutheran Church was established in Lihue, Kauai. Lutheran missionary activity in exotic locales like Hawaii often took one of two forms: the mission station or the *volkskirche*. Mission stations were contained communities that could serve as a springboard for missionary activity. Often the station was physically enclosed by a wall or fencing. Believers could sojourn outside the walls of the mission to spread the word—teaching and preaching. Individuals who demonstrated an interest in converting were brought back to the compound. Safe from their old life and outside forces, they could explore the new community that conversion would bring to them, developing new relationships and learning more about the Lutheran faith or learning the language of the missionaries.

Another strategy was what was termed the *volkskirche*, or folk church, which developed during the twentieth century. The volkskirche approach rejected the isolationist aspects of the mission station and sought instead to work more closely with the groups that one intended to evangelize. It emphasized a more syncretic approach to conversion, in which previous family, tribal, or cultural values were subsumed into the overarching Christian framework.

In the twentieth century, Lutherans have shifted their energy away from missionary work and focused increasingly on pursuing a more unified approach to Lutheranism here at home. The LCMS has remained an important player on the national level in the Lutheran Church. In the 1970s, overtures were made to move toward a merger of the LCMS with the Association of Evangelical Lutheran Churches. Three hundred congregations left the LCMS to join the AELC. They hoped, eventually, to unify with the American Lutheran Church and the Lutheran Church in America. By the 1980s, after considerable study and dialog, the Commission for a New Lutheran Church was formed. It recommended a merger of the various Lutheran groups, which would become the fourth largest Protestant denomination in the United States.

In May 1988, the three churches did merge, and a new church, the Evangelical Lutheran Church in America, was born. Church leaders compared the new body to a mosaic, given the many different ethnic backgrounds of the Lutherans that made up its membership. In a very real sense, the unity that escaped the Lutherans in the nineteenth century was finally achieved in the twentieth.

On some levels, contemporary Lutherans still struggle with some of the same questions that plagued the Lutheran Church in the nineteenth century. To what extent should they honor the traditional elements of their inheritance and to what extent should they adapt themselves to the contemporary landscape? To what extent can one reconcile reason and religion? To what extent should the modern insights of biblical criticism inform one's faith? But these questions demonstrate, in another sense, the extent to which they have remained loyal to the central legacy of their founder Martin Luther. As Martin Luther was willing to stand firm in the convictions of his own faith against extraordinary pressure and insurmountable obstacles, today's American Lutherans stand firm in the conviction of the importance of justification before God and the critical role Christ plays in receiving that justification. American Lutherans continue to be the voice of Martin Luther, reminding the rest of America what individual religious conviction can achieve in a changing world.

13

EVOLUTION OF THE
BLACK CHURCH

The story of the Black Church begins in Africa. Although many Americans fail to realize it, Christianity has a long, deep history in Africa. Beginning with the story of the Ethiopian eunuch in the Acts of the Apostles, Christianity has grown and flourished on the African continent (Acts 8:26–40). Psalm 68 prophesized that Ethiopia would soon "stretch her hands out to God" (68:31). But even before the development of the scriptural canon, religion was deeply rooted in African soil in the form of African traditional religions.

African traditional religions take many forms, and any generalization is likely to prove overly simplistic, but many of these religious traditions can be characterized as fundamentally monotheistic with polytheistic dimensions, or as "monarchial polytheism." They emphasize connection with the legacies provided by ancestors, the histories of distinct cultural and tribal groups, and the importance of family and clan. These are belief systems that guide family relationships and day-to-day life, that instruct one in relationships to the land and to others, and that see the expression of the divinity in the phenomenon of the created world.

Christianity was introduced into the rich mixture of African traditional religions. The rich imagery of the Egyptians informs the art of the Coptic Christians. The deep roots of Judaism mingle with those of African traditional religions. Christianity arrives as a third force, into the already complex religious landscape of Africa, and it, too, leaves indelible marks on the lives of the African people.

The earliest Christian development can be found in Egypt, when John Mark, writer of the gospel, established a church, perhaps as early as 42 CE. One of the Roman generals, St. Maurice, was a black African who refused to lead his troops against fellow Christians. In Ethiopia, Ezana, king of Axum, who has been called the African Constantine, was the first Christian ruler. St. Pachomius is said to have sent a monk, Abba Yohannes, to Ethiopia. Thus, when Christian missionaries "brought" Christianity to Africa in the fifteenth and sixteenth centuries, they had little idea of the rich Christian history the continent already held.

What these Christians also brought to Africa was the European hunger for slaves. The Portuguese, as early as 1442, had taken slaves back with them. Slaves who were baptized were sometimes returned, and, soon, evangelization reached the Congo, where the king and queen were soon baptized. The Congo was declared the first Christian state in West Africa.

With the missionaries came the slavers, and the diaspora. The numbers are startling. Of the five and half million slaves imported to the Americas between 1532 and 1870, 37 percent came out of Angola; 38 percent came from the two Bights—Bight of Biafra and Bight of Benin; 12 percent came out of the Gold Coast; and the remaining 13 percent came out of Senegambia and Sierra Leone.

The Americas consumed the lives of slaves. Some 399,000 went to British Colonial America, over 1.5 million to Spanish America, over 1.5 million each to the British Caribbean and the Dutch Caribbean. But by far the largest number went to Brazil, where over 3.6 million were sent.

A third wave of Christianity swept through Africa in the late 1700s, when British abolitionists founded the colony of Sierra Leone for slaves returning to Africa. In 1787, some 411 ex-slaves landed in the Province of Freedom. In 1792, another 1,190 sailed up the river. By 1820, the descendents of ex-slaves had founded churches in Liberia. The slaves who were brought to America and those who returned to Africa knew a continent that already had a long and complex history of Christianity, one that would combine Christianity with African traditional religions in the New World and the Old.

Slavery necessitates domination of the mind as much as the body if it is to be sustainable, and, so, it comes as little surprise that those who survived transport from Africa to America faced an immediate form of what can only be termed religious imperialism. Their African names, African language, African culture, and African religion had to be eradicated to reinforce the new way of life. Traditionally, it is the elderly and women who serve as the "culture bearers," the ones who reinforce with children and the young the importance of observing cultural traditions. The majority of the slaves were young males. African women, what few there were, were most often deliberately separated from the men. Nor did many survive to an old age, given the hard life of slavery and the meager supports available to those who were no longer economically productive. Large groups of young men, without elderly people or women, often from different tribes or languages groups, found it difficult to sustain any sense of cultural identity.

Usually, only the forms of Christian worship embraced by the slave owners and local clergy were deemed acceptable. Biblical interpretation often emphasized the need for obedience and acceptance of one's lot in life and the great virtue of a strong sense of duty. Publicly, slaves picked up denominational affiliations just like they picked up names from their owners, and they became recognized as Methodist, Baptist, Anglican, or Catholic.

But even in the early days, a tension existed between Christianity and slavery. Many Christians owned slaves, including Protestant clergy and Catholic priests, seeing no contradiction between the two institutions. In fact, as noted above, traditional Christian beliefs could be incorporated into the socialization of slaves. But baptism of slaves raised a whole set of other questions. Did it acknowledge that slaves had souls as viable and valuable as their owners'? Did it mean they had a right to rest on the Sabbath? Who would minister to them? Certainly white ministers had plenty of "more important" responsibilities without taking on ministry to slaves. To complicate things further, many of the most active abolitionists saw their work as religiously informed, such as the Quakers discussed in chapter 7.

Thus, African American religion, from its earliest days, developed along two bifurcated streams. One was an underground river, allowing them to reinforce the beliefs that slaves brought with them from Africa. This type of cultural survival meant the development of secret ceremonies, the "Invisible Institution," that could pass unnoticed by the inquisitive eyes of slave owners. The second was a heartfelt embrace of Christianity, which also had deep roots in African history. But this must be a Christianity that was informed by and reflected the experience of Africans in the American landscape, that understood their troubles, their sorrow, their pain, and their hope.

Sometimes secret meetings were called by word of mouth. At times, when their absence was least likely to be noted, slaves would slip away, under cover of darkness, into the nearby forest or wood to meet. There they would celebrate elements of their lost heritage—dancing and singing, praising the divine, free from the constant observation they lived with. They employed various strategies to avoid detection, sometimes hanging blankets to muffle the sound of their gathering or turning a kettle upside down to fragment the sound waves. But relatively little is known about such gatherings, in part because serious scholarship on the subject is just beginning, and in part because of their secret nature and the oral tradition they relied upon.

The emphasis on religious conversion and religious experience over doctrinal compliance or biblical study meant that revivals appealed more to illiterate whites and to slaves. Slaves were usually forbidden to learn to read. The more physical elements of such worship, including dancing and singing, were familiar from African traditional religions but were also transmuted into new forms of Christian worship. With the emergence of the Great Awakening, a spirit of revivalism spread across the nation, and the revival spirit was embraced not only by white Christians but by African American Christians as well. Roving preachers like George Whitefield were happy to report on the number of Negroes who had attended their sermons. Evangelical ministers in the South encouraged the evangelization of the Negro population. Presbyterians, Methodists, and Baptists encouraged revivals in the South. Both slaves and free blacks seemed to prefer the Baptist and Methodist revivals, and by 1797, the Methodists boasted a black membership of 12,215, mostly in Maryland, Virginia, and North Carolina. The Methodists even encouraged some black men to serve as lay preachers themselves. African Baptist churches began to emerge around 1800, usually affiliated with white congregations and under the supervision of white ministers.

It was also around the turn of the nineteenth century that some Protestant clergymen began to develop the plantation mission. Since plantations were often isolated, surrounded by large amounts of land under agricultural production, it was often impossible for slaves to get to worship services. Missionaries like Charles Colcock Jones undertook this work and championed it through writing and publishing. He advocated the formation of local associations to minimize the resistance of local landowners and held up the work of Pietists, the Moravians or German Lutherans, as exemplary.

Several denominations pursued plantation missions, the Baptists, Presbyterians, and Episcopalians among them. The Methodist Episcopal Church may have been the most effective, for while statistics are not entirely reliable, between 1846 and 1861, they are said to have increased their black membership from around 120,000 to over 200,000. Similarly, the Baptist Church reported an increase from 200,000 to 400,000. But these radical increases in black membership brought problems. Many churches had segregated seating sections for blacks. With ever-increasing numbers, they often simply outgrew the available segregated seating, forcing white congregations to come to terms with their own racism. Were they willing to sit next to blacks in the central areas of the church?

Such challenges reached a boiling point in the Methodist Episcopal Church. It may, in fact, have been the effectiveness of the Methodist tradition in the area of revivals and plantation missions, along with its willingness to allow black men to serve as lay preachers, that led to its contribution to the first successful black Methodist churches. Arguably, the first black Methodist church was established in Wilmington, Delaware, in 1807. But it had its roots years earlier, in a group known as the Free African Society and its forerunners Absolom Jones (d. 1818) and Richard Allen (1760–1831).

Jones was born a field slave but was later recruited to serve in his master's house. There, he learned to read and developed a hunger for education. At sixteen, he was sold, and his new master took him to Philadelphia to work as a delivery boy. His new master permitted him to attend night school and, eventually, to purchase his own freedom. In Philadelphia, Jones came to know Richard Allen.

Allen had also been born a slave. Early in life, he was sold to a family near Dover, Delaware. Living with that family, he experienced a profound conversion and dedicated his life to Christ. He subsequently became a Methodist. Ordained a preacher by the Methodists, Allen managed to convert his own master, who then allowed him and his brother to purchase their freedom.

Allen joined the congregation of St. George's Methodist Episcopal Church at a time when many of the black members of the congregation were increasingly dissatisfied. Allen himself was convinced of the validity of the Methodist tradition, the possibility of achieving sanctification through both a gradual process of pious living and the certainty of justification he had experienced in his conversion. Allen envisioned an environment where he could pursue animated preaching, singing, interaction with the congregation, and the freedom to have worship services that honored and reflected the riches of African heritage.

His preaching began to attract larger and larger numbers of black believers, but Allen increasingly felt restricted by the practices of the white congregation and its leadership. Blacks were usually buried in separate cemeteries. Many churches required separate seating areas for black church members. One morning, during a prayer service, Jones and other blacks were asked to leave the central sanctuary and sit in a segregated area. They did more than that. They walked out of St. George's Episcopal Methodist Church never to return.

They did not immediately establish their own congregation. Instead, Jones and Allen established what they called the Free African Society. The society was not a religious society, per se, but a society without religion that encouraged its members to live "an orderly and sober life" and to support one another, widows, and children. Thus, the Free African Society could meet the most pressing needs of the black community without antagonizing both whites and dissenting blacks by establishing a religious congregation. In addition to offering support to, and demanding a high moral tone from, its members, the society became involved in abolitionist work, took a census of free blacks, and established a school house. The Free African Society also became a model for other black religious groups, reflecting the need of the black community for both religious leadership and help in facing the everyday challenges exacerbated by racism, poverty, and the fragmentation of families.

Because the Quakers played such a large role in abolitionist activity in Philadelphia at that time, it is natural that they became interested in the Free African Society. When some members of the group began to move toward a religious mode of worship that replicated a Quaker meeting, Allen, with his deep-seated Methodist beliefs, could not condone the shift, and he separated from the group. As a gesture of reconciliation, the society built a church, St. Thomas's African Episcopal Church, and Allen was named its pastor. On July 29, 1794, Methodist Bishop Francis Asbury endorsed the group, preaching at Mother Bethel. The African Methodist Church had begun.

Allen left to head up the Bethel group and soon gathered other congregations under his wing. In 1800, a group from Salem, Massachusetts, joined Allen's church. Members of the Union Church of Africa joined in 1813. A group in Baltimore, Maryland, organized the Baltimore African Church and joined Allen's church in 1816. Allen's leadership was consecrated when he was named the first black bishop of the AME Church in 1816.

Allen's church became known as a reliable stop on the Underground Railroad. He carried his abolitionism into his role as bishop, and slave owners were denied membership in his churches. This set the tone for later members of the AME Church to adopt strict resolutions against slavery and to maintain an unquestioned moral stance against the practice of slavery.

But Allen's AME Church was not the only church formed during that time period. The AME Zion traces its roots to the same period. The AME Zion grew out of the Methodist John Street Church in New York City. John Street, like other churches, had seating problems given the number of blacks that were joining the congregation. Some white member of the community recommended building a separate chapel for ministry to black members, effectively splitting the congregation along racial lines. A woodworker's shop was secured to serve as a chapel. On September 8, 1800, it was incorporated as the Zion Church under the religious leadership of Abraham Thompson, June Scott, and Thomas Miller. After witnessing the break made by congregations in Philadelphia and Baltimore, the black congregation decided to break entirely with the white congregation. Two decades later, on August 11, 1820, the group decided to form the African Methodist Episcopal Church in America, which later became known as the African Methodist Episcopal Zion Church.

The Baptist Church also welcomed black membership prior to the turn of the nineteenth century. One estimate suggests that black membership in the Baptist Church increased by twenty-two thousand between 1793 and 1813. As was the case with the Methodists, many of the conversions came on the heels of revivals and preaching by Baptist ministers. Black Churches soon began to form in the Baptist tradition. In 1812, Joseph Willis, an African American Baptist preacher, formed the first Baptist church in Louisiana at Bayou Chicot and became its first pastor. Willis went on to become the first moderator of the Louisiana Baptist Association.

In Kentucky, three hundred blacks met regularly under the guidance of a slave known as "Old Captain." But the South Kentucky Association refused to ordain him. Old Captain continued his ministry without their sanction. An African-born slave in Virginia who converted to the Baptist faith and preached for forty years, he eventually converted his owner's son.

Of all the denominations, the Baptists were the most willing to allow blacks to preach. Black preachers and ministers were active not only in rural areas but in urban areas as well. Shortly before 1800, African Baptist churches began to form and send clergy to the associations' meetings. But by the 1820s, it was decided that such churches should remain under the supervision of white pastors. The extent to which white pastors actually supervised varied widely, though, and some black congregations remained effectively autonomous, in practice if not in theory.

At around the same time, shortly after 1800, some black congregations were established among the Episcopalians and the Presbyterians. Most African Americans found these denominational traditions too formal and much less fluid than the Methodist or Baptist traditions. In 1807, the first black Presbyterian church was formed in Philadelphia, but even as late as 1861, the Presbyterians still accepted slaveholders into their congregations and disagreed on whether slavery was a civil or religious matter.

The first black Episcopal church was headed up by Absolom Jones. After the Free African Society built St. Thomas's African Episcopal Church and Allen departed with the Bethel group, the congregation of St. Thomas was accepted into the Episcopal Church in 1794. Jones became the church's first deacon in 1795.

Even as Presbyterians and Episcopalians accepted black congregations and black members, they practiced a form of civil segregation that kept black and white members largely apart. Most churches reserved a separate seating section for black members or relegated them to balconies or galleries. Discriminatory practices within the churches themselves made them less appealing to black members. And separation of the two groups often resulted in black members' being effectively driven out from positions of power or authority, which remained overwhelmingly in the hands of white males.

But the importance of the establishment of independent Black Churches in the early part of the nineteenth century should not be underestimated, in part because it provided a stream of articulate black leadership that contributed immensely to the abolitionist cause and helped to galvanize national opinion to support efforts in the Civil War to bring an end to slavery. Nor can the leadership of an individual like Richard Allen be emphasized enough, even though his own racial policies, which called for separatism and black willingness to take responsibility for black social problems, are unlikely to be popular today. The civil freedom he sought through his abolitionist activity was combined with a deep commitment to the project of personal holiness and personal commitment to the religious life.

While many African Americans pursued Christianity as their primary form of religious practice, the adoption of the Christian outlook was not the sole response of Africans on American soil. Many others channeled their religious beliefs through traditions that held a greater connection to African traditional religions. Some did so through maintaining a relatively pure form of religious practice that had its roots in the soil of Africa, and others did so through a creative syncretism that joined Christianity and African beliefs in a new religious form. Some of the most intriguing forms blended African traditional religions with Roman Catholicism.

Roman Catholic interaction with African Americans has a deep history, particularly in the South. As early as 1725, the Society of Jesus, or the Jesuits, had established a residence in New Orleans, Louisiana. By 1727, the Ursulines, a Roman Catholic women's religious order devoted to teaching, had opened a school in New Orleans. The Ursulines opened their school to French, Native American, and African girls alike. Their work was remarkably effective. By 1750, the literacy rate for women in New Orleans was 71 percent. More women than men could read in New Orleans, while elsewhere women's literacy rate was roughly half that of men's.

High rates of literacy and the presence of large numbers of free people of color contributed to the ability to organize. By the nineteenth century, Henriette Delille (1813–1862), who was a daughter of one of the oldest, most respected families in New Orleans, founded the Sisters of the Holy Family, considered the second-oldest Catholic religious order for women of color.

The oldest was founded by Marie Almaide Maxis Duchemin, later known as Mother Theresa Maxis, in Baltimore, Maryland, in 1829. Together with Elizabeth Lange, Marie Magdalen Balas, and Rosine Boegue, Duchemin founded the Oblate Sisters of Providence to allow young "girls of color" to consecrate their lives to God. As free and French-speaking women of color, they found support for their efforts from Archbishop James Whitfield.

While wealthier free people of color had the sophistication and support to found religious orders and participate in established institutions, many impoverished blacks or slaves turned to intriguing mixtures of African and European belief systems. Among these groups are Vodou and Santería. Vodou, sometimes spelled voudoun, vodu, or voodoo, conjures up stereotyped images for many Americans today of dolls with pins stuck in them or glazed zombies. Actually, vodou is a term for an African traditional religion that originated in West Africa and came to the United States through the slave trade. Based on the Fon word for "spirit," vodou presents a world infused with spiritual energy in a belief system that may be as much as ten thousand years old. In vodou, which is monotheistic with polytheistic dimensions, a creator god, Papa Bon Dieux, inspires spirits known as Iwa or Ioa to intercede in human affairs. Singing, dancing, and certain trance states allow greater communication with the Ioa, who begin to take on a relationship to individuals like that of a patron saint.

Since the socialization of slaves demanded they be stripped of their African identity, including their language, religion, and name, many slaveholders outlawed the practice of vodou or other African traditional religions. The religion of vodou itself was demonized and painted as inherently evil and contrary to Christian beliefs and ideals. Only in the late twentieth century did reliable research provide greater understanding of vodou and related African American religious streams. The belief system is still known as vodou in Haiti and select Caribbean islands. Elements of vodou can be found integrated into Candomble Jege-Nago in Brazil; Obeah in Jamaica and Trinidad Tobago; Santería in Cuba and other Caribbean Islands, as well as Argentina, Venezuela, Colombia, and Mexico; Dahomean in Africa; and voodoo in Louisiana. Elements of Christianity, primarily Catholicism, have been blended into some of these streams.

Santería is one of the most intriguing of these syncretic streams. Santería is strongest in Cuba and among those Africans whose background can be traced to the Yoruba. The Yoruba people lived in what is now the southwestern corner of Nigeria, along the border of Dahomey. They were concentrated in cities like Oyo, Benin, and Yagba. In regular battles between the Yoruba and Dahomey, many Yoruba were enslaved and shipped to slave ports in Cuba and Brazil. In 1851, the Fon kingdom of Dahomey invaded the traditional lands of the Yoruba. The Oyo Empire collapsed, and hundreds of thousands of Yoruba were enslaved in the aftermath.

Huge numbers of Yoruba were consumed by the sugar trade in Cuba. Over three hundred fifty years of slavery in Cuba, some five to seven hundred thousand Africans were imported. Many of these were Yoruba. Spanish law required that slaves entering the Indies be baptized Roman Catholic, and the slave code of 1789 required that they be catechized as Catholics. The church organized blacks into clubs called *cabildos* for religious education, usually grouping blacks from the same nation or region together. These societies soon expanded to become mutual-aid societies, to provide needed social services, and to care for the most vulnerable members of the community. Out of the Yoruba cabildos Santería emerged.

Santería, which means "the way of the saints," blends Catholic and Yoruba beliefs. In a sense, the Yoruba beliefs were submerged beneath a veneer of Roman Catholicism. It may have begun as a form of deception, to disguise Yoruba beliefs and practices and make them appear acceptable to Roman Catholic slaveholders. But it quickly became a solidly established religious practice in its own right.

Understanding Santería begins with understanding the power of the *orishas.* Orishas are powerful spiritual entities who can be either supremely helpful to humans or extremely dangerous. As with the loa, the believer develops a relationship with an orisha, who hopefully becomes a spiritual guardian and protector. The belief in orishas quickly blended with the Roman Catholic belief in saints, especially the idea of a patron saint, and, soon, the Catholic saint and the orisha were simply considered different manifestations of the same spiritual entity. Thus, through what appeared to be pious devotion to the saints, one could unleash the power of the orisha.

Each orisha is associated with a spectrum of qualities or characteristics. Each is correlated to a particular saint, to a principle like illness, death, or fatherhood, and to a number, a color, certain foods, a certain dance movement, and an emblem. One can pay homage to the orishas through a wide variety of practices, which might include dance, animal sacrifice to appease their hunger, or the use of selected botanicals.

Numerous theories have emerged as to why Santería survived when so many other forms of African traditional belief systems were obliterated through slavery. Some speculate that it was because the Yoruba were urban dwellers and, thus, took readily to life in the cities of the New World. Others attribute it to the high number of free people of color in Cuba. Census figures show that one-third to one-half of Cuba's population with African descent were free people of color. This relative autonomy may have allowed better economic status and economic support for worship services and practices. Others attribute it to differences between Roman Catholic and Protestant catechesis. Roman Catholics, with their emphasis on the sacrament of baptism, may not have been as rigid about correct doctrinal belief. In their eagerness to save souls through baptism, they may have allowed more people in with only marginal religious training or education. Some insist that the survival and prevalence of Santería can be attributed primarily to the fact that Roman Catholic clergy were particularly obtuse, a perspective that some Roman Catholics might suggest is still true today.

Regardless of the reason, the syncretic beliefs we call Santería did survive and continue to influence areas that have a significant Cuban population or that once had large number of Yoruba slaves. So, one sees the ongoing practice of Santería in the Caribbean, in Miami, Florida, and in New York. A recent ruling of the Supreme Court protected animal sacrifice as an essential part of the practice of the religion, and while many practitioners will not instruct someone who is not of African descent, increasing numbers of scholars, both black and white, are recognizing and extracting the riches of the religious streams associated with vodou and Santería.

The United States still has not given slavery the amount of scholarship and study it deserves, and research into African American history remains challenged by a lack of materials, resources, and funding. Research into African American religious history is no exception to this general rule. Additionally, historical work is hampered by the relative paucity of written documents relating to African history, and most historians must cast a much wider net in order to construct such histories, including looking at the stories told by textiles, folk tradition, ritual, and dance. But study of the role of African Americans in American religious history is one of the most dynamic and promising areas of historical research.

In a sense, the story of the Black Church begins and ends with African traditional religions. While the slave system and the evangelical eagerness of Christian missionaries sought to strip African identity from those who experienced such a tragic passage to these shores, the deep roots of African heritage were strong enough to withstand the centuries of attack. Today's

African Americans are no longer required to make a choice between African heritage and belief in Christianity. The history of African traditional religions is being told. The secrets of the "Invisible Institution" of slave religion are being uncovered. The heroic role of figures like Richard Allen in founding the first all-black congregations and demanding autonomy is being recognized. The viability and beauty of belief systems such as vodou and Santería are being recognized.

Recognition of the unique needs of African Americans in terms of religious identity, community services, and aid to the community is increasing. Scholarship is being focused on the relationship between religion and leadership in the Black Church, looking, for instance, at the river priests who guided the people on the Niger River. The religiously inspired led slave revolts in protest of the inhuman treatment African Americans experienced under slavery. More recently, figures like Martin Luther King Jr. and Malcolm X showed the world that the tie between religious conviction and leadership continues in black history. That strong connection promises that future generations of inspired political and communal leadership are likely to emerge from the ongoing evolution of the black church in America.

14

BAPTISTS AND BAPTISM

Many consider the Baptist tradition as American as apple pie, but like so many other American religious traditions, it has its earliest roots on the other side of the Atlantic. It is difficult to say when the tradition we know as Baptist came into being, but most scholars place its beginnings in England in the seventeenth century. In the turbulent days following the Reformation, many believers felt their convictions challenged and sought new understanding of their religious faith. In England, Henry VIII and his daughter Elizabeth I of England had firmly established the Church of England as the sole church of the state.

With the translation of the Bible into English and the teachings of many of the Reformers, such as Martin Luther and John Calvin, available, many English believers began to challenge the newly established Church of England as the sole avenue of reform. Some of these, who demanded a more "pure" church in terms of doctrine and practice came to be known as the Puritans and are discussed in chapter 2. Others felt it was impossible to reform the church from within and that true reform required them to separate from the existing church. These groups came to be known as Separatists.

The Separatists were a diverse group and would later evolve into Baptists, Presbyterians, Congregationalists, and Quakers, among others. One segment of the Separatists began to emphasize what they termed a "believer's baptism." Since the time of Augustine of Hippo, the Catholic Church had followed a practice of infant baptism. Some of the Separatists began to challenge this idea and to call for baptism to be practiced only when a person came to believe fully. Many of those who supported believer's baptism came to be known as Anabaptists. The Baptists rejected the name Anabaptists, but in the confusion of the day, as distinct religious traditions emerged and evolved, few distinctions were made, and they were often mistakenly referred to as such. Early adherents to the Baptist tradition preferred to be called the Brethren or the Brethren of the Baptized Way. But their focus on the importance of baptism and on the believer's baptism, eventually led to their simply being called Baptists.

The two major groups that would later evolve into what we now know as the Baptist tradition were called the General Baptists and the Particular Baptists. General Baptists were so called because they accepted the idea of the general atonement. From this perspective, Christ died for the sins of the human race, for all people in general. What one must do in order to achieve salvation was to believe. The Particular Baptists believed that Christ's death only guaranteed the salvation of a particular group, a group known as the elect. This perspective incorporated the Augustinian view of predestination as championed and further developed by Calvin. The Particular Baptists accepted many of Calvin's views.

The first General Baptist church was founded in Amsterdam. John Smyth (1570–1612) was an ordained minister in the Church of England who was educated at Cambridge University. Over time, he found himself more and more drawn to the perspectives of the Separatists. He joined a small Separatist congregation in Gainsborough, near London. King James I was rigorously persecuting anyone who failed to participate in the Church of England, and, soon, the Gainsborough congregation felt they should leave England and move to Amsterdam, Holland, in search of greater religious tolerance. Smyth and a wealthy layman by the name of Thomas Helwys (c. 1550–1616) became the leaders of this expatriate group.

While in Amsterdam, they encountered a group of Mennonites, who take their name from Menno Simons (c. 1496–1561). The Mennonites were Anabaptists, and Smyth and Helwys's contact with them was significant because Mennonites not only practiced the believer's baptism but believed in full-immersion baptism, both of which would later be incorporated into Baptist belief. There are also distinct differences between the groups. The Baptists have never adopted the pacifism, communal ownership of property, or optimistic view of human nature that the Mennonites hold. Smyth went so far as to request that his group be accepted into the Mennonite community, but Helwys and others refused to join. Regardless, in the first decade of the seventeenth century, the Mennonites prompted Smyth into greater reflection on his own theological principals. He determined to model his community of believers as closely as possible on the life of Christ's followers in the New Testament.

In 1608 and 1609, Smyth decided to disband his Amsterdam congregation and form a new one. This was to be an intentional community, in which only those who had publicly professed their faith would participate. He arranged to have himself and other members of the new church baptized. By 1611, he had determined that he would lead a group of believers back to England. He and his ten followers established a Baptist church there on his return. Emphasizing general atonement, believer's baptism, and religious liberty, their views found fertile ground, and forty years later almost fifty individual congregations had been established in the London area.

Helwys also returned to England and established a church in 1612. After his return, Helwys wrote a book on freedom of conscience entitled *A Short Declaration of the Mystery of Iniquity*. There was some early division between Baptists concerning which doctrine of predestination would prevail. As noted above, the Particular Baptists tended to favor a Calvinistic interpretation of predestination, with salvation being granted only to a particular group, the elect. Other Baptists favored a more Arminian view. James Arminius (1560–1609) was a Dutch Reformed theologian who published "Five Arminian Articles" in 1610. From an Arminian perspective, salvation came not exclusively through grace, which a strict Augustinian perspective would suggest, but through living a holy life. In *A Short Declaration of the Mystery of Iniquity*, Helwys adopted language that suggested a more Arminian interpretation of predestination. Iniquity, in Helwys's view, was the oppression he had experienced in terms of religious freedom in England. In the book, Helwys challenged the divine right of the king to rule, suggesting the king was but a mortal man. The book came to be considered one of the classics of Baptist history but did little for its author. As a result of his outspoken views, Helwys was arrested later that year. Locked away in Newgate Prison, he died in 1616.

A generation later, the Particular Baptists had also grown and developed. Most trace the history of the Particular Baptists back to a congregation headed up by pastors John Lathrop and Henry Jessey. Discussions of the theological importance of baptism led to divisions within the congregation, and one group withdrew in 1633. Five years later, another group left to join the previous dissenters. Subsequently, all of the dissenting members submitted to a believer's baptism, and historians consider that group the first Particular Baptist church. Several more Particular Baptist churches developed over the next twenty years, and by 1640, at least two of the congregations had formally adopted immersion as the most appropriate form of baptism.

It was also during this period that Baptists began to develop some of their own organizational infrastructure. The General Baptists formed associations to determine and maintain doctrinal practice among member congregations. They developed the General Assembly, a national meeting where representatives from different churches could meet and exchange views. Particular Baptists resisted such organizational participation, zealously guarding their religious liberty and determined to keep authority within the congregation itself. Such congregational "autonomy" is one of the central beliefs associated with the Baptist tradition. When combined with believer's baptism, baptism by immersion, reliance on scripture, and freedom of conscience, you have a framework for Baptist belief that continues even today.

One of the most famous of the early Baptist believers was John Bunyan (1628–1688), the author of *The Pilgrim's Progress*. Bunyan was born at Harrowden, near Bedford, England. Bunyan elected to take a believer's baptism, as an adult, and held most of the basic beliefs of the Baptist tradition. He believed fiercely in scripture, in the congregational approach to the government of the church, and in justification by faith alone. His beliefs in terms of the Doctrine of Grace followed the lines of the Particular Baptists. But Bunyan opposed closed membership for the church and the practice of closed communion. He believed all should be called to God's table and God's church and that religion should not be a basis for division between "the holy and the holy." Bunyan's religious enthusiasm and zealous preaching led to his arrest for preaching without a license. It was during his imprisonment that he produced his best-known books.

By the 1640s, the Particular Baptists had produced their first confession of faith. That confession was later clarified to make it clear that Baptists were not the same as Quakers, then reissued in 1652. A second confession was produced in 1677, which was modeled on the Westminster Confession and celebrated ties between the Puritans and the early Baptists. The following year, the General Baptists issued "The Orthodox Creed." This was a statement produced in the hope of protecting Christians from error in their beliefs about Christ. Eleven years later, in 1689, the Act of Toleration was issued and, for the first time, Baptists in England had a chance for true religious freedom. One might think that would encourage Baptists to remain in England, but many still elected to seek religious freedom in other lands, including America.

One of the most significant early developments of the Baptist Church in America was the establishment of the Philadelphia Baptist Association in 1707. Here Baptists found that they could affirm the presence of other congregations without jeopardizing their cherished independence. Generally, participation in associations allowed Baptists to address four areas that they could not necessarily pursue in individual congregations. First, they could promote communication and fellowship between member churches. Second, they could provide affirmation and witness to the beliefs that they shared. Third, they could support one another in terms of delicate doctrinal questions or financial necessity. Finally, they could support ministries that were beyond the individual congregation, such as the establishment of theological schools, the training of ministers, publishing, and missionary work. But these associations served in an advisory capacity rather than as leadership for the individual member churches.

Given their participation in the Separatists movement in England, it comes as no surprise that Baptists were among the early religious refugees to make their way to American soil. Throughout the seventeenth century, Baptists emigrated to New England. Among them was Roger Williams (c. 1600–1683), who, although he did not remain Baptist, founded Providence, Rhode Island, and the First Baptist Church of America in 1639. Originally intending to be a minister in Salem, Massachusetts, his denunciation of the Massachusetts charter meant conflict with civil authorities. When he refused to retract his views, he was banished. Purchasing land from the Narragansett Indians, he recruited other colonists to follow, and, soon, the city of Providence was begun. John Clarke (1609–1676) founded a church shortly thereafter in Newport, Rhode Island. Both Williams and Clarke were Puritan Separatists, who, in keeping with the beliefs of the Particular Baptists, incorporated Calvinist doctrine and belief into their religious perspective.

As early as 1656, Baptists had appeared in New York. By the mid-1680s, Baptist churches had been formed in Pennsylvania, New Jersey, and Delaware. In the 1680s and 1690s, Baptists began to settle in the middle and Southern colonies. By 1682, a Baptist church had been founded in Charleston, South Carolina.

The Baptists saw spectacular growth in the period between 1700 and 1800. In 1700, only twenty-four Baptist churches had been established in the American colonies. By 1800, the Baptists could be considered the largest denomination in America. The year 1715 saw a Baptist church established in Virginia, and 1727 brought the Baptist tradition to North Carolina. But the most significant growth in the South came in 1755, after two Baptist preachers established a church in Sandy Creek, North Carolina. Shubal Steams and Daniel Marshall began to use the church as a home base and to practice a kind of circuit riding, traveling across the South, preaching and baptizing. They laid a good foundation for the future development of the Baptist Church in the South. In addition to individual conversions and the establishment of individual churches, there were large increases in church membership. Over one hundred congregations that had identified themselves as members of the Congregationalist Church changed their identification to Baptist.

As noted above, the Philadelphia Baptist Association was founded in 1707. By 1755, it had established a home missions program, but because many Baptists remained cautious about any incursion on the autonomy of their individual congregations, they remained open to other approaches to mission work. In 1792, William Carey (1761–1834) led a group who founded the Baptist Missionary Society in England. Andrew Fuller (1754–1815), a prominent pastor, supported this missionary work. The society did not require any supervisory capacity for churches participating in mission work. Rather, participants were given the freedom to form their own independent societies or to participate financially. The model quickly became popular, and most churches eventually relegated their missionary activity to independent societies.

In May 1814, another significant move forward in missionary activity came with the founding of the General Missionary Convention. With the full name the General Missionary Convention of the Baptist Denomination in the United States of America for Foreign Missions, it was meant to coordinate mission activity and consolidate efforts. Since Baptist belief emphasizes unmediated communication with God for the individual and the independence of the local congregation, the convention was not intended to set doctrinal matters in terms of theological interpretation. Instead, its energy would be focused on raising money for further missionary work.

Initially, thirty-three representatives from all over the country met in Philadelphia, Pennsylvania, for the convention. But the convention would be divided in 1845, when Southern adherents would become the Southern Baptist Convention and Northern adherents would become members of the American Baptist Missionary Union, which operated out of Boston, Massachusetts.

In 1824, the Baptist General Tract Society was formed just for the purpose of publishing and distributing published works. With offices originally in Washington, D.C., its leadership moved to Philadelphia in 1826. In 1840, its name was changed to the American Baptist Publication Society.

In 1832, the American Baptist Home Mission Society came into existence. More and more land began to be incorporated into the United States as the nation moved west, and American Baptists decided they need a mission society that could watch over missionary activity in the West.

The General Missionary Convention had its work cut out for it. Holding together a diverse group with strong feelings about congregational autonomy is not an easy task. The United States is much larger and more diverse than many other nations, and, so, organizing at the national level meant finding ways to overcome differences in culture, economics, and politics.

Several issues divided Northern and Southern Baptists. One involved what was known as the Landmark movement, which was important to Baptists in the South. This movement, which was led by J. R. Graves (1820–1893) among others, stressed the idea that the Baptist Church was the only "true church" in light of the New Testament. It also encouraged isolationism, suggesting that Baptists compromised their own beliefs when they entered into relationships with non-Baptists. One implication of the Landmark movement was that the movement's members resisted any form of church government that could not be found and recognized in the pages of the New Testament. This made the congregational structure and history of the Baptist Church somewhat problematic. Traditionally, Baptist congregations regularly exchanged views with other Baptist congregations. Landmarkians argued that Baptist congregations should not engage regularly with other Baptist congregations and certainly should not pursue relationships with non-Baptist congregations. Some believe that the popularity of this form of Baptist belief in the South is related to the high levels of anti-Catholic sentiment in the region. Ultimately, the Landmarkians left the Southern Baptist Convention to form the American Baptist Association in 1905 and the Baptist Bible Fellowship in the 1950s.

There were also differences of opinion as to how missionary money should be spent. The Baptist societies noted above all had headquarters in the North but derived revenue from both the North and South. Most of the missionaries were sent to the upper part of the Mississippi River valley. Many Southern Baptists felt those efforts might be more fruitfully directed to the Southeast or to the American Southwest. Problems in communication between North and South and newspaper articles in the religious press that exaggerated differences only served to aggravate the situation.

Additionally, the Northerners seemed to prefer a very loose denominational organization, primarily linked by the payment of dues and individual societies that each specialized in a specific ministry. Southern churches would have preferred an organization that operated more like an association, with numerous ministries operating under the umbrella of one administrative organization. But these differences were not as difficult to overcome as those related to the issue of slavery.

Often, but not always, differing views of slavery fell along a North-South divide. Some Baptists leaders were actively engaged in abolitionist activity, and abolitionist sentiment continued to grow in the North.

Throughout the 1840s, debate flourished as to the church's position with regard to the question of slavery. The constitutions of the societies, whether Southerners could receive missionary appointment, and how and when societies could mete out discipline to individual churches all revolved around the issue of slavery.

In 1844, Georgia Baptists asked the Home Mission Society to appoint a slaveholder as a missionary. They nominated fellow slaveholder James E. Reeve to the society. His appointment was turned down. The Alabama Baptist Convention then asked to appoint a slaveholder as a missionary. The society turned them down. The Virginia Baptists then called for a meeting of all the Baptists in the South. During that meeting, the Baptists from the South decided to break with the existing group and formed the Southern Baptist Convention in Augusta, Georgia, in 1845. The remaining Northern elements would later reorganize to form the Northern Baptist Convention in 1907. But since 1845, the Baptists have had three separate bodies, originally identified as Northern, Southern, and colored.

The Southern Baptist Convention, as it emerged, made up two boards. First, there was a board devoted to foreign mission work, which was based in Richmond, Virginia. Second, there was a home mission board based in Marion, Alabama. A constitution was drafted and circulated, and the following year, at a convention in Richmond, it was adopted.

Over the course of the Civil War, both the Southern Baptist Convention and the Northern Baptists supported mission work in the South. Bibles and other materials were sent into the South. But the most devastating impact of the war was the destruction of Southern churches. Many were leveled or irreparably damaged in the course of fighting and occupation. Additionally, the Southern economy was in shambles by the end of the Civil War, and humanitarian aid was continually needed.

The Civil War had a profound impact on the Southern Baptist Convention, as Southerners recovered from the brutal impact of war, Reconstruction, and a shattered society. It was not until the late 1870s and early 1880s that the convention was able to return to a relative state of normal operations. After the war, Northern Baptists asked the Southerners to return to the organization established prior to 1845, but the Southerners declined.

In 1866, Virginia Baptists let it be known that they would rather continue their own work "in our own way." Their sentiments set the tone for other members of the Southern convention, and, soon, it became apparent that rather than a temporary division based on the slavery issue, a permanent institution had been established in the form of the Southern Baptist Convention, which would continue into the future.

From the time the Southern Baptist Convention was established in 1845, it had a strong sense of mission and strongly supported missionary activities. The Foreign Mission Board began work in China and elsewhere in Asia, the Middle East, Liberia, and Mexico. A domestic board was set up to oversee missionary work among Southern whites, slaves, free blacks, Native Americans, and Chinese immigrants in California. The convention's Domestic Home Mission Board agreed to accept assistance from its equivalent in the North, the American Baptist Home Mission Society of New York. But some Northern Baptists saw the South itself as a mission field and sent missionaries to help rebuild Southern churches after the war and to support freed blacks in their transition from slavery.

In 1882, the Southern Baptist Convention decided to reassert its dominance over mission work in the South. It established a new Home Mission Board in Atlanta, Georgia, and appointed Isaac Taylor Tichenor to run it. Tichenor was a Confederate Army veteran and a champion of industry. He had previously served as president of Alabama's State Agricultural and Mechanical College. Tichenor focused a significant part of his boundless energy on reclaiming Southern Baptist churches that had been temporarily run by the Northern convention.

The Home Mission Board established its own publication, *Our Home Field*, and kept supporters updated on progress on numerous fronts. By the latter part of the nineteenth century, the board seemed to consider Native Americans a dying breed among whom the need for evangelization was largely over. Instead, work was needed in education. The board optimistically pursued missionary work in Cuba, hoping to disestablish the entrenched Roman Catholic Church there and bring a new level of religious freedom to the island. Attention would be focused on incoming immigrants, whose need to be assimilated and "Christianized" was clear. In addition, missions were pursued among Southern blacks in the hopes of ameliorating some of the hostility that remained in the aftermath of the Civil War. The board also pursued missions in Southern cities and in mountainous regions of the South, such as the Appalachians.

But while these diverse missions were pursued, the Southern Baptist Convention saw its true power as lying in the hands of white Southerners. Tichenor played an important part in consolidating the institutional aspects of the Southern Baptist Convention. Two key moves in that regard were the establishment of the Woman's Missionary Union and the Sunday School Board.

The Woman's Missionary Union was established in 1888. From the middle of the nineteenth century on, women had established local mission societies in the Baptist Church. Some enterprising women passed out cir-culars to encourage women to collect funds for mission work both foreign and domestic. The Foreign Mission Board quickly realized the potential for such a pattern of collection and provided boxes specifically for that purpose. In the early 1880s, the wives of preachers and representatives who attended the Southern Baptist Convention began meeting informally while their husbands attended the meetings. Soon, members of the convention began to call for a more formal structure through which women might participate in the support of mission work. In 1888, the Woman's Missionary Union was established as an auxiliary to state conventions and denominational boards.

But the Woman's Missionary Union was different from those state and denominational boards. For one, its influence was conventionwide, not re-stricted to a particular locality. As they sent the money they collected to the state conventions, the conventions were able to use part of the funds for their pressing needs before passing the remaining funds on to the Home Mission Board or the Foreign Mission Board. The Women's Missionary Union also supported the Sunday School Board. As the Sunday school movement swept across Protestant America, the Baptists kept in step. The Woman's Missionary Board allied with the Sunday School Board in the plan to have the Sunday School Board become the sole provider of texts for re-ligious instruction. They also collaborated with the Sunday School Board in preparing texts that combined educational information with information about missionary work.

In 1907, the Woman's Missionary Union opened the Baptist Woman's Missionary Union Training School in Louisville, Kentucky. Since the Southern Baptist Convention had also established the Southern Baptist Theological Seminary there, women could study alongside their male coun-terparts in seminary classes. Women attending the training school received instruction in running a settlement house, with an emphasis on social work and social gospel.

In addition to the training school and the seminary in Louisville, the Southern Baptist Convention built up a substantial network of schools to provide seminary education. These include the Southeastern Seminary in Wake Forest, North Carolina, the Southwestern Baptist Theological Semi-nary in Ft. Worth, Texas, the Golden Gate Baptist Seminary in Mill Valley, California, the Midwestern Baptist Theological Seminary in Kansas City, Missouri, and the New Orleans Baptist Theological Seminary in Louisiana. From its modest beginnings with the Baptist General Tract Society, the con-vention now runs one of the biggest religious publishing companies in

America, Life Way Christian Resources, which originated with the Sunday School Board's work in the nineteenth century.

Southern Baptists are now considered the largest Protestant group in America. They represent over forty thousand individual churches and twelve hundred local associations. While the largest number of their believers is still in the Southern states, they now spread nationwide. Arguably, their most famous spokesman is Billy Graham, who has instructed generations of Southerners in his own approach to the gospel life.

The division that resulted in the establishment of the Southern Baptist Convention was not the only split the denomination would experience. In 1932, the General Association of Regular Baptist Churches split from the Northern Baptist Convention, and in 1940, the Conservative Baptist Churches did the same. The Northern Baptist Convention itself is now known as the American Baptist Churches in the United States. Other Baptists groups have emerged from ethnic or national affiliation, such as the Baptist General Conference, which grew out of the Swedish Baptists, and the North American Baptist Conference, which grew out of the German Baptists. Over fifty Baptists groups are recognized in the United States today.

The Baptists have a saying among themselves. When you get two Baptists together, you get three different opinions. More recently, divisions have emerged among Baptists regarding the level of authority that should be given to pastors. Many Baptists traditionally subscribed to the Lutheran idea of the priesthood of all believers. But the Southern Baptists have increasingly elevated the authority of the pastor over that of the priesthood of all believers. Disagreements have also arisen consistently over what approach to take in the interpretation of scripture. The introduction of the historical critical method in the study of biblical texts sparked a great deal of discussion and controversy in numerous Christian denominations, and the Baptists were among them. Given the primary role of biblical authority in the Baptist tradition, interpretation of scripture has become a highly politicized area.

Today, many Americans associate Baptist religious perspectives with a fundamentalist outlook, a charge that may be very accurate in some cases and very inaccurate in others. Those who make sweeping generalizations about the Baptist tradition often fail to realize the degree to which that tradition has become a delta, a religious river that branches into multiple streams with multiple perspectives. Today's Baptist churches stretch from ultraconservative to liberal, with everything in between. But most share a perspective, framed by differing stances or interpretations, rooted in the core beliefs of the tradition. As in the earliest days of the tradition, we still find adherence to the believer's baptism, baptism by immersion, reliance on scripture, freedom of conscience, and a belief in congregational autonomy. To this day, we also find among the Baptists individuals who are willing to move against the current, to face political difficulty or intellectual challenge, just as the early Separatists did in England, in order to stand firm in their belief and in the convictions that have emerged from that belief.

15

PENTECOSTALS AND
THE HOLINESS MOVEMENT

Although not all scholars agree, an increasing number believes that Pentecostalism is a descendent of the holiness movement, which, in turn, had its origins in the Methodist tradition. John Wesley, the founder of Methodism, discussed in chapter 4, had a particular interest in spirituality and religious experience. His was a lifelong pursuit of holiness, informed by some of the greatest writers in Western spirituality. Those familiar with Methodist tradition will also likely be familiar with Wesley's Aldersgate experience, in which Wesley, in his own words, felt his "heart strangely warmed." Many consider Aldersgate a critical moment of conversion in the life of John Wesley. Yet, Wesley did not consider himself to have achieved spiritual perfection through this experience. Rather, he went on to develop a twofold approach, which recognized the validity of both sudden or abrupt conversion and of a slower process of gradual conversion that emerged out of the determined pursuit of a life of holiness and Christian perfection. Wesley spent almost forty years continually revising one tract he had written, "A Plain Account of Christian Perfection as Believed and Taught by the Reverend John Wesley." This short work became, in effect, a manifesto for the holiness groups that grew out of the Methodist tradition.

In Wesley's understanding, Christian perfection was most commonly attained through a gradual process, a gradual growth through grace. But it could also come suddenly through a "second work of grace." John Fletcher, who was Wesley's heir apparent as the leader of Methodism, considered this second blessing a "baptism in the Holy Spirit." When the Methodist Church formally came to America in 1784, Wesley's second work of grace came with it, and the first American publication of the *Book of Discipline* of the Methodist Church in 1788 contained a complete copy of Wesley's "Plain

Account of Christian Perfection." Methodism grew rapidly on American soil as Americans embraced Wesley's "heart religion" over the more dry, abstract, and intellectualized forms of faith dominant at the time.

Methodism also rode into greater popularity through the power of Methodist preachers and the growing movement of religious revivals across the country. The most famous of these was the camp meeting at Cane Ridge. Starting in June 1800, three Presbyterian ministers held revivals that ran over the course of three summers in Logan County, Kentucky. Cane Ridge, held in 1801 in Bourbon County, was the high point of this flurry of revivals. Estimates of attendance range from ten to twenty-five thousand people, and the Cane Ridge camp meeting went on for over a year. Preachers exhorted believers to embrace God with all their hearts. Attendees responded with dramatic displays of religious inspiration—trembling and shaking, crawling on all fours, going into trances, swooning and singing. Some were "slain in the spirit" or "smitten of the Lord," falling down as if unconscious. Others spoke in tongues, making garbled noises that could not be understood as normal speech.

But the meeting at Cane Ridge was not the only event that contributed to the growing interest in holiness and perfection in nineteenth-century America. Figures like Charles G. Finney also contributed. Finney was Presbyterian, but nothing in that strict Calvinist background prepared him for the sudden conversion he experienced. He considered the experience, to use Fletcher's term, a "baptism in the Holy Spirit," and he subsequently became certain that one could achieve sanctification in this life. Throughout the 1820s, Finney led revivals, preached, and evangelized. Eventually, he was hired by Oberlin College in Ohio, and Finney developed a second theological approach to holiness and perfection in what is sometimes referred to as his Oberlin theology. Many of the terms he used to expound that theology would reflect the ideas of the later Pentecostal movement.

Among Methodists who continued to expound the importance of perfection and holiness was Phoebe Palmer. In 1835, Palmer's sister began to hold weekly meetings in her home, which she called the Tuesday Meetings for Promotion of Holiness. Soon, Palmer was leading the meetings, convinced there was a "shorter way" to achieve perfection than the slow gradual work of sanctification. She and her husband, Dr. Walter Palmer, became the highly visible leaders of a holiness movement, traveling the country to appear at lectures, revivals, and church meetings.

As a result of their celebrity, a magazine was founded to distribute the Palmers' thoughts and teachings. The Boston-based monthly, titled the

Guide to Christian Perfection, and later titled the *Guide to Holiness,* was the first publication devoted to the holiness movement. Its circulation reached as many as thirty thousand copies at the height of its popularity. In 1858, a Presbyterian minister decided to extend the message of the holiness movement beyond the Methodists. He wrote a book titled *The Higher Christian Life.* It became a best seller. His book, along with A. B. Earle's *The Rest of Faith* and Jesse T. Peck's *The Central Idea of Christianity,* kept the ideas of the holiness movement percolating in the American conscience.

With the rising tensions that preceded the Civil War, the attention of many religious denominations shifted from the pursuit of holiness to the question of slavery. As noted in chapters four and fourteen, both the Baptists and the Methodists experienced splits in their denomination over the issue. The last great revival before the Civil War occurred in 1858. The revival began in New York City. Thousands of urban workers joined together to sing hymns and pray. Interest in the holiness movement shifted to the North, as Southerners became increasingly preoccupied with slavery, the devastating impact of the Civil War, and the more pressing concerns that accompanied war and defeat. In the immediate aftermath of the war, between 1865 and 1867, the South experienced a short revival of the holiness spirit. Spurred on by bishops of the Methodist Episcopal Church, believers began once again to focus on sanctification in the grim aftermath of war.

The next significant development in the holiness movement, however, came not from the South but from the North. In 1866, J. A. Wood and Harriet E. Drake began organizing a camp meeting. Soon, Wood had recruited two ministers, William Osborn of New Jersey and John Inskip of New York. Ultimately, thirteen Methodist ministers signed up to participate in a large meeting in Philadelphia, Pennsylvania, in June 1867. At the Philadelphia meeting, they jointly agreed to hold a camp meeting in July of the same year. A call was put out to everyone, regardless of denomination, with a special invitation to those who felt "isolated" as a result of their beliefs about holiness. The subsequent camp meeting, which began on July 17, 1867, is considered by many to be the start of the modern holiness movement in America. The meeting was a great success, and at the end of the meeting, Inskip was chosen to lead a new organization, the National Camp Meeting Association for the Promotion of Holiness.

The association was kept busy organizing camp meetings in Pennsylvania, New York, and other states. Over the next sixteen years, fifty-two national camp meetings were scheduled. As many as twenty thousand attended one of the meetings, which even welcomed a U.S. president. The Methodist

Church, dominant in the holiness movement, began to urge its pastors to reassert Wesley's doctrine of Christian perfection. A flurry of publications dedicated to Christian holiness began to appear.

The holiness movement had a curious ability to transcend race lines in nineteenth-century America. In 1786, Richard Allen founded the African Methodist Church, as discussed in chapter 13. In 1821, James Varick and his companions founded the African Methodist Episcopal Church in America, which would later become the African Methodist Episcopal Church of Zion. Because of their roots in the Methodist Church, both groups remained receptive to the teachings of the holiness movement, especially in light of Wesley's teachings on sanctification. By the late 1870s, many black churches were entering into the holiness movement, and in 1877, a revival was held at Allen's Bethel Church in Philadelphia. This Holiness Conference, offered in June 1877, seems remarkably progressive from today's perspective. It was interracial, interdenominational, and gender inclusive, allowing women to participate and exercise spiritual leadership.

By the 1880s, the South was once again ready to embrace the holiness movement, and a series of revivals were scheduled. Inskip, working in his role as president of the National Holiness Association, preached in Savannah and Augusta, Georgia, organized a holiness association for the state, and met with leaders of the Methodist North Georgia Conference. The establishment of holiness associations became something of a movement. State-based and regional associations sprang up, and activity increased at several Methodist district conferences.

The holiness movement reached its peak in the 1880s. While the Methodists were central to the movement, it had also reached Presbyterians, Baptists, and Congregationalists. But within the Methodist tradition itself, it was not without controversy. In part, the resistance the movement encountered had to do with the interdenominational practices of the National Holiness Association, which some Methodists viewed as contrary to traditional practice. But more disturbing still to many conservative Methodist leaders was a trend toward "come-outism," urging members to "come out" of the Methodist church, that was originating in a radical branch of the Holiness Movement.

Congregations embracing the holiness movement began to spring up. In 1880, Daniel S. Warner organized a Church of God congregation in Anderson, Indiana. Shortly thereafter, another believer, S. B. Shaw, started a group known as the Primitive Holiness Mission. But in 1887, John P. Brooks wrote a book entitled *The Divine Church*. In that book, he criticized the Methodist Church as drifting too far away from a rigorous practice of the faith, saying it had become "soft," lost its spiritual rigor, and was now overly concerned with polity and the construction of grand buildings. A new radical stream of holiness began to emerge. Adherents identified themselves by their objections to the formality of the Methodist Church and to the pleasures of the world. This radical group became increasingly worrisome to established Methodist leaders, particularly when its theological interpretations stretched to new teachings that had never been part of Methodist tradition or theology.

By 1885, the movement to denounce holiness began to grow in the Southern Methodist Church. One Georgia Methodist, Atticus Greene Haygood, called for a return to the gradual process of sanctification as the only true Methodist approach. Haygood assumed a leadership role in the group that would eventually undermine the holiness movement. In 1884, a theologian at Vanderbilt University had openly challenged the holiness interpretation of sanctification. Soon, a series of books denouncing the holiness view of sanctification were published. Preachers who supported the holiness movement began to find themselves sent out to pasture, assigned to small, rural churches.

Those who did embrace the holiness movement began to feel less and less comfortable in the Methodist Church. In 1894, at the General Conference of the Methodist Episcopal Church, Haygood, who had risen to the chair of bishop, issued a statement denouncing the holiness tradition. A rule was invoked, Rule 301, which allowed resident ministers the power to refuse access to their congregations to outside evangelists. Many holiness preachers suddenly found themselves without an audience. Adherents to the holiness movement were suddenly confronted with the decision of whether to abandon their holiness beliefs or "come-out" and abandon their affiliation with the Methodist Church.

Some elected to stay within the Methodist Church and try to change it from within. Others left and began to establish new churches in the holiness tradition, such as the Church of the Nazarene, founded in 1895 by J. P. Widney. But those who elected to leave the Methodist Church often had significantly different understandings of just what constituted holiness, and by 1905, numerous different denominations had emerged. In a single seven-year period, twenty-three new holiness denominations were started. The movement itself fragmented. But in the fragmented pieces of the holiness movement was the foundation for a much larger movement that would have a powerful effect on the American religious landscape, the Pentecostal movement.

As noted above, over twenty different holiness denominations emerged out of the reaction to the 1894 General Conference of the Southern

Methodist Church. Only a few of those followed a stream we would today identify as Pentecostal. Whereas the earlier stream of the holiness movement had emphasized its relationship to Wesley's theology and the "second blessing" of a sudden form of sanctification, some leaders now began to make more and more reference to the Pentecost, and the "Pentecostal" dimensions of such religious transformation. One of the most radical of these was Isaiah Reed, who founded the Iowa Holiness Association. The association flourished and attracted members from Missouri and Nebraska. It soon had a larger roster of members than the national association. Iowa became a hotbed of radical holiness thought and practice.

In 1895, Benjamin Hardin Irwin, a member of the Iowa Holiness Association, founded the Fire-Baptized Holiness Church. Entranced with John Fletcher's "baptism of burning love," his study led him to the conclusion that a third kind of sanctification existed, and he began to seek a "baptism of fire." In October 1895, he claimed that experience and immediately began preaching on it. Soon, his churches were overflowing with demonstrative believers, who also achieved the baptism of fire with great regularity. The majority of the holiness movement did not accept Irwin's teaching and continued with the "second blessing" approach they had followed for so long. But Irwin's movement grew and expanded in the Midwest and South. By 1898, he had established state organizations in Iowa, Kansas, Texas, Oklahoma, South Carolina, North Carolina, Georgia, Florida, and Virginia. He called for a national convention in South Carolina, where he was named general overseer. The following year he established a journal, the *Live Coals of Fire*, which asserted the baptism of fire followed sanctification. The journal's influence helped to provide fertile ground for the subsequent development of the Pentecostal movement.

Irwin's radical enthusiasm led to his own decline. He soon decided that fourth, fifth, and sixth baptisms were also necessary, moving him and his followers further and further away from the mainstream of the holiness movement. Some critics began to call for yet another baptism, this time a "baptism of common sense." When it was subsequently discovered that Irwin's personal life was far from above reproach, he resigned as overseer, and his church began a long decline. In spite of his failure, Irwin created a climate that would be receptive to many of the teachings of the Pentecostal movement, which developed thereafter. One of his elders, W. H. Fulford, went on to become president of a splinter church, The United Holy Church of America.

Numerous conservative holiness denominations sustained the spirit of the holiness movement, including the Church of the Nazarene, the Pilgrim

Holiness Church, the Wesleyan Methodist Church, the Christian and Missionary Alliance, and the Free Methodist Church. But perhaps the most popular was the Church of God. The Church of God was founded in 1880 by D. S. Warner in Anderson, Indiana, as noted above. Several groups began to use the term Church of God to signal their dissatisfaction with the Methodist reaction to the holiness movement. After 1906, some of these groups would come to be known as Pentecostals.

The year 1906 is somewhat of a watershed in the history of Pentecostalism in this country. In April of that year, California's *Los Angeles Times* published a derogatory article describing a revival meeting held on Azusa Street. The revival, led by William Joseph Seymour, was held in an abandoned African Methodist Episcopal church. Seymour, an African American preacher who had been influenced by Charles Fox Parham, believed in powerful manifestations of the power of the Holy Spirit and emphasized the same in his preaching. When Seymour began giving regular sermons at the old African Methodist Episcopal church, a revival developed. Like Parham, Seymour believed in glossolalia, or speaking in tongues, and soon after his revival began, numerous participants began receiving that gift. The *Los Angeles Times* ridiculed such practices, but its coverage had an unintended effect. Rather than discouraging the revival, it cause it to grow, as those seriously engaged with holiness approaches gravitated toward others of like mind and curiosity seekers gathered to watch the believers.

The revival went on for three and a half years, with highly emotive forms of spirituality becoming the norm during that time. Believers wept, shouted, danced, swooned, sang, spoke in tongues, and went into trance states. Seymour and his principal supporters would spend time between services in an upstairs area that came to be known as the "Pentecostal upper room." Perhaps because of that designation, an article in the *Way of Faith* proclaimed, "Pentecost has come to Los Angeles, the American Jerusalem."[1] The name stuck, and, soon, the demonstrative type of religious practice associated with Azusa Street came to be known as Pentecostalism.

Some of those associated with the holiness movement became concerned by the excessive emotionalism and displays associated with the revival on Azusa Street. Seymour himself attempted to curb the displays of speaking in tongues, although he was unable to do so. But the dramatic aspects of the revival, combined with extensive coverage by newspapers, meant that the impact of the revival reached far beyond the city of Los Angeles. Ministers from New York, Chicago, and the Midwest came to observe and took stories back with them to their congregations. Pastors from as far away as Oslo, Norway, brought Pentecostal prayer forms back with them to their home churches.

Azusa Street is widely recognized as the beginning of the international Pentecostal movement. Perhaps nowhere was the news of the Azusa Revival greeted with more interest than in the American South. Members of holiness congregations circulated writings by Seymour and embraced the profound devotional experience of Pentecostalism. One of the key figures in bringing Pentecostalism to the South was Gaston Barnabas Cashwell of Dunn, North Carolina. Cashwell had given up a future as a minister in the Methodist Church in order to join a holiness church. When he heard reports of Seymour's revival in Los Angeles, he became determined to see the revival first hand. Traveling to the West Coast, he attended the revival and asked Seymour to "lay hands" on him. He returned to North Carolina filled with the spirit.

Back in North Carolina, he promptly rented an old warehouse, invited all the ministers of the Fire-Baptized Holiness Church, the Pentecostal Holiness Church, and the Free-Will Baptist Church to attend. Thousands of people came to the warehouse to learn more about the movement where believers "talked in tongues," and many of the clergy had profound Pentecostal experiences in the course of the meeting. Members of more mainline denominations, Baptists, Methodists, and Presbyterians, also embraced the Pentecostal experience.

Cashwell was extremely effective in bringing the leaders of various churches associated with the holiness movement to adopt Pentecostalism. These included the Pentecostal Holiness Church, the Fire-Baptized Holiness Church, the Tabernacle Pentecostal Church, the Church of God in Christ, and the Church of God. He even converted B. H. Irwin, the founder of the baptism-in-fire movement described above.

The Pentecostal movement had soon established itself firmly in the hearts and faith-lives of thousands of Southerners. As it crossed racial lines and economic divisions and unified divided denominations, no one had ever seen anything like it. Nor did the growth of the Pentecostal movement stop at the coasts of America. Methodist pastor Thomas Ball Barratt took Pentecostalism back to Norway with him. Among his converts was a German named Jonathan Paul, who formed a Pentecostal denomination known as the Muhlheim Association. Italian immigrants in the United States embraced the movement and, soon, transferred it back to their homeland. Two young Swedish converts, Daniel Berg and Gunnar Vingren, took the movement to Brazil in 1910. A Methodist missionary and physician named Willis C. Hoover brought Pentecostalism to the Methodists of Chile. John Lake (1870–1935), took Pentecostalism to South Africa. A Russian-born Baptist pastor named Ivan Efimovich Voronaev took the movement to Russia and the Slavic lands. Methodist and Presbyterian missionaries later took Pentecostalism into Korea. William Kumuyi, decades later, brought Pentecostalism to his Nigerian homeland. In a few short decades, Pentecostalism was established as a worldwide religious phenomenon.

The road to the establishment of Pentecostalism as an accepted part of the American religious landscape was not smooth, however. As quickly as the movement spread to other nations, it evoked opposition from established denominations. Religious leaders from numerous denominations denounced the movement, just as leaders had denounced the emotionalism of the Great Awakening generations before. Curiously, some of the bitterest opposition came from churches in the holiness movement.

One opponent was Alma White, who headed up the Pillar of Fire Church. White believed that speaking in tongues was the work of the devil and published his views in a book titled *Demons and Tongues*. W. B. Godbey, a holiness preacher, dismissed the movement as "spiritualism," the equivalent of speaking to the dead. H. A. Ironside thought the practices more appropriate for the "madhouse," and H. J. Stolee dismissed them as mob hysteria or hallucinations. Others simply called speaking in tongues "gibberish."[2]

Many of the leaders of the Pentecostal movement responded to these attacks with publications of their own, and a flurry of books defending Pentecostal practice emerged. As early as 1907, Charles Parham was defending speaking in tongues in his book *Kol Kar Bomidhar: A Voice Crying in the Wilderness*. G. F. Taylor penned *The Spirit and the Bride*, and David Wesley Myland produced *The Latter Rain Covenant and Pentecostal Power* in 1910. But even as these Pentecostal leaders defended the practice of speaking in tongues and the emotionalized spiritual responses associated with the Pentecostal movement, a greater division was emerging in terms of how one understood sanctification as a "second work of grace."

One of the most basic splits in doctrinal interpretation in the Pentecostal movement came in the form of the "Finished Work" controversy. In the early stages of the movement, most saw sanctification as a second blessing, a cleansing or purification that prepared one for greater interaction with the Spirit. This perspective was pretty much in keeping with the Wesleyan understanding of sanctification and reflected the Methodist roots of the movement. But with its rapid growth, converts from many different denominations came quickly into the Pentecostal movement. They were less likely to assume a Wesleyan understanding of sanctification. Many saw only two stages as necessary—conversion and the baptism of the Holy Spirit. A group led by William H. Durham of Chicago sought to replace the understanding of sanctification as a second blessing with what he termed the "Doctrine of the Finished Work."

Durham denied that conversion left any "residue of sin" in the believer, as Wesley had cautioned. Instead, in Durham's view, sanctification happened in the instant of conversion. One therefore had no need of sanctification as a second blessing or later development. In robust style, Durham took his challenges directly to Seymour in the Azusa Street Mission and denounced other interpretations. A theological battlefield opened up within the ranks of the Pentecostal movement, with each side denouncing the other's views. Durham's sudden death in July 1912 was viewed a confirmation of his error by his opponents. But hundreds of independent churches adopted Durham's views, and the belief became well grounded in certain streams of Pentecostalism.

Eventually, those churches that had embraced the Finished Work doctrine began to feel the need to organize into something resembling a denominational structure. Others felt the same impulse, including members of the Church of God in Christ, which had been founded in Tennessee by C. H. Mason. Two of those dissatisfied with Mason's leadership, E. N. Bell and H. G. Rodgers, led splinter groups related to the Church of God. They decided to organize a new group that would not be dependent on Mason and called a general council in April 1914 in Hot Springs, Arkansas. Three hundred laymen and clergy came to the council, where they approved a constitution founding a denomination called the General Council of the Assemblies of God. Adopting a Finished Work doctrine, they formally distanced themselves from the Wesleyan tradition.

Other innovations were introduced. Earlier groups had followed the episcopal framework of the Methodist tradition. These groups opted for a structure that was closer to the Baptists, with most control remaining at the level of the individual congregation. Segregation also grew out of the split. The Church of God remained primarily black, while the newly established Assemblies of God was overwhelmingly white. A separate tradition of African American Pentecostals developed in the split's wake. The split due to the Finished Works controversy was profound, and from 1914 on, the Pentecostal movement was divided between those who followed the more Methodist holiness tradition and those who followed the Finished Work tradition.

The development of Pentecostalism in America reflects many of the characteristics of the development of the groups that influenced it, the Methodists and the Baptists. In their earliest stages, they were viewed with a great deal of suspicion, their religious innovations were denounced, and they met with considerable prejudice. Rumors painted members to be even more extreme than they actually were and dismissed adherents to the holiness tradition as "Holy Rollers."

In part, the suspicion was based on those who conflated the emerging Pentecostal tradition with the snake handling that developed in Alabama, Kentucky, and Tennessee. George Hensley championed that movement, asserting that the handling of snakes was a sign that one was redeemed in Christ and that faith in the Lord would protect the handler. The Pentecostal Holiness Church and the Church of God both denounced the practice, but it continued in rural areas in specific congregations.

Others distrusted the Pentecostal tradition because of its willingness to allow women to preach in church. Pentecostals cited Joel 2:28, which clearly states, "Your sons and your daughters shall prophesy." Today, one out of six ordained ministers in the Assemblies of God is a woman, and 17 percent of the ministers in the Pentecostal Holiness Church are female. Since women preachers such as Mary Woodworth Etter and Aimee Semple McPherson had high profiles and were widely known for their preaching and faith healing, the prominent role of women was clear even to outsiders.

Many preachers in the Pentecostal tradition emphasized the role of faith in healing and offered healing as a mark of spiritual progress. This emphasis on faith healing, combined with proscriptions against alcohol, tobacco, dancing, movies, and makeup, made the tradition unappealing to many Americans. But the group continued to achieve rapid growth in spite of these elements. By the 1940s, over thirty-six different Pentecostal churches had been founded. Today, the larger groups include the Assemblies of God, the Church of God in Christ, the Church of God, the Pentecostal Assemblies of the World, and the Pentecostal Holiness Church. The Church of God, the largest, boasts almost seven million members, and the Assemblies of God has over two million.

Many Americans today are most familiar with the Pentecostals through the charismatic movement. Many individuals who were already established in more mainline religious traditions, both Protestant and Catholic, were intrigued by the spiritual vitality of the Pentecostals. Many of them began to integrate elements of Pentecostal worship into their traditional liturgy and prayer life. These groups became known as charismatics.

In the 1960s, a group of Catholics at Duquesne University began reporting incidents of glossolalia, or speaking in tongues. Soon reports were coming out of Notre Dame University as well. Catholic Church authorities began examining the movement as a possible form of enrichment for the church. Ultimately, that gave rise to the Catholic Charismatic Renewal, which has emphasized a greater relationship with the Holy Spirit in the framework of Roman Catholic tradition.

The Protestants, too, have proven themselves receptive to Pentecostal views. One interdenominational journal, *Christian Life,* reports on Pentecostal experiences among members of diverse religious traditions. Even the holiness movement, which had so firmly denounced Pentecostalism in its infancy, began to show signs of a thaw in its relations to the Pentecostals in the 1960s, and a "new climate of understanding" has grown and developed.

By the 1980s, many leaders of the Pentecostal movement referred to what they termed a "third wave," coming after the first wave of the "classical" Pentecostals and the second wave of the charismatic movement. This third wave, it was predicted, would enter mainline denominations silently as leaders of traditional denominations accepted the gifts of the Spirit. Rather than leaving those congregations, members of the third wave remained in place, bringing their own Pentecostal perspective and gifts into their tradition. Not all Pentecostals or Neo-Pentecostals supported such a move, but the hunger of those in traditional churches for forms of worship that honor the emotional aspects of their relationship with the divine, the strong association of such worship with the Holy Spirit, and the enrichment such practices can provide mean that the Pentecostal tradition will continue to interact with mainline denominations in a powerful and dynamic way. From Wesley, through the holiness movement, through the early days of Pentecostalism, that interdenominational dynamism has been a long time coming and serves as an ongoing source of powerful prayer and praise.

NOTES

1. Frank Bartleman, *How Pentecost came to Los Angeles,* 1925, cited in Vinson Synan, *The Holiness-Pentecostal Tradition* (Grand Rapids, MI: William B. Eerdmans Publishing Company, 1997), 99.

2. See more detailed discussion in Synan, *Tradition,* 146. I am indebted to Synan for the general perspective informing this chapter.

16

THE CALIFORNIA MISSIONS AND THE HISPANIC SOUTHWEST

While numerous Christian traditions crept ever westward across the United States following settlement and missionary activity, Catholicism had been making its presence known in California and the American Southwest for centuries. After the "discovery" of the New World by Spanish explorers in the late fifteenth century, Ferdinand and Isabella of Spain assumed dominion over it. Pope Alexander VI, in a diplomatic move to avoid division, awarded half of the New World to Spain and half to Portugal. While the Portuguese concentrated on Latin America, the Spanish developed a vast colonial system that stretched from Central America, through Mexico, and into the western United States. A viceroy of New Spain was appointed in Mexico City to oversee the civil, religious, and military affairs of the Spanish crown in the New World.

Spanish exploration and immigration from Mexico northward followed three streams. The first headed north to the Rio Grande River, then northeast to establish cities such as San Antonio, Texas. A second stream headed due north, following the Rio Grande up the Camino Réal, as the Spanish trading route later came to be known, and Spanish settlements grew up along both banks of the long and sinuous river. These northern areas came to be known as Nuevo Mexico. Finally, a stream of exploration and immigration followed the Pacific Coast, into the lush landscape that would come to be known as California.

Originally, California was believed to be a large island, and the Gulf of California was thought to be a strait, separating California from the mainland. As early as 1542, sea expeditions had been launched up the California coast, attempting to find a new route to the Orient. Spanish explorers made notes about geographical features and the natives, and they assigned Spanish names to everything they encountered. By 1579, Sir Francis Drake was attempting to claim the land for England. From a port north of San Francisco, he named the land Nova Albion, New England, and declared it property of Queen Elizabeth. But the Spanish blocked any further English settlement, and California remained predominantly under Spanish dominion.

Exploration continued into the early seventeenth century, but there were few resources and little demand for colonizing the area known as California between 1600 and 1769. But in 1769, everything changed. In June of that year, Father Junípero Serra climbed onto a mule to lead a pack train into San Diego. Eventually, Serra would be portrayed as a saint by some and a demon by others. Serra had been born in Mallorca, Spain, in 1713. He was a scholar, a teacher, and a solid administrator. He taught philosophy for fifteen years at Palma before being sent to America. Once in Mexico, he taught at the College of San Fernando, worked among Native Americans for three years in Sierra Gorda, then returned to Mexico City. When responsibility for missions in Baja California had just been transferred to the Franciscans, of which he was a member, Serra was tapped as the leader for the missionary efforts.

Earlier sailing missions, Cabrillo in 1542 and Vizcaíno in 1602, had mapped the California coast as far as Monterey. Areas north of that had been explored by Russian fur traders between 1740 and 1765, and they began to establish settlements along what is now known as the Russian River. This incursion made the settling of California a greater priority for the Spanish, lest the Russian encroachment continue to move south. Don Gaspár de Portolá was assigned military leadership of the 1769 expedition, and Serra was assigned to lead the missionary efforts.

The group was divided into two seagoing parties and two land expeditions. Serra and Portolá traveled in the second land expedition. Their first encounters with Native Americans were not promising. The Spanish seized all possible food along the path they traveled, and some Native American communities were left to starve in their wake. But by July 16, 1769, Father Serra raised a cross in San Diego to establish the first of the California missions, San Diego de Alcalá. By June 3, 1770, they had established a second mission in Monterey and named it after St. Charles Borromeo.

These two widely separated missions—they were six hundred fifty miles apart—in San Diego and what they believed was Monterey became the endpoints for a time. The Spanish hoped to establish missions between them, each one day's ride from another. But the Spanish faced immense logistical problems in establishing further missions. Ships of the period could carry relatively little in terms of food or supplies and were subject to Pacific storms. The inland route did not have adequate water. Nor did New Spain, itself a colony, have vast resources to be used for the colonization of outlying regions. Relationships with the Native Americans were uncertain, as was the nature of the reception that Spanish soldiers or colonists might receive at their hands. However, in 1774, Juan Bautista de Anza pioneered a pack route that would enable regular reinforcement by mule train.

Once the pack route as a means of support for the missions had been established, the individual missions could be developed. Development radiated out from the first two missions in San Diego and Monterey, which could be supplied to some extent by sea. Once San Francisco Bay had been discovered, two missions were established there, and three were opened along the Santa Barbara Channel. In 1784, the death of Father Serra meant a change in the leadership of the missions. Father Fermín Lasuén, who had already demonstrated administrative skill in the missions, was tapped as the next leader. He added nine more missions to the mission chain and continued his work on the missions until his death at age eighty-three. Between the two of them, Serra and Lasuén guided the missions for thirty-four years. Within a half a century, twenty missions had been established on the California coast, and the land known as California was irrevocably changed.

While the Franciscans celebrated their efforts to bring Catholicism to the Native Americans of California, the impact of colonization on the peoples of California was devastating. Prior to colonization, California was home to more Native Americans per square mile than any other part of the country. Among the all-but-vanished tribes of California are the Cabazon people, the Chemehuevi people, and the Achomawi, Karok, Modoc, Okwanachu, Tolow, and Yurok tribes. Monterey was once home to the Ohlone or Costanoan, the Esselen, and the Salinan peoples. But few Americans today could name a single Californian tribe. Initial encounters were often friendly, but as Native American tribes began to realize that the missions were permanent incursions into their traditional tribal lands, many resisted, some violently.

Most devastating to the Native American populations, however, was not the military presence of the Spanish but what the Spanish brought with them in terms of epidemic and disease. Native Americans had no immunity to European diseases. As such, diseases that were often relatively mild for Europeans, common childhood conditions such as measles and chicken pox, proved disastrous to native populations. They died by the thousands, and mission graveyards for Indians remain as testament to the devastation. In addition, venereal disease, which often accompanies any influx of sailors or soldiers into an area, killed many of the natives.

Given the encroachment they increasingly recognized, the devastation that came with European illness, and the highly structured way of life demanded at the missions, few Native Americans found the Franciscans or the Christianity they offered attractive in the early days of the missions. In the first five years, only 491 infants were baptized, 462 adults converted, and sixty-two marriages celebrated. Even those who initially accepted life in the mission compound often found the life unbearable. Overworked and underfed, they frequently fled back to their native villages disillusioned.

Most histories suggest that the Native Americans "consented" to life on the missions, but that consent was often coerced by poverty, starvation, or inequality of power. Once they had joined the life at the mission, it is clear that they were expected to remain at the mission for the remainder of their lives and never leave mission grounds without express permission.

Life in the missions was completely foreign to the Native American way of life. Native Americans provided virtually all of the labor required to build the mission buildings. Whereas they were used to building in wood or reed, these were massive structures of adobe and stone. Men were expected to spend a specified number of hours a day producing adobe bricks and roof tiles, constructing walls, or working in the fields. Women were expected to contribute through weaving, carding and spinning wool, and grinding corn. Systematic agriculture was developed in the area surrounding the missions, and missionary priests oversaw the planting of bananas, oranges, olives, figs, and vineyards. Thousands of cattle were bred, along with chickens, sheep, goats, horses, and donkeys. Mission communities included numerous workrooms for weaving or making pottery, for carpentry or for study. Storerooms contained previous year's crops of wheat, corn, and beans.

Life on the mission was regimented. Residents were expected to attend numerous prayer services every day. Other tribes, who had resisted mission life, regularly raided the stores of the mission and challenged adherence to the new way of life. But raiding parties were sporadic, and some Native Americans welcomed the mission as a source of regular food. Those who did, however, were at much higher risk of contracting European diseases. Periodically, large-scale revolts broke out, and the Native Americans burned down mission structures, ran off the herds, and destroyed the crops in the fields.

In spite of these obstacles, the missions grew and became relatively stable communities for over a century. Other than the decimation of the Native American population through overwork and disease, the most serious blow to mission life came after the Mexican Revolution, when the people of Mexico decided to eject all Spanish nationals. Most of the members of religious orders who ran the California missions were natives of Spain. The

Franciscan padres held the land of California in trust for the Native Americans. In 1830, only twenty-one pieces of land were in the hands of private landholders.

The revolutionary government in Mexico, eager to eject Spanish nationals and open up the land of the missions to private ownership, decided in 1833 and 1834 to pass decrees that required their secularization. Secularization meant they could expel the missionaries who ran them, confiscate any funds the mission might have, and take possession of the land and the vast herds of livestock under mission control. The buildings were divided, with some becoming public and some remaining religious. The land was turned over to the Native Americans, but many had little conception of property rights and were quickly defrauded of ownership of the land by speculators.

The effect on the missions was reminiscent of the devastation of the Roman Catholic Church in France over the course of the French Revolution. It was nothing short of disastrous. When the revolutionary government decided to secularize the missions in 1834, they were home to over thirty thousand Native Americans, almost half a million cattle, more than three hundred thousand sheep, and over sixty thousand horses and mules. After secularization, there remained only 4,450 Native Americans and less than thirty thousand head of cattle. Over an astonishingly short period of time, the orchards went to seed, the fields went unplowed, herds disappeared, and storerooms were emptied.

Few periods of American religious history are as controversial from a contemporary perspective as the development of the California missions. Traditional accounts of the missions portrayed the Native American populations of California as "heathens." One Russian in 1816, reflecting the racism rampant at the time, called them "ugly, stupid and savage." There is little doubt that the Catholic priests and brothers who ran the missions saw themselves as doing the work of God, bringing the light of Christ to those desperately in need of the church's teachings. But there is also little doubt that many of them regarded the Native American residents as childlike and incapable of adult morality. Most had little or no understanding of Native American tradition and religious beliefs or of Native American language and culture. In an age that celebrated colonial imperialism, the Franciscan friars who ran many of the missions could see themselves as brave pioneers, doing the work of God in the fields of the Lord.

In the twentieth century, particularly in the aftermath of the American Indian Movement, the work of the California missions has been reassessed from a Native American perspective. Junípero Serra, initially seen as a hero, has been loudly condemned by Native American scholars and historians as one who promoted slavery and genocide. Contemporary critics point out that no attempt was made to preserve the existing Native American cultures in California, forever depriving us of knowledge of many of them as a result. They see the Native Americans' labor in the construction of the missions as exploitation, the cost demanded of a conquered people, enforced militarily and inescapable for most of the Native Americans who resided in the missions as nothing more than slaves, stripped of their own belief systems and systematically exterminated by overwork and disease.

In countering these charges, many assert that the Native Americans actually fared better under Spanish rule than they did under the later rule of the United States. Under the U.S. government, Native Americans were driven off all of the lands in California, not just those close to the missions, and restricted to small reservations on land that was basically uninhabitable. Americans also brought more diseases that proved fatal to thousands of Native Americans in California.

After California came under American jurisdiction, in the 1850s and 1860s the Federal Land Commission reviewed the property rights of the missions, and Congress returned many of the lands to the Roman Catholic Church. But the church at the time had few resources to support the missions, and many of them were leased out for use as farms or for agricultural storage. The buildings themselves fell into disrepair. In the twentieth century, the historical value of the missions and their architectural significance began to be recognized. As a result, a restoration movement developed, and the majority of the Spanish missions have now been restored and are open to the public.

While the western stream of Spanish exploration and immigration resulted in the development of the California missions, the central stream moved up the Rio Grande valley into the area known as Nuevo Mexico and recognized today as the state of New Mexico. A different relationship played out between the Spanish colonial settlers that moved *al Norte* (to the north) and the Native American residents of New Mexico.

The earliest Spanish foray into what is now known as New Mexico was an expedition headed up by Francisco Vásquez de Coronado in 1540, almost two hundred years before George Washington was born. Coronado had heard stories of seven cities of gold and struck out in search of the cities, and in search of the gold. He never found gold, but he made his way north of what is now Albuquerque and met the inhabitants of a dozen pueblos. New Mexican pueblos are unlike many other Native American communities in that they are established agricultural communities that have remained in the same place in distinctive architectural structures for centuries. But the culture of each pueblo, as they were called by the Spanish, is unique, with significant variations in language and systems of belief. After the Spanish requisitioned grain and drove the Native Americans from one of the pueblos to commandeer housing, the natives rebelled. Coronado ultimately returned to New Spain, broke and disillusioned, with even less gold than he had set out with.

The next substantial Spanish expedition was that of Juan de Oñate. De Oñate was a seasoned campaigner against native tribes, having fought against the Chichimecs for twenty years. When he left for New Mexico in 1598, with approval from both the viceroy and the king, he took nearly two hundred soldiers and their families, along with oxen, horses, and supplies. He also had instructions that the missionary work of the church was the most important aspect of his trip, beyond building houses and settling the Rio Grande valley. Moving up the river valley, they were warmly greeted by the people of San Juan Pueblo and established San Gabriel as New Mexico's first capital. Then, disaster struck.

Juan de Zaldívar, Oñate's nephew and second in command, was killed at Acoma Pueblo, west of modern-day Albuquerque, along with ten of his men. Oñate launched a brutal attack on the pueblo in retribution, led by Vincente de Zaldívar, younger brother of the slain commander. When Zaldívar returned from Acoma, victorious, with hundreds of the people of Acoma Pueblo dead and a few captives trailing behind him, Oñate took revenge. Men over twenty-five were to have one foot cut off and serve twenty-five years of "personal servitude." Men between twelve and twenty-five would serve twenty years of servitude. Women over twelve would serve twenty years. And sixty young women from Acoma would be sent to Mexico to serve in convents. Two Hopi Indians captured at Acoma both lost their right hands and were sent out to tell other natives what Spanish retribution looked like.

The battle at Acoma changed the entire climate of the Spanish presence in New Mexico. New Mexico's natives became increasingly hostile, and their movements more and more limited. Oñate failed to turn up any of those things that might catch the interest of the crown—no big deposits of gold or silver, no pearls or riches. In 1607, he was suspended from office by the Spanish crown.

But the memory of his harsh treatment of the people of Acoma lived on, as did the structures of injustice that rankled the Native American population of New Mexico. Oñate established what is called the *encomienda* system, in which the peoples of lands conquered by Spain were required to pay tribute in grain or other goods to the representatives of the Spanish crown. The tribute was essentially an annual tax. Even less just was the system of *repartimiento,* which meant that Spanish landowners could ask the governor for laborers from nearby pueblos to work Spanish lands. The system was often abused, and resentment toward the system was added to the legacy of mistrust of New Mexico's Native American population.

But, in the period after Oñate's removal from office, missionary activity in New Mexico blossomed. Some historians even refer to it as the Great Missionary Era. Over two hundred fifty Franciscan friars were sent to convert the Pueblo peoples to Catholicism between 1610 and 1680. The Spanish crown "invested" a million pesos in supplying the missionaries, helping them to build churches. New Mexico became known as the territory of Saint Francis.

Similar to the missions in California, the Franciscan missions erected a group of buildings nearby each pueblo and requisitioned the Pueblo natives to provide most of the labor. They offended Pueblo men by asking them to build walls, which in Pueblo culture was specifically women's work. They commandeered Pueblo labor as cooks, sacristans, altar servers, porters, maids, and general servants. The Franciscans demeaned Pueblo beliefs, almost never having adequate understanding of Pueblo languages or existing belief systems. Since Pueblo beliefs emphasized the role of harmony, the Pueblos were more receptive to the possibility of adding Catholic beliefs to their existing array of beliefs. Many saw parallels between their kachinas and the Catholic saints, resulting in a syncretism in some ways similar to Santería.

But tensions continued on a deeper level, and these were exacerbated by a drought that hit after 1650. Without rain, crops were imperiled, and hunger was widespread for both Native Americans and Spanish colonials. In 1675, Gov. Juan Francisco Trevino launch an ill-advised campaign against the shamans of various pueblos, denouncing them as idolaters. He arrested forty-seven and hung three. Another committed suicide. A group of Tewa warriors gathered and confronted the governor, demanding the release of the shamans. When the shamans were released, among their number was an intense young man named Popé.

The year 1680 brought Popé's revenge. Under his leadership, the pueblos successfully planned and executed an overthrow of the Spanish in New Mexico. The Pueblo Revolt brought relatively modest losses by today's standards. Twenty-one Franciscan friars were killed, and four hundred Spanish colonists lost their lives. But the revolt had a huge impact on the Spanish Empire. Never before in its history had Spain lost an entire province to a revolt by indigenous peoples, and it could not afford to see the idea replicated in other parts of the empire. The revolt also endangered the entire northern frontier.

After the bloodbath, the Pueblo people streamed to the rivers to purify themselves and wash away their baptisms. But the Spanish were not about to let the matter rest. Inspired by the reconquest of Spanish lands from the Moors, Don Diego de Vargas led two hundred Spanish soldiers back to Santa Fe in 1692. The Spanish, along with their language and their culture, returned to New Mexico permanently. The return of de Vargas is still celebrated each fall in the Santa Fe Fiesta.

After de Vargas's reconquest, New Mexico settled into a relatively peaceful period under Spanish colonial rule. Two garrisons were established, one in El Paso and one in Santa Fe, each housing soldiers and supplies. New Mexico was considered essential to protect the northern border of New Spain, and the Spanish were particularly sensitive to incursions by the French. The French had a long-established presence in Louisiana, and New Mexicans knew the periodic arrival of trappers and traders. Security was also threatened by raiding parties from nomadic tribes, such as the Comanche or Apache and the Navajo.

In 1803, Napoleon sold the Louisiana Territory to the United States, and the American presence suddenly moved much closer to New Mexico. By 1806, Zebulon Pike had been dispatched to explore the southwestern areas of the Louisiana Purchase. Changes were afoot in Mexico as well. In 1821, the Mexican Revolution brought the ejection of Spanish nationals, and local priests replaced the largely Spanish-born Franciscans who had managed churches throughout the state. Ecclesial responsibility for New Mexico lay in Durango, Mexico, and promising young men would make the long and arduous journey to Durango in order to be trained for the priesthood. New Mexican Catholicism developed unique characteristics, blending the culture of Castile in distant Spain, the colonial imprint of its time as a Spanish colony, and the perspectives of native-born Hispanics, who understood well the texture of the land and its peoples.

Perhaps the best-known and most widely studied conflicts in New Mexico's religious history came with the annexation of increasing areas of land to the growing United States. By 1846, Col. Stephen Watts Kearny had received orders to seize the Far Southwest for the United States. With some sixteen hundred men, he left Ft. Leavenworth on the Santa Fe Trail. By August, he had entered the streets of Santa Fe, largely unopposed, and New Mexico became a territory of the United States.

With the change in civil government came a change in the administration of the church. The Catholic Church in New Mexico, which had been under the jurisdiction of the bishop of Durango, Mexico, shifted to the jurisdiction of the American bishops in Baltimore, Maryland. They lost little time in appointing a vicar apostolic to the area. But they made what could be considered a significant error in judgment. Knowing nothing of the Spanish distrust of the French for centuries in New Mexico, they appointed a French priest as the first leader of the American Catholic Church.

Jean Baptiste Lamy, who would become the first archbishop of Santa Fe, came from a family steeped in traditional, obedient French Catholicism. All but one of his siblings entered religious life. His brothers Louis and Jean Baptiste entered the priesthood, and his sister Marguerite became a Sister of Mercy. His remaining brother, Etienne, married and had two children. Etienne's family was no less devout. One of his children became a priest, the other a nun.

Lamy was chosen for the vicar apostolic of New Mexico precisely because his family background would have produced someone with what the Vatican then saw as most desirable personal virtues and political views. Lamy had a conservative, loyal background, and he had inherited the French clergy's distrust of liberalism and the dynamic changes the French Revolution had brought to the French political landscape.

Joseph Machebeuf, Lamy's vicar general and later the first bishop of Denver, Colorado, also came from a conservative French family. When Lamy and Machebeuf arrived in Santa Fe in 1852, they brought a deep distrust of the Republican ethos that had killed so many priests in France and disrupted the lives of so many of their friends and family. Within a year of his arrival, Lamy, the new French bishop, had displaced six priests and run off the vicar, who angrily left for Durango. Machebeuf would later write that three-quarters of the clergy in New Mexico were Auvergnats, originating from the same province in France that was home to him and Lamy. But the Hispanic clergy of New Mexico understandably considered the placement of so many French priests an assault on Hispanics by a French ecclesiastical hierarchy.

Tensions between the native Hispanic clergy and the new French hierarchy came to a head in the new bishop's relationship with the priest who shepherded the small northern New Mexico community of Taos, Antonio Jose Martínez. A distorted version of their conflict later served as the basis for Willa Cather's novel *Death Comes for the Archbishop*. Martínez was a remarkable figure, who has been compared to Benjamin Franklin. Born in 1793 in the small village of Santa Rosa de Abiquiú, he was a member of a provincial family long known in the area. He married young and had a daughter, but after his wife died, he decided to pursue the priesthood and traveled to Durango to study. There, he identified deeply with the two priests who had played critical roles in the Mexican Revolution, Miguel Hidalgo y Costilla and José María Morelos. He returned to New Mexico determined to be not only a religious leader to his people but a political leader as well.

By the time Lamy and Machebeuf arrived, Martínez was considered one of the most influential men in the territory. He had become the *cura encargado,* or pastor in charge of the church in Taos; he had opened a school and a seminary; he had served as a delegate for the planning of the territorial government and in the newly formed legislature. But Martínez seemed to have no idea that the new French hierarchy might not relish such political involvement. Martínez's liberal views and civic involvement might have reminded them of the secularized priests who chose to serve the French government after the Revolution in France. Martínez's actions were laudatory in New Mexico's new democratic landscape, but they seemed very contrary to the docile, obedient spirituality emphasized in the French church of the time.

The disagreement began when Bishop Lamy appointed a Spanish-born priest, Damaso Taladrid, to replace Martínez in Taos. Martínez argued with the younger priest, who published a derogatory article about Martínez in the *Santa Fe Gazette.* Martínez responded in kind by publishing a denunciation of foreign priests, asserting the right of the legislature to write to the pope if dissatisfied with local church leadership, and complaining of unfair regulation of church business. Lamy wrote to Martínez responding to the charges and three days later suspended him from the priesthood. Martínez responded by dictating the requirements for a suspension under canon law, asserting that he had received a lifetime appointment and could not be suspended.

By the summer of 1857, the population of Taos was divided, depending on whether one supported the new pastor or the old. In an attempt at appeasement, Lamy removed the younger Taladrid from office. Instead, he appointed a native New Mexican priest, José Eulógio Ortiz to the position. But Martínez continued to perform marriages and baptisms, insisting he was still *cura proprio* of the parish. Shortly thereafter, Lamy began formal proceedings of excommunication.

Admonitions were read three Sundays in a row, and on the fourth Sunday, Machebeuf sang the High Mass and read the instrument of excommunication. In all probability, it was meant to be medicinal, to spur Martínez to comply with Lamy's original suspension and to return him to the fold. But Martínez was unrepentant and continued to perform marriages and baptisms. In 1859, he issued a letter of protest against his French bishop, suggesting it would be better if the people of Taos elected their priests. Ten years after his excommunication, Martínez died, still unreconciled to the church of New Mexico.

The conflict between the French clergy appointed by the American bishops and the native Hispanic clergy is a painful chapter in New Mexico's history. The events of the 1850s continue to divide scholars and residents of New Mexico, as the relationship between conquering Americans and conquered Hispanics sorts itself out. But it also took centuries to sort out the relationship between the Native American peoples of New Mexico and the Spanish, after their arrival and colonization, and similar angst accompanied the development of the California missions and the relationship between the Spanish and the Native Americans in California. In some ways, the dynamic between these groups repeats in miniature the dynamic that is seen again and again in American religious history. One group, established, experiences incursion from another group, be it in the form of contact events, immigration, or military conquest. A period of adaptation follows, and, in many cases, the invader becomes the established group, only to have its equilibrium upset by yet another religious upstart. It is a pattern that is not limited to the past but will likely continue in the future as the American religious landscape absorbs new groups and once again experiences the impact and recognition lags that follow change. Ideally, those who make up the American religious landscape can learn from the painful conflicts of the past and use that knowledge to develop a more harmonious and tolerant religious landscape in the future.

17

RAIDS, GHOSTS, AND RENEWAL

Confrontations between Spanish settlers in California and New Mexico and the Native Americans that inhabited those lands took place centuries ago. Today, many Americans fail to learn the history of those distant centuries or shy away from the painful truths that become evident when one studies the widespread extermination of the indigenous peoples of the American landscape. The building of the United States of America is also the story of the dismantling of the Native American way of life, the rich life lived prior to large-scale immigration by Europeans. The building of America also entailed the destruction of a people, an act sanctified by Christian religious beliefs, and the transformation of Native American belief systems as they struggled to integrate the impact of their own devastation. No one can claim exact figures, but some estimates hold that prior to the arrival of Europeans, the North American continent was home to over five million Native Americans. By the turn of the twentieth century, their numbers had dropped to approximately two hundred fifty thousand. In other words, 95 percent of Native Americans had disappeared.

While the Spanish pressured Native American populations from the South, moving up from Mexico into Texas, New Mexico, Arizona, and California, other groups brought pressure to other geographical areas. Russian trappers and traders moved down the coast of California from the north, establishing communities and trade routes. French settlements pushed up the Mississippi River valley. But by far the greatest pressure came from the continual waves of Americans moving west as the country pursued its sense of Manifest Destiny, the belief that the United States was destined by God to rule from coast to coast.

Some events radically accelerated the numbers of Europeans moving into the American West. As early as 1850, gold had been discovered in Colorado, a few miles from what is now the city of Denver. By 1858, a full-fledge gold rush had begun and thousands of Americans, mostly single men, flocked to Colorado in search of fortune. Mining towns grew up quickly, with names like Central City and Golden City. But along with the increase in whites living in the hills and foothills of the Rocky Mountains came increased interactions with the Comanche, Kiowa, Cheyenne, and Arapahoe who had long called the area home. The Plains Indians did not always gracefully accept the presence of new white settlers in their lands, and those traveling across the vast grassy plains of eastern Colorado were particularly vulnerable to attack. The telegraph line between Denver and Julesburg, in northeastern Colorado, was cut time and time again, and raiding parties regularly swept down on wagon trains. Soon, settlers became hesitant to travel between St. Louis, Missouri, and Denver. Reports of battles between Native Americans and settlers were sensationalized in Denver papers, and tensions between the two groups grew.

In September 1864, a Cheyenne chief named Black Kettle decided to begin peace talks with the whites. He sent word to the commander of Ft. Lyon and said that representatives of four tribes, the Arapaho, Comanche, Kiowa, and Sioux, all wanted to meet to discuss the possibility of peace with the whites. On September 26, the chiefs rode into Denver. Colorado governor John Evan did not endorse the talks. Too many atrocities, he said, had been committed by the Arapaho and Cheyenne. One vocal supporter of Evan's view was Col. John Chivington, who had previously served as a presiding elder for the Rocky Mountain District of the Kansas-Nebraska Methodist Conference. Chivington urged military conquest of the indigenous peoples. With such antagonistic views prevailing, the talks failed to produce any concrete results.

But the chiefs of the Cheyenne and Arapaho still had faith in Gen. Ned Wynkoop and moved their communities to the Big Bend of Sand Creek, fifty miles from the outpost he commanded at Ft. Lyon. Wynkoop permitted trading with the fort and helped those camped nearby with supplies during lean times. Given the political views of the governor and his supporters, Wynkoop's actions soon came under fire, and he was replaced by Maj. Scott J. Anthony. Anthony publicly announced he would continue Wynkoop's policy but privately was eager to send troops against the tribes.

Chivington decided to pursue political office and ran for territorial congress. He was defeated and, after his defeat, turned his energies toward the pursuit of a different kind of notoriety. As a colonel, he gave orders to the First and Third Regiments of Colorado to prepare to march. These were not well-trained or professional troops but a motley collection of poorly trained and ill-equipped men serving in what today we might term a militia. With their mismatched weaponry, a force of men on farm horses, riding alongside men on elegant riding horses, set out for Ft. Lyon. They reached it on November 28. Chivington announced to his troops that they would immediately march on Cheyenne leader Black Kettle's community at Sand Creek.

Only one officer voiced substantial objection to the plan. Capt. Silas Soule had been a veteran of the Civil War battles in New Mexico and felt attack was inappropriate. He reminded Chivington that these were non-combatants, who had placed themselves under the protection of General Wynkoop and, thus, the U.S. Army. Chivington's response to the objection was to threaten Soule with court martial.

In the early morning hours of November 29, Chivington's troops reached Black Kettle's encampment. They rode into the village made up of 115 Cheyenne bleached-hide lodges and 8 Arapaho lodges. Black Kettle emerged holding a pole with an American flag on it and a white flag of surrender fluttering beneath it. He yelled to his people not to be frightened, that the attack was some kind of mistake. As he spoke, the members of the First and Third Regiments ran his people down, shooting and bayoneting women, children, and elderly men. The killing spree continued for hours, with soldiers killing toddlers with rifle fire, parading parts cut from the bodies for one another, and mutilating the dead. The only soldiers who did not participate in the carnage were those under the command of Captain Soule. Soule refused to allow his men to fire a single shot.

There are no accurate records of the number killed at the Sand Creek Massacre. Estimates run anywhere from two hundred to six hundred. Most of those killed were women, children, and elderly persons. Only six were taken prisoner, two women and four children. It is believed that a few escaped on foot, with Black Kettle among them. After the long day of killing and carnage, Chivington ordered the village burned to the ground.

The Denver *Rocky Mountain News* proclaimed Chivington's actions at Sand Creek "among the brilliant feats of arms" in warfare against the Native Americans. Many of Denver's white citizens applauded Chivington's massacre at Sand Creek. Others, disturbed by the brutal assault on women and children, sought justice for those whose blood had drenched the soil at Sand Creek.

General Wynkoop denounced the killings and Chivington's leadership. Several unnamed "high officials" demanded an investigation, and, ultimately, no fewer than three separate investigations were launched. One was by the U.S. Congress, another by the Army Department, and a third by the commandant of the Military District of Colorado. Few were willing to testify against Chivington and his troops in the subsequent hearings, but Captain Soule came forth. He identified individuals who participated in the atrocities, giving their names and linking them to specific actions. After his testimony, Soule was murdered—assassinated in broad daylight on Lawrence Street in Denver—by one of the regiment's soldiers.

Ultimately, the investigations resulted in censures—for Governor Evans, for Major Anthony at Ft. Lyon, and for Colonel Chivington. Most of the blame was laid at the feet of Chivington, but the Methodist elder seemed oddly unrepentant for his part in the slaughter. He later wrote that the Native Americans deserved to be "whipped" because they had "threatened" the army post.

The slaughter known as the Sand Creek Massacre, of course, did nothing to improve the relationships between whites in the Colorado Territory and the Native Americans still in the area. The antagonism between the two groups increased. Cheyenne, Arapaho, Sioux, Kiowa, and Comanche all began to make more frequent raids on white settlers and travelers. The attacks temporarily slowed the flood of immigrants coming through St. Louis to the West. But the slowdown was only temporary, and the subsequent discovery of huge veins of silver in the Rocky Mountains only served as more incentive for more waves of settlers. The white population in cities like Denver continued to expand, and the Native American tribes indigenous to the area continued to feel more and more pressure to retreat from traditional lands, to cede dominion over the land to the endless flow of immigrants.

The Civil War temporarily delayed the coming of the railroad to Denver, as men and supplies were diverted to the war effort, but after the end of the Civil War, the railroad made its way through Colorado. Once railroad tracks were laid and immigrants arrived by the trainload, the possibility for any reversal of fortunes seemed increasingly unlikely. But just as things grew most desperate for the Native Americans in the American Rockies, a movement arose that seemed to offer new hope and a possibility of redemption, the Ghost Dance.

The Native Americans had met ongoing encroachment by whites for centuries with armed revolt. For example, the years 1622 and 1644 saw the Powhatan revolts. In 1715, the Yamasee war erupted. In 1763, the Delaware revolted. The Shawnee followed suit in 1763. And the Creek Indians' millenarian movement sprang up in 1813. But the flow of white settlers continued, and the position of most Native Americans continued to decline. By the end of the nineteenth century, many tribes had been relegated to reservations, often poor land far from their traditional lands. Treaties offered little protection, and hunger and disease became predators as powerful as the white armies.

Today, many historians see the Ghost Dance as a kind of spiritual revolt as Native Americans struggled to sustain their identity in the face of genocide and widespread disruption of their culture. The Ghost Dance could be considered a spiritual revolution that quickly spread among Native Americans throughout the western half of the United States.

The dance seems to have originated with a Paiute Indian named Wovoka, also called Jack Wilson. Wovoka announced to the Indian nations that he was appointed a new Christ figure and had come to prepare them for salvation. He invited representatives of all the tribes to meet with him in Nevada to learn of the salvation that could be obtained through dancing the Ghost Dance and singing Ghost Dance songs.

Wovoka told them that he had traveled to the spirit world and talked to the Creator. The Creator had related a prophecy in which a new earth would arise, coming from the west and pushing the white men back to their original lands beyond the ocean. Once the new earth covered the land, sweet grass would grow, and the buffalo and wild horses would return. Those who participated in the Ghost Dance would be elevated, lifted up as if by wings, as the soil for this new earth was laid down. They would be reunited with all lost family members, friends, and ancestors, who would then return to the new world with them. After the return, Native Americans would once again live in harmony with the wild horses and the buffalo.

News of the Ghost Dance soon spread quickly through almost all the tribes west of the Missouri and swept through the Lakota bands—the Oglala, Brule, Hunkpapa, Minneconjou, Oohenonpa, Itzipco, and Sihasapa. Soon, many were donning the special shirts that marked one as a dancer, singing the Ghost Dance songs, and dancing. The Ghost Dance shirts had special symbols that were believed to protect the dancer from the bullets of white soldiers. One observer noted that none of those participating wore hats. On questioning, she found that as a rite of purification, dancers removed everything that had been manufactured by the white man and, instead, donned the specially made shirts and dresses. For men, the Ghost Dance shirts and leggings were made of matching material and painted in red, some with stripes. Feathers were tied to the sleeves to flutter in the wind, reminiscent of the flight the dancers would make while the new earth was laid down. For women, there were white dresses. The area around the neck of the dresses was painted blue, and figures were scattered over them, figures that included bows and arrows, along with the sun, moon, and stars, birds, and other natural images.

After being addressed by the high priest, the dancers formed a circle, standing one behind the other, and placed their hands on the person in front of them. They marched and chanted, crying "Father, I come." Then, grasping handfuls of dust, they threw it into the air and joined their hands together over their heads. Standing still, they called on the Great Spirit to allow communication with the dead. A rest period and another talk by the high priest followed. Then, once again, a circle was formed. Facing the center and taking one another's hands, they swang back and forth at increasing speed, chanting, "Father I come. Mother I come. Brother I come."

They danced until exhausted, then fell. Those losing consciousness, it was believed, would be granted visions or healed from sickness. As more and more dropped into unconsciousness, the dancing stopped and dancers were seated. Then, the fallen began to recover consciousness and to tell the stories of their visions. After another rest period, the cycle of dances would be repeated, up to three or four times a day.

Historians have taken numerous approaches to understanding the rapid spread and intense power of the Ghost Dance. Many have portrayed it as the "last hurrah" of a defeated people, singing their swan song before the complete collapse of Native American culture across the nation. But more recently, historians have begun to challenge that view of the Ghost Dance. That view, they assert, portrays the Native Americans as passive victims, who reacted to the active agency of the whites, rather than as active participants in carving out their own identities in the wake of contact events with Europeans.

From this perspective, both Europeans and Native Americans were abruptly pushed into a New World. The world the Native Americans had known was forever changed by the arrival of Europeans—Europeans had also arrived in a new land. The impact of the changes that followed the arrival of Europeans—the loss of traditional lands, the death of thousands of Native Americans to measles and chicken pox, the military losses—meant adjustment to a whole new way of life. Some historians have suggested that these changes also precipitated their entering a new religious world as old systems of belief broke down, new and more potent Gods were sought, and native belief defined itself against the incursions of Christianity.[1] Some religious leaders or shamans within the tribes advocated intensive purification rites in the aftermath of contact events, as if the white man could be cleaned away like vermin. Shamans suggested a pure return to the old ways of the tribes and a rejection of anything manufactured by white men or tainted by them. They denounced the use of alcohol, the separation from traditional lands, and the lack of respect demonstrated toward ancestors. Divisions emerged within tribes as some attacked those tribal members who consorted with whites or advocated adoption of white customs.

From this perspective, the envisioning of an idealized future, such as that promised by the Ghost Dance after the return to the land, could be considered a vision of the people after they completed the difficult transition of integrating the changes that came with the American colonization of their lands. Rather than being the fantasies of a defeated people, movements such as the Ghost Dance can be seen as imaging that could pull the belief systems of native peoples forward into a future more promising than the painful past they had known. These movements became, in effect, collective rites of passage as the tribes moved through a change in social status. In the language of anthropologists Victor Turner and Arnold van Gennep, they moved from the first social status, into a liminal stage, and then into a redefined social status or reality.[2]

The Ghost Dance then could be considered a kind of rite of passage, performed collectively by large numbers of people across tribal divisions, on the way to a new social reality. The removal of those items associated with whites, the symbolic disrobing and donning of special garments, became purification rites. The withdrawal from those possessions or customs associated with whites was not merely a destructive impulse but a means of asserting their own Native American identity, by first purifying themselves of the influence of whites.

This also suggests that the responses of Native Americans to white encroachment should not be considered in isolation but alongside similar religious movements in other racial groups. They might be compared, as historian Joel Martin suggests, to African American slave revolts, or to some of the visionary traditions that sprang up among white Americans as they struggled to redefine themselves in the American context.[3] Martin goes so far as to suggest that they could also be compared to fundamentalism. Both are movements that look back to the past for a less complex understanding and way of life in the face of challenges posed by adaptation to the modern world. Today, from a postmodern perspective, many scholars would view the Native Americans alongside other third world groups as those that developed religiously inspired models of resistance to colonial encroachment and conquest.

Today, we no longer have to rely on educated whites to interpret the actions and history of the native peoples of America. Instead, we have a rising group of Native American scholars and historians who bring their unique cultural perspective to their work in history and the study of religion. Historian Vine Deloria Jr. emphasizes that Native American belief systems are based in a sense of kinship that extends to people, lands, and other life forms.[4] The land that one springs from becomes a kind of mother in that the type of land one lives in shapes one's thought and outlook, shapes what one becomes. With kinship comes responsibility, and Native American belief systems emphasize the dignity of all forms of life and the need to treat each with respect. These beliefs also mean that within families one must be careful to show the appropriate respect for family relationships. One who is outside of the complex web of relationships or who does not honor the kinship of other life forms and treat all with dignity and respect, from a Native American perspective, does not really exist. What white scholars have often interpreted as animism or totemism is actually awareness and honoring of the kinship relationship between the human being and other life forms.

Thus, the wholesale slaughter of the buffalo by whites would have been unthinkable to the Plains Indians. Respect for the buffalo meant taking their lives only when necessary and carefully utilizing all of what the buffalo provided. Whites, in comparison, shot buffalo by the thousands from passing train windows, not even bothering to stop for the skins or the meat. The violation of basic Native American religious beliefs that this represents is profound. The disregard for relatedness contradicts the very foundational relationships established by kinship.

But without the articulate education provided by scholars like Deloria, few Americans in the American West of the nineteenth century had any understanding of Native American belief systems or values. And few could envision the spread of the Ghost Dance as a purification process and a rite of passage for Native Americans moving toward a new identity in the aftermath of insurmountable loss.

In October 1890, news of Wovoka reached Lakota chief Sitting Bull at Standing Rock. Sitting Bull was known for his defeat of Gen. George Armstrong Custer at the Battle of Little Bighorn in 1876. Intrigued by what he heard, Sitting Bull invited Kicking Bear, who brought news of the movement, to teach the Ghost Dance to his people. James Mclaughlin, the government agent stationed at Standing Rock, had little or no understanding of the elements that informed the dance. McLaughlin considered the dance indecent and disgusting, calling it absurd. As more and more Native Americans gathered to participate in the dance, many whites became uneasy, fearing that they were gathering for military purposes and that the dance was leading up to some form of attack or massive rebellion.

McLaughlin ordered Kicking Bear removed from Standing Rock. He also telegraphed officials in Washington, D.C., demanding that U.S. troops be sent for the protection of white settlers and laying the blame for the new form of religion on Sitting Bull. One man sensed that they were overreacting. Valentine McGillycuddy, who had formerly served as an Indian agent, compared the Ghost Dance to the ascension robes of the Seventh Day Adventists and asked why, if it was all right for the Adventists to don their garments, it was not all right for the native peoples to gather for the Ghost Dance. McGillycuddy's question was moot.

On December 12, Indian police received an order to arrest Sitting Bull. In the early hours of the morning, just before dawn, over three dozen Indian police officers surrounded his cabin. A squadron of cavalry had also been called and waited as backup a few miles away. Native American lieutenant Bull Head went into the cabin to find Sitting Bull asleep. Waking, he agreed to accompany the police. While he was dressing, a group of Ghost Dancers gathered outside the cabin. Soon, they outnumbered the police, and fear began to build. A dancer named Catch-the-Bear grabbed a rifle and shot Bull Head. When Head attempted to fire back on his assailant, he accidentally shot Sitting Bull. Another policeman misinterpreted the actions and shot Sitting Bull in the head. Fighting broke out between the dancers and the police. Six police and seven of Sitting Bull's warriors were killed before the backup unit of cavalry could get to the scene to stop the fighting.

North of Standing Rock, in the Cheyenne River Reservation, another group of Ghost Dancers, Miniconjou Lakota led by Big Foot, encountered a large group of U.S. Army troops. Apprehensive, they stopped. They were joined by a group of Hunkpapa Lakota, who relayed the story of Sitting Bull's murder the previous day. Fearing that they, too, would be killed, Big Foot directed his people to travel south to an area east of Pine Ridge, over two hundred miles across snow-covered prairie.

Gen. Nelson Miles ordered the arrest of Big Foot, and the military pursued the fleeing Lakota. The army searched the Badlands and, finally, located the group on December 28, 1890. The Seventh Cavalry, under the command of Maj. Samuel Whitside, accepted Big Foot's surrender. They were joined in their camp at Wounded Knee Creek by troops under the command of Col. James W. Forsyth.

The cavalry established two separate camps for their native prisoners. Just over a hundred warriors were put in one camp, and the two hundred fifty women and children who accompanied them were put into a separate camp. They were guarded by 470 U.S. troops and some thirty scouts. On the morning of December 29, Forsyth ordered his men to disarm Big Foot's group. They searched the women's camp first, treating the women roughly, lifting their skirts and laughing, taking every conceivable weapon, including the women's sewing tools. Then, they searched the men's group and gathered about forty rifles.

No one knows exactly what happened to provoke violence. It is thought that one of the Sioux warriors refused to turn over his rifle, and in a struggle for control of the gun, it fired. Firing on both sides broke out. Approximately half of the warriors were shot in the first exchange of fire, while others fled to the women's camp to protect the women and children. A group of rapid-fire cannons, which could fire over fifty shells a minute, were focused on the camp from the surrounding hills. When the fighting broke out, the gunners began firing on the women's camp. Shrapnel from the shells felled the women and children. Bodies were found scattered as far as three miles from the camp.

The shooting was indiscriminate. Not only were women and children gunned down in the melee but dozens of cavalry soldiers lost their lives and another forty were injured. Estimates of Native American casualties vary, but it is believed that around three hundred men, women, and children died in the massacre at Wounded Knee. It is known that 146 were buried in a large communal grave after being stripped of their clothing and personal items by soldiers seeking souvenirs. But the exact number of casualties can never be known, as many Lakota families had recovered the bodies of family members for tribal burial before the burial party got to the scene.

General Miles heartily disapproved of the actions at Wounded Knee and had Forsyth removed from office. Most of the casualties were women and children. Of the men who were killed, many were unarmed. And he had lost over thirty soldiers. But Forsyth seemed oblivious to the idea that anything inappropriate had occurred. He considered his troops actions to be "gallant conduct." General Miles's perspective did not prevail. The army awarded the Medal of Honor to three officers and fifteen enlisted men for their actions at Wounded Knee, and Forsyth was reinstated. Eventually, he became a general.

Some view the actions of the Seventh Cavalry as revenge for their losses at Little Big Horn. It was, after all, the Seventh Cavalry that lost three hundred men under the leadership of General Custer on June 25, 1876. A Lakota survivor of Wounded Knee told of one soldier yelling "Remember Custer" before killing an old woman.

The U.S. Army awarded more medals to soldiers at Wounded Knee than to those at any other single battle in history, and while the Lakota people have formally requested an apology for the massacre at Wounded Knee, none has ever been made. Native American activists continue to request that the medal awarded to soldiers at Wounded Knee be withdrawn. Many consider Wounded Knee the last battle of the Indian Wars, the end of the military conquest of Native Americans by U.S. troops.

For many Native Americans, the massacre at Wounded Knee has become emblematic of the genocide experienced after the arrival of Europeans on the North American continent. This slaughter of women and children by U.S. troops serves as a symbol of the far greater loss of 95 percent of the Native American population.

In 1972, a group of Native American activists seized the small town of Wounded Knee, South Dakota, at the site of the massacre. Dennis Banks, Russell Means, Carter Camp, and other activists held off federal marshals and tribal police for seventy-two days. Some championed their actions as the herald of a new age in relations between whites and Native Americans, while others, including other Native Americans, decried holding the town as simply dangerous showmanship.

Their dramatic actions and the flurry of responses to them suggest that both white and Native Americans still have not completed the hard work of integration.

While romanticized versions of Native American life appear periodically in films and on television, and while New Age thinkers celebrate aspects of Native American belief, the majority of Americans still have little understanding of Native American cultures and beliefs. Few Americans can even name the tribes that once inhabited the areas where they have built their towns and cities. American Indians continue to face dire social problems, including high rates of substance abuse, suicide, and economic struggle.

While some Native American groups, such as the Pueblos in New Mexico, appear to have developed syncretic belief systems that blend their traditional beliefs with elements of Christianity, others hold steadfastly to native beliefs and resist any infiltration of Christian belief. However, with the heyday of the missionary movement over, fewer Christians are trying to convert the Native Americans wholesale to Christian denominations.

Since the activism of the 1970s, a steady stream of Native American literature, scholarship, and art has been produced, and many Native Americans feel that they are once again finding their voice after centuries of being quieted by colonial expansion, military persecution, and religious insensitivity. But the reconciliation of native peoples to various denominational approaches to Christianity is far from achieved. There remains great work to be done, and many still doubt whether white Americans who pride themselves on being devout Christians will ever demonstrate the level of respect and dignity for others that Native American belief systems value so highly. Ironically, as environmental concerns grow ever greater and environmental degradation becomes an ever-growing threat worldwide, Americans may ultimately be forced to develop a greater understanding of the complex web of kinship relationships with all life forms that Native Americans have understood and honored for so long.

NOTES

1. See discussion in Joel W. Martin, "Before and beyond the Sioux Ghost Dance: Native American Prophetic Movements and the Study of Religion," *Journal of the American Academy of Religion* LIX, no. 4, winter 1991.

2. Victor W. Turner, *The Ritual Process: Structure and Anti-Structure* (Chicago: Aldine Publishing Company, 1969); Arnold van Gennep, *The Rites of Passage,* trans. Monika B. Vizedom and Gabrielle L. Caffee (Chicago: University of Chicago Press, [1960] 1980).

3. Martin, "Sioux Ghost Dance," 694.

4. Vine Deloria Jr., *For This Land: Writings on Religion in America* (New York: Routledge, 1999), 130–31.

18

MORMON COUNTRY

While many of the traditions previously examined had their roots in other nations, the Mormon religion is uniquely American. Like others, the name by which it is commonly known, Mormonism, did not originate with the Mormons themselves. Like the names for the Baptists and the Methodists, it was a term that nonmembers used to describe the group. The correct name is the Church of Jesus Christ of the Latter-Day Saints, but, eventually, the term "Mormon" came to be widely accepted. Mormonism was born and bred on American soil, beginning in Sharon, Vermont, with the birth of the man recognized as its founder, Joseph Smith (1805–1844). Smith was born on December 23, 1805. He spent his childhood working on farms in Vermont and New York. Because of his family's poverty, the children helped earn income through agricultural work. This work, combined with frequent moves, made standard education inaccessible to Smith, but he was taught at home in reading, writing, and arithmetic. By the time he reached adolescence, Smith and his family were living in Palmyra, New York.

While Smith was young, local farmers in the area engaged the services of a diviner to locate water. The man promised to also locate buried treasure and was hired at three dollars a day. When the treasure failed to materialize, the diviner moved on. In spite of his brief tenure, the diviner left a profound impression on young Smith, who was soon using the diviner's methods to locate lost tools.

It was also in adolescence that Smith began receiving divine visions. As early as age fourteen, he reported a direct revelation from God. Smith asked God which of the various religious traditions around he should follow. Spending time in solitude in the woods near the farm, he experienced visions of both Christ and God the Father, who told him to resist joining other churches. Smith honored the request.

In 1823, Smith began to experience regular visits by an entity he described as an angel named Moroni. Moroni told Smith of ancient records of God's interactions with the natives of America. Smith's divine visions and clairvoyance became well known, and, soon, he was asked to travel to the Susquehanna Valley outside of Damascus, New York, to look for treasure. No treasure was found in material terms, but Smith found a romantic treasure in the form of the daughter of the man in whose house he had boarded. Emma Hale, the daughter of Isaac Hale, had captured his heart.

Smith took a job at a nearby farm in order to remain close to Emma. He began attending school to improve his prospects and slowly began to court Miss Hale. Eventually, he won her over, but her father was decidedly against the match. His resistance may have been due, in part, to the fact that in 1826 Smith's disgruntled treasure hunters had filed charges against him as an imposter. Smith was found guilty, although there is no record of a jail term or sentence. By 1827, Smith had convinced Emma to elope with him. After spending some time with his parents in New York, the couple returned to seek the forgiveness of Emma's father.

By the following year, 1827, Smith had received the record described by Moroni and began translating the contents. The angel had directed him to a location near his family farm in Palmyra. When he dug in the spot indicated, he found a set of golden plates covered with writing. With the help of two stones he had found, he could translate the writing on the plates. Emma served as scribe, writing down the translations. The fruit of their labors was the manuscript entitled the Book of Mormon.

Over the course of two and a half years, Smith continued working on his translation. By 1830, it was complete and ready for publication. Many Americans were shocked by the contents of the Book of Mormon. They doubted Smith's assertions that a group of Jewish families had settled in America in the seventh century before Christ and their descendents were the Native Americans. But at the time, theories about the "lost tribes of Israel" were common, and the framework of the Book of Mormon built on established ideas from the New Testament. A few days after the publication of the book, Smith founded the first congregation of the Church of Jesus Christ of the Latter-Day Saints and assumed the role of its first president.

Smith traveled back to Palmyra, where he soon converted his parents and his brothers and began to find others receptive to his new religion. Smith, in many ways, made the proposition an attractive one. He shied away from teaching about fire and brimstone or focusing on hell and damnation.

Instead, he frequently used humor to charm his audience and began to gain the reputation of being a fine orator. He also taught that at the center of every human being was a spark of the divine that could be drawn upon to transform that human.

In 1831, a preacher in Kirtland, Ohio, decided to convert to Mormonism. He brought his entire congregation with him into the growing church, and Kirtland soon became recognized as a center for Mormon religious life. A community grew up in the area around Kirtland. Headquarters for a new national church were established, a temple was built, and a tithe of 10 percent of their income was assigned to all members.

But while the church continued to expand and members of the church prospered through hard work, they increasingly came under attack from their non-Mormon neighbors. The publication of the Book of Mormon had been greeted by many Christian pastors as blasphemy, and neighbors around Kirtland were suspicious of this new group and new religion. Soon, rumors that Smith had propositioned a teenage girl provoked a mob. Smith was tarred and feathered. In the aftermath of that assault, he became determined to find a new place for his growing church, a place he called Zion.

During the 1830s, a community of Mormons had been established in Independence, Missouri, and Smith hoped that Missouri might prove home to his tribe. However, the group in Independence began to experience similar harassment from non-Mormons. Soon, its members were driven out of town and forced to found a new settlement, which they called Far West. Attacks by non-Mormons sprang up in Far West as well, and Smith decided to head up a group of men who would travel to Missouri and defend their vulnerable fellow Mormons. When Smith and his men arrived in Missouri, they received a surprise. The Missouri state militia had been called up, and the Mormons were greatly outnumbered by armed men.

Although Smith surrendered to Missouri authorities, he was charged with treason on the basis of leading an armed force into Missouri. He was imprisoned and, soon, charged with conspiracy to commit murder as well. A non-Mormon had been killed in one of the exchanges with the Mormons. During the time he was imprisoned, non-Mormons launched another attack on the settlement called Far West, and the members of the community were driven toward the Mississippi River. Smith bribed his jailor with a bottle of whiskey and eight hundred dollars in cash and rode to join his retreating group.

In 1839, fifteen thousand Mormons crossed the Mississippi River and began to settle in Illinois. Politicians, eager to secure this new block of votes, welcomed the Mormons. Smith established himself in a settlement founded by the Mormons and named Nauvoo. Soon, he had regained his social standing and was commissioned as a lieutenant general in the local militia. At thirty-eight, he was pleased by the figure he cut in a military uniform. He decided that he would run for the office of the president of the United States.

But Smith had not garnered universal support, even within the ranks of his own religion. He tended toward the autocratic in his exercise of authority. His divine claims of authority had ruffled the feathers of some of his fellow Mormons and strained his marriage. His marriage was also strained by his interest in other women. As early as 1831, Smith may have been considering the possibility of polygamy in the Mormon Church. While he discussed the possibility with close aides, he refrained from making any public declarations.

He did begin to propose a practice of "celestial" marriages—an eternal, spiritualized union that took precedence over earthly marriage, and began proposing the same to a number of women. He also began elaborating on the role of a woman's husband in assuring her salvation. Women's salvation would be dependent on their husbands and not something that could be individually achieved. Polygamy would be accepted. Men could take multiple wives, but women must only marry one man.

Smith met with significant resistance on the question of polygamy. His own wife was vehemently opposed, and since many of the women to whom he had proposed "celestial" marriages were already married, many of their husbands were less than supportive of the new practice. In 1844, the Mormons split into two groups. Husbands of the women drawn into "celestial" marriage helped to organize the split and began attacking Smith and his views. They established a newspaper and began a public relations campaign against Smith's new policies.

Enraged by the editorials in the paper, Smith ordered the printing press destroyed. He was subsequently charged by the governor of Illinois with violating the First Amendment of the Constitution of the United States. The state militia was called up and took Smith into custody. Smith was taken to a jail in Carthage, Illinois, and imprisoned along with his brother, Hyrum, and several other Mormon leaders. On the second day of his imprisonment, vigilantes stormed the jail and fired upon the prisoners. Smith defended himself with a revolver and tried to escape through a window. He was shot in the back by one of the vigilantes attacking the jail. Falling out the window, he met more shots from the crowd gathered outside the jail. Although he survived the first round of shots and the fall, members of the crowd continued to fire on him. On June 27, 1844, Smith died in front of the Carthage jail. He was thirty-eight years of age.

After Smith's death, the leadership of the Mormon Church was assumed by Brigham Young (1801–1877), who became a towering figure in Mormon history. Like Smith, Young was born in Vermont and grew up in an agricultural region, learning first hand the work it takes to carve a living out of the land. He was the ninth of eleven children, and his mother died of tuberculosis when he was fourteen. When his father remarried, Young decided to leave home. He moved to Auburn, New York, to live with a sister and became a master carpenter. In 1823, he relocated again, this time to Port Byron, New York, where he found work repairing canal boats. A year later, he married Miriam Angeline Works and, together with his wife, joined the Methodist Church. He spent four years in Port Byron, then moved on to Oswego, New York, a port city on Lake Ontario. There he became involved with a group of religious devotees. But over time, he decided it was best if he was closer to his father and other family members and decided to move in 1828. He settled in Mendon in Monroe County.

In 1830, Joseph Smith published the Book of Mormon. Smith's brother, Samuel, came through Mendon County distributing copies of the book. One copy was given to Phineas Young, Brigham's brother, who was a Methodist pastor. The book was circulated through the Young family—first to his father, then his sister, then to Brigham. Not one to rush in to things, Young spent two years examining the tenets of the Mormon faith before he decided to convert. When he converted, most of his family members converted with him. The same year he converted, 1832, his wife died of tuberculosis. Young left his daughters with friends and traveled to Kirtland, Ohio, to meet Joseph Smith. Inspired by his newfound religious belief and Smith, Young decided to become a Mormon missionary and began a series of trips around New York and Canada. In 1833, he led some of those he had converted to Kirtland, where he heard Smith preach. He decided he should relocate his family to Kirtland. There, he met Mary Ann Angell, who became his second wife in 1834.

The year 1834 brought the persecution of Mormons in Missouri, and Young and his brother marched behind Smith when he went to aid his fellow believers. Having come to the attention of Smith and the church leadership, who recognized his dedication and devout belief, Young was ordained a member of the original Quorum of the Twelve Apostles in 1835 and participated the following year in the dedication of the Mormon temple in Kirtland. Smith began to assign specific duties to Young, and when other members of the church challenged Smith's leadership, Young was so adamant in defending Smith that Smith's critics became furious with him.

He was forced to flee with his family to the other Mormon community, Far West.

By 1838, the situation of the Mormons in Ohio and Missouri had become untenable. Threats of violence hung over the group, and they were targets for crime. Since Smith had been imprisoned, along with his brother and Sidney Rigdon, Young became the senior member of the Quorum of the Twelve. He assumed responsibility for evacuating all Mormon families from Missouri. He oversaw the composition of the Missouri Covenant to guarantee that families without horses or wagons would be transported by other Mormons and oversaw the relocation of somewhere between eight and twelve thousand people.

Settling his family in Nauvoo in 1839, Young took a mission trip to England with other members of the Quorum of the Twelve. Directing a missionary team, he oversaw the baptism of over seven thousand individuals, distributed copies of the Book of Mormon, and helped another thousand to emigrate and move to Nauvoo. On his return to Illinois, Young became the president of the Quorum of the Twelve, second in command only to Smith.

Smith indicated to Young and other members of the quorum that he felt the Mormons should establish a base in the Rocky Mountains. He also oversaw the establishment, by Young, of a Council of Fifty to govern the Mormons. After Smith's death, Young continued to prepare the group for a move to the West. Another covenant was issued, the Nauvoo Covenant, to ensure that those without means of transportation would be able to accompany those who did own wagons and draft animals. More violence against the Mormons erupted in September 1845. Fearing additional violence, Smith instructed the group to prepare for departure in February 1846.

The scope of the undertaking was massive. Young personally led the venture, and it is estimated that sixteen thousand people set out under that leadership. They traveled first to what is now Florence, Nebraska, on the Missouri River. The group was broken up into smaller and more manageable groups to sit out the winter before attempting to move into the Rocky Mountains. In April 1847, Young set out with a smaller advance group.

In June 1847, Young met Jim Bridger near the Little Sandy River. Bridger, called by some the last of the mountain men, was a trapper, trader, and guide who had spent over twenty years roaming the Rocky Mountains. In 1825, while exploring the Bear River south of Cache Valley, Bridger had come across the Great Salt Lake. He mistakenly believed it to be part of the Pacific Ocean because of the salt water, but he had spent the winter of 1825 and 1826 on the shores of the huge lake. Later, he returned to spend some of his winters in the Salt Lake Valley.

Bridger suggested to Young that the Mormons might settle in Salt Lake Valley. Bridger drew a map for Young, and Young was impressed by Bridger's knowledge of the area. Bridger led Young and his advance party to Salt Lake in the late spring and early summer of 1847. When Young arrived in the Salt Lake Valley, in July 1847, he announced that it would be the new home for the Mormons and selected the spot for the temple. Land in the area was surveyed, gardens built, and farms laid out. He named the new community Great Salt Lake City, Great Basin, North America. By December of the same year, he had returned to the winter quarters on the banks of the Missouri. The following spring, he led thirty-five hundred Mormons back to Salt Lake City. The growth of the city had begun.

Young immersed himself in the building of the city of Salt Lake. As president of the church, he began to develop the civic and religious infrastructure that would support the growth of the Mormon Church. He divided the city land into ten-acre blocks, assigning them to various families and assigning one to the temple. By 1853, construction of a temple was begun in the heart of the city. Farms were laid out in five- and ten-acre plots, and teams worked together to develop a system of canals and ditches for use in irrigating crops. Roads were built. Timber was logged in the nearby mountains. Fences were constructed. In 1849, Young divided the city into nineteen wards.

Young decided to name the area the State of Deseret and to appoint himself governor. Then, he turned his attention to supporting those who continued to undertake the long journey to Salt Lake. He set up different types of communities. Some would be temporary gathering places. Others would be focused on the production of food or needed goods. Some would be missionary communities to proselytize to the Native Americans. The final type of community would provide housing and agricultural areas for the new immigrants as they moved from the East. By the time of his death, almost four hundred colonies had been established.

Overall, the Mormons had relatively good relationships with Native Americans in the area. Young advocated offering support to the natives, avoiding violence, and pursuing their conversion. Land was offered for farms. His relative success led to his being appointed governor of the territory of Utah and the superintendent of Indian affairs of the Utah Territory by President Millard Fillmore. But by the time James Buchanan had become president, more and more politicians were becoming concerned about Young and his Mormons. Surprised by the massive amount of immigration, having little understanding of the nature and structure of the Mormon Church, some began to challenge the theocracy that was growing in the Utah desert. In 1857, President Buchanan appointed Alfred Cummings of Georgia to be territorial governor and sent a large military force to Utah to make sure that American laws prevailed in the region. Young was not informed, and when his scouts reported the movement of large numbers of troops toward Salt Lake, he feared another outbreak of violence like those that had plagued the Mormons in Missouri and Ohio. He instructed the Mormons to mobilize and prepare to defend their city. Fortunately, an influential non-Mormon interceded and established a line of communication between Young and the military leadership. A peaceful agreement was reached, and the army established Camp Floyd forty miles outside of Salt Lake City. Territorial governors ruled in name only, while Young retained the actual power of leadership for the majority of the people of Salt Lake.

The year 1857 also brought one of the few possible scars to Young's reputation with the assertion of his involvement in what came to be known as the Mountain Meadows Massacre. On September 11, 1857, a group of white settlers traveling three hundred miles south of Salt Lake City were attacked. It is not clear who was responsible for the attack. Some lay the blame on the Paiute Indians. Others believe the Paiutes were allies with and sent by the Mormons and that the Mormons offered them the wagon train's cattle as an inducement. Still other accounts say that the murders were carried out by Mormons, who masqueraded as Indians.

No less a figure than Mark Twain reported on the massacre and placed the blame squarely on the Mormons. Twain, in his book *Roughing It,* reported that Mormons dressed as Indians had attacked the wagon train. Members of the wagon train had circled the wagons and defended themselves for five days. At that point, the "Mormons" donned regular clothing and, carrying a white flag, went down to meet with the members of the train. After convincing members to come out from behind their barricades, they systematically killed them. It is estimated that 120 men, women, and children died in the Mountain Meadows Massacre.

One pioneering member of the Church of the Latter-Day Saints, John D. Lee, was eventually tried and executed for the crime. But the church has always denied any involvement in the massacre and that Young had anything to do with the event. Some accounts suggest that Young was the one who ordered the attack. Suspicion against the Mormons was increased by the Mormon doctrine of blood atonement, which holds that an especially grievous sin can only be atoned for with the spilling of the sinner's blood.

Some historians speculate that this may have been used in some way as jus-tification for the massacre.

Other theories hold that the settlers who were attacked had previously attacked the Mormons, poisoning wells and boasting that they had been part of a group called the "Missouri Wildcats" that had been involved in the murder of Joseph Smith. Yet another theory suggests that members of the wagon train were from a region in Arkansas where Mormon apostle Parley P. Pratt had been murdered. Still others suggest that Young wanted to pro-voke an incident between Indians and the U.S. Army because of his own concerns about the federal troops marching toward Salt Lake. A letter Young wrote to an Indian missionary stresses the need for cooperation with the tribe and suggests that, without the tribe's assistance, the federal troops would wipe out both the Native Americans and the Mormons. Some may think the Mormon response to the approaching troops somewhat reac-tionary, but given the experiences of both groups—the massacres of Native Americans and the mob violence the Mormons had encountered—and the fact that federal troops were marching on Salt Lake, some level of alarm is more than understandable. In 1999, the president of the Mormons, Gordon B. Hinckley, offered some words of reconciliation to the descendents of those killed in the Mountain Meadows Massacre, but the church has never acknowledged any complicity in the massacre itself. It is unlikely that the full story of the Mountain Meadows Massacre will ever be known.

Regardless of the many challenges the Mormons faced—hostilities in Ohio and Missouri, the dangers of the overland trek to Utah, the U.S. gov-ernment's initial wariness of their theocratic structure, and beliefs that clearly set them apart from mainline religious groups—they have grown and prospered. In part, that is due to the extraordinary amount of missionary ac-tivity they have undertaken since their founding in 1830.

As noted above, Brigham Young participated in missionary activity in England after joining the church. The first group of Mormon missionaries to travel to England left in 1837. A later group arrived in England in 1850. By that time, the Mormons could claim thirty thousand members in Great Britain, and England became a springboard for more missionary activity in Europe. In the early 1850s, missions were launched to Scandinavia, Italy, Switzerland, and Germany. Later work ventured into Holland, Iceland, and Belgium.

In 1843, Addison Pratt and a group of other missionaries had traveled to the Pacific Islands. By 1849, George Barber and Benjamin Richey had begun missionary work in Calcutta, India. They were followed by Maurice

White and William Willes. In 1852, Brigham Young sent off missionaries to Thailand, then called Siam. More expansive development of missionary activity in the Far East would have to wait until the twentieth century, when the Mormons moved into Japan, Korea, China, and the Philippines.

Members of the Mormon Church undertake missionary activity as a matter of course, and neatly dressed pairs of Mormon missionaries have become a common sight in many cities. This consistent missionary activity has helped to make the Church of the Latter-Day Saints one of the fastest growing in American history. By the turn of the twenty-first century, it was estimated that the church had over eleven million members throughout the world. It has established some twenty thousand churches and one hundred temples in one hundred fifty different nations.

But the Mormons remain controversial on many levels. Many of their practices have remained too far outside those of mainline religious denominations, and they continue to attract scrutiny and distrust. Many Americans disapproved of the Mormon practice of polygamy, and felt it undermined traditional Christian values. Eventually, the U.S. Congress passed legislation that prohibited the practice. Mormons appealed all the way to the Supreme Court, but the court ruled against the Mormons and laid a foundation for the constitutionality of laws that prohibit polygamy.

Many Mormons resented the intrusion of federal regulation into their personal lives, and many discretely refrained from compliance. In 1904, sitting president of the church, Joseph F. Smith, issued an official statement prohibiting plural marriages, threatening excommunication to those who insisted on continuing the practice. One group, the United Order Effort, elected to retain the practice of polygamy and was excommunicated from the Church of the Latter-Day Saints. The group boasts a membership of approximately ten thousand people. Other splinter groups in Utah, Arizona, and New Mexico, not officially related to the Church of the Latter-Day Saints, are thought to practice polygamy still, and periodically news stories emerge of law enforcement's attempts to bring them into compliance with federal prohibitions.

Some aspects of Mormon faith and practice are very much in line with mainline Christian values, such as the Mormon emphasis on family. Family is considered extremely important in the Mormon tradition, and large families are not uncommon. Families participate in the church through the "ward" or "branch," which roughly correlates to a church in other religions. Each of these is led by a male bishop and offers two different levels of priesthood, the Aaronic priesthood and the Melchizedek priesthood, both of which are restricted to men. Women participate in the Relief Society, which mimics the organizational structure of the larger church. Wards are organized together in stakes, which somewhat resemble Roman Catholic dioceses, and each stake is presided over by a president. Subsequent levels of hierarchy include the Area Authorities and the First and Second Quorum of Seventies, which are sometimes called the General Authorities. The First Quorum of the Seventies assists the twelve apostles. Finally, the highest governing body, as instituted in the days of Joseph Smith, is the Quorum of the Twelve, which is presided over by the First Presidency, a supreme council of three high priests, composed of the president and his counselors.

The theological position taken by founder Joseph Smith is sometimes called "restorationism." This refers to the establishment of the Church of the Latter-Day Saints by Smith as a restoration of the true church. From this perspective, the "true church" ceased to exist in the second century of the common era, until it was restored by Smith. Over the years, numerous other groups have established themselves as believers in restorationism, and, today, over one hundred denominations share the belief. The groups vary in size, with some being as small as under one hundred members. Others have hundreds of thousands of members or even millions.

One of the largest restorationist groups is the Community of Christ, previously known as the Reorganized Church of Jesus Christ of the Latter-Day Saints, which has approximately a quarter of a million members. Formed in 1860, it is descended from those Mormons who elected not to travel to Utah under Brigham Young's leadership. The Community of Christ accepts some and rejects other beliefs and practices of the Latter-Day Saints Church. For example, it allows both men and women to participate in the priesthood.

The Mormon tradition challenges commonly held beliefs in Christianity. Mormons believe that scripture is not limited to the Bible. Joseph Smith's Book of Mormon and two other texts, *Doctrine and Covenants* and *The Pearl of Great Price*, also inform and shape their tradition. Nor do the Mormons subscribe strictly to a Trinitarian Christian perspective. Smith advocated a plurality of God, and that God, Christ, and the Holy Ghost were distinct persons and distinct gods. Further, the Mormon beliefs about God emphasize humanity over divinity, and a complex world of spirit brothers and sisters populates their theological landscape. Early Mormon thinkers asserted that Christ practiced polygamy and that among his wives were Mary and Martha of Bethany and Mary Magdalene. They maintain, as well, a distinction between the Holy Ghost, which serves as the third member of the Godhead, and the Holy Spirit, which could be considered a spirit of intelligence that permeates the created world.

Recently, controversy over Mormon practice has erupted over their practice of baptizing the dead. Salvation is not assured through Christ's atonement but requires works and baptism in water. To assure the salvation of their ancestors, the Mormons have avidly pursued the study of genealogy, and they house centers for genealogical research across the country. But when they have charitably extended the practice of baptizing the dead to those Jewish individuals who died in the Holocaust or to other deceased members of different religions, they have come under significant scrutiny and criticism.

In spite of the variances with established Trinitarian Christianity, the order, family values, and zeal of Mormon believers, combined with their ongoing missionary activity, has led Mormonism to be considered one of the fastest-growing religions in the world. Their significant financial resources, ability to blend civic and theological structure, canny understanding of politics, and obvious devotion all guarantee that the Church of Jesus Christ of the Latter-Day Saints will continue to make its own unique contribution to the American religious landscape.

19

GOLD MOUNTAIN

As Europeans moved westward across the United States in greater and greater numbers, and Hispanics moved northward in streams into California, New Mexico, and Texas, yet another group began to arrive in America in the nineteenth century in greater and greater numbers. With the discovery of gold in California and the labor demand created by work on the railroad, Chinese immigration increased dramatically. So did immigration of Asians from numerous other areas.

By 1848, the United States had annexed or militarily conquered land from the Atlantic to the Pacific, and one morning in January 1848, the western part of the United States was irrevocably changed. James Marshall, who headed a crew for businessman John Sutter, had begun construction of a mill on the south fork of the American River. Something in the bottom of a ditch caught his eye, and a few minutes later he had confirmed his suspicions. It was gold. Soon, Sutter's men were quietly panning for gold, but news of the find could not be kept quiet for long. The result was the California Gold Rush, which dramatically changed the California landscape. By April 1849, some thirty thousand Americans were traveling to California to look for gold. Over the course of the year, eighty thousand came into California, almost all of them men, more than half under twenty. Two-thirds came from the United States and a third from all over the globe—from lands as diverse as Germany, Mexico, Ireland, Russia, Italy, the West Indies, and Australia.

One of the first foreigners to make his way to Sutter's Mill in the search for gold was a young Chinese man named Chun Ming. Chun Ming struck it rich and wrote back to China so that everyone could celebrate his success. The Chinese began to refer to America as "Gold Mountain," and more and more young Chinese men were eager to try their hand in the gold fields of California.

The increase in numbers is startling. Just over three hundred immigrated in 1849, and four hundred fifty arrived in 1850. In 1852, twenty thousand came to California.

Many of the men came from Guangdong Province in south central China and were used to long, hard days of work with minimal reward. Spurred on by merchants who loaned them money for their passage, they arrived in increasing numbers. Some headed strait into the gold fields; others stayed in Sacramento or San Francisco, opening laundries and restaurants.

The Chinese miners and workers brought with them the system of thought known as Confucianism. The term Confucianism derives from an anglicized pronunciation of the name K'ung Fu Tzu, or Confucius (551–479 BCE), the founder of Confucianism who was born in Shantung Province. K'ung Fu Tzu wandered the landscape of China, learning and studying. After a small group of devotees began to follow him, he turned to teaching in the last years of his life. Beginning in China, Confucianism slowly spread to Korea, Japan, and Vietnam.

Strictly speaking, the tradition Confucius has passed down is not a religion, although scholars today believe it has religious foundations. Some characterize it instead as a social philosophy, or a civil religion, due to its focus on the interaction of different members of society. But Confucianism has never had many of the trappings of other religions, such as stately churches or classes of priests.

The teachings of Confucius center on moral interaction, rules for appropriate conduct, the shape of proper social relationships, and the wisdom gained through the moral life. Many of the principles emphasized in Confucianism are derived from older writings, which are sometimes referred to as the Five Classics and the Four Books. The Five Classics include the *I Ching*, or Book of Changes, the *Shu Ching*, or Book of History, the *Shih Ching*, Book of Poetry, *Li Chi*, Book of Rites, and the *Ch'un Ch'iu*, or Spring and Autumn Annals. These volumes are deeply ingrained in Chinese thought and culture. The *I Ching* instructs one in a form of divination and was popularized in the United States, in part, by Carl Jung. The *Shu Ching* provides historical foundations for Chinese identity, and the *Shih Ching* gives voice to the poetic nature of the Chinese. The *Li Chi* is probably closest to what many consider the main thrust of Confucianism, because of its focus on rules of conduct. The text itself was destroyed, but it is believed that large sections have been preserved in other writings. Only the *Ch'un*

Ch'iu was formulated by Confucius and outlines historical events from the eight to fifth centuries before the common era.

In addition to the Five Classics, one is expected to be familiar with the Four Books, or *Shih Shu*. These are compilations of sayings compiled by Confucius, along with comments written by subsequent followers. One, *Lun Yu*, addresses morality and politics. Others, *Ta Hsueh* and *Chung Yung*, have Confucius's thought systematically arranged and combined with the reflections and explanations of later believers. Finally, the *Mencius*, or Book of Mencius, gives the thought and reflection of a man considered one of Confucius's most illuminated disciples, noted below.

Confucian thought emphasizes duty or loyalty to oneself and to others and an altruism that is grounded in the goodness of the human heart. Like Christianity, Confucianism emphasizes the Golden Rule and consideration of others. But Confucianism emphasizes that such consideration takes place within a clear hierarchy of social relationships and advocates a rather altruistic attitude toward leaders or sovereign rulers, elevating the virtues of obedience and honor. He also charges leaders with the need for serious cultivation of their own wisdom in order to remain worthy of the respect due to them.

Following the death of its founder, Confucianism split into two schools. One, headed by Mencius, noted above, emphasized that human nature is primarily good and that only the degradation and evil encountered in life degrades that goodness. Morality becomes a search for the means to return to one's original goodness. An opposing stream was developed by Hsun-tzu (Hsun K'uang, c. 300–235 BCE). It emphasized, like Augustine of Hippo, the fallen nature of the human being. But, Hsun-tzu challenged, humans can redeem that dark and fallen nature by learning to channel their desires and by practicing rules of social propriety and restraint. He emphasized the role of music and rites in forming moral character and the need for ritual in moral formation.

By the time of the Han Dynasty (206 BCE—220 CE), Confucian systems had been accepted as orthodox practice for subjects of Emperor Wu (140–187 BCE). Over the course of the next two thousand years, Confucian beliefs became deeply ingrained in Chinese culture. In the Qing, or Ch'ing, Dynasty (1644–1911), Confucian thought experienced something of a renaissance in China. Scholars of the time felt that Confucian thought had become distorted and recommended a return to the purer forms of Confucian thought practiced during the Han Dynasty, before the beliefs of Buddhism and Taoism had begun to infiltrate the belief system. These scholars launched a new generation of studies into the texts and thought of

Confucianism, using methods newly available in terms of history and developing sciences.

Thus, in the middle of the nineteenth century, as Chinese men immigrated to California in search of the promise of Gold Mountain, they brought with them Confucian beliefs, whether explicitly or implicitly, through their deep veins in Chinese culture. But along with that infrastructure of Confucian practice and belief, they brought many of the virtues associated with Confucianism—a respect for leadership, a capacity for obedience and hard work, a desire to maintain harmonious relationships, and a certain underlying altruism in human affairs. As such, the Chinese were soon recognized as promising workers for the monumental task of completing the first transcontinental railroad.

The completion of the transcontinental railroad had been temporarily sidelined by the demands of the Civil War. North and South both had other priorities for men and resources during the tempestuous time of the war. Even with the cloud of war hovering overhead, lobbyists from the Western states traveled to Washington, D.C., to enlist the help of the federal government in the construction of the vital link of the railroad. In 1861, an enterprising man named Theodore Judah convinced four Sacramento merchants to fund the beginning of a train line through the Sierra Nevada mountains. The four, Leland Stanford, Charles Crocker, Mark Hopkins, and Collis P. Huntington, ponied up their contributions, and Judah traveled to Washington to try to convince Congress to approve the Pacific Railroad Act. On June 20, 1862, his work paid off, and the newly formed Central Pacific Railroad was awarded the contract to build the western line of the transcontinental railroad. Judah never lived to see his dream completed. He died from yellow fever contracted en route to New York to secure additional funding.

Once funding was secured, the mammoth project began. The goal was to take the railroad from the coast of California, through the Sierra Nevada mountains, and across the western desert to an as yet undetermined meeting place, where the western line would join the eastern line of the Union Pacific. Initial work moved relatively quickly, but workers soon entered the Sierras. Charles Crocker, who headed up the effort, found that American workers were not entirely reliable when faced with the tough conditions demanded by work on railroad construction. Only about 60 percent stayed on after beginning work. He suggested to his superintendent of construction, James Strobridge, the use of Chinese workers on the project. Strobridge rejected the idea, but Crocker's insistence ruled the day.

Soon after, eleven thousand Chinese workers were employed by the Central Pacific, and more were recruited in China. Leadership on the railroad soon realized the many strengths the workers brought to the job. They organized easily and bathed regularly. They drank only boiled water and, so, had fewer health problems. They worked systematically and efficiently and usually without complaint.

Working in the Sierras brought special challenges. A passage for the railroad literally had to be cut from stone, and tons of rock had to be blasted and removed to form the narrow route of passage. Small and light, Chinese workers were willing to be dropped over the edge of cliffs in baskets, where they would place explosives in crevices to blast out a shelf for the tracks. Besides the dangers of explosive work, Chinese workers faced the daunting snows of the Sierras, and at times drifts reached as high as sixty feet. Many of the workers lost their lives to avalanches, snow slides, or the collapse of tunnels under the snow.

By the spring of 1867, the Chinese workers had realized that their own working conditions were distinctly different from white workers. They worked longer hours, received more dangerous assignments, and had to cover the cost of their own food. They decided to strike. Crocker threatened to replace the entire crew with freed slaves but, ultimately, was forced to renegotiate the conditions under which the Chinese worked.

In September 1868, the Chinese and American workers under Crocker's leadership accomplished their goal. The Central Pacific line broke through the High Sierra and onto the plains of the Nevada desert. Newspapers generously thanked "John Chinaman" for his patience and hard work, but the gratitude felt toward Chinese immigrants would not last for long.

By 1871, anti-Chinese sentiment had reached violent proportions. In October of that year, a diverse group of Americans and Europeans attacked Los Angeles's Chinatown. When the violence subsided, twenty-three Chinese immigrants had been hung, stabbed, dragged behind horses, or shot. Over three hundred thousand Chinese immigrants had come to America since the early days of the Gold Rush, and hostility toward them grew with every wave of immigration.

Six years later, when depression brought hard economic times to the region, politicians found Asians a likely scapegoat for frustration. Dennis Kearney founded the Workingmen's Party with the express goal of ejecting the Chinese from the Pacific Coast. The party didn't last, but the anti-Chinese sentiment did, and violent events similar to the siege in Los Angeles were soon cropping up all over the West—in Rock Springs, Wyoming, and Tacoma and Seattle, Washington. By 1882, western politicians had passed the Chinese Exclusion Act, and the number of Chinese entering

America was virtually brought to a standstill. More systematic forms of discrimination soon followed; the Chinese were forbidden to reenter the United States after visits home and were required to carry certificates of eligibility if they chose to remain in the States. The Chinese failed to find the kind of organized social structure, respect, and honor dictated by their Confucian beliefs. Instead, they encountered exploitation, discrimination, and violence. One worker, returning home, categorized Americans at large as "barbarians."

The passage of the Chinese Exclusion Act, with the subsequent dramatic decrease in Chinese immigration, was followed by the first significant wave of immigration from Japan, which began in 1885. The first wave was spurred by the concept of *dekasigi*, meaning to leave one's homeland in order to find profitable work elsewhere, then to return with significant funds. The first dekasigi immigration wave brought Japanese immigrants to the Hawaiian Islands during the period from 1885 to 1894, with later immigration to the West Coast. Many of these immigrants came from areas in Japan where the dominant form of Buddhism was Jodo Shinshu Honganji-ha. Accordingly, requests were submitted to the Honganji-ha mother temple in Japan for permission to establish Buddhist temples in Hawaii and San Francisco. In 1899, two missionary priests, Rev. Dr. Shuye Sonoda and Rev. Kakuryo Nishijima, arrived in San Francisco, marking the official beginning of the Buddhist Churches of America.

The Buddhism that followed Japanese immigrants to America descended from the teachings of Guatama Buddha (c. 560 BCE—c. 480 BCE). The name Buddha means "the enlightened one." It was given to the prince of a small kingdom in India whose personal name, Siddhartha, translates to "he who will accomplish." Accounts of Buddha's life are difficult to ground historically because they have become embedded in legend over the centuries, but a traditional portrait has emerged. Prior to his birth, his mother, Maya, had a dream of a white elephant announcing the arrival of her son. Siddhartha began life as the pampered son of a local dignitary. Noting, with displeasure, his son's tendency toward a contemplative life, Siddhartha's father sought to tempt him with a myriad of luxuries. His son was married young and introduced to court life. But Siddhartha rejected these worldly ways and left home, traveling and searching for enlightenment. Inspired by a wandering monk, he vowed to relinquish his wealth, family, and inheritance to search for religious truth. He examined the beliefs of Hinduism but could not reconcile himself to the caste system. After six years of further searching, he received enlightenment in 528 BCE, while sitting under a pipal tree near Gaya, in the Indian state of Bihar.

After his enlightenment, Buddha began to integrate his experience and teach followers, many of whom became monks under his tutelage. The teaching he espoused begins with what are called the Four Noble Truths. All life entails suffering. Suffering is caused by selfishness. Humans can transcend suffering. The means of transcending suffering is the practice of the Eightfold Path. The Eightfold Path consists of right understanding, right purpose, right speech, right conduct, right livelihood, right effort, right awareness, and right meditation. Practice of the Eightfold Path is informed by the Five Precepts, which, like the Ten Commandments of Christianity and Judaism, guide action. These precepts include no killing or doing harm to living creatures, no stealing, no improper pleasurable indulgence in sexuality, no lying, and no use of intoxicating agents.

By the third century before the common era, Buddhism was adopted by Emperor Ashsoka, who met a monk named Nigrodha shortly after participating in a bloody revolt and witnessing many killings in an effort to retain control of the land of the Kalingas. Nigrodha convinced him to embrace a path of peace. He ordered that stone pillars be built across the land with sayings of the Buddha inscribed upon them. He also sent missionaries all across India and to many distant lands, including Egypt and Greece. The Christian patristic figure Origen reports his missionaries in what is now Great Britain.

In the first century, as legend tells us, the Chinese emperor Ming Ti had a dream. Complying with the dream, he sent men down the Silk Road, the trade route. His representatives came back with a portrait of Buddha and a copy of the Sutra, or new scriptures. By the time of the Han Dynasty, approximately 150 CE, it is believed, a Buddhist community had been established in China. Over time, the belief system spread as well to Korea, Japan, and Vietnam.

As it spread, different streams of Buddhism developed. Among them was a school that emphasized meditation and has alternatively been called Ch'an, Son, Dhynana, or Zen Buddhism. It is believed that a monk named Bodhidharma traveled to China in 520 CE. He brought with him a "silent transmission" and became the first patriarch of the school. Convinced that the limits of language could not contain the impact of true enlightenment, Bodhidharma simply displayed a flower. One monk, Kashyapa, understood without words, and silent transmission began. Zen Buddhism is known for a focus on meditation, a diminishment of the value of words in training, and the use of paradox or nonlogical language to further the understanding of the proficient.

With the arrival of increasing numbers of Japanese immigrants in the United States, more and more forms of Buddhism were brought to the mainland. Japanese Buddhists sometimes divide the history of Buddhist development in America into several periods, which are given the names of various generations of Japanese immigrants. The first generation is called Issei, the second generation is called Nisei, and the third generation is called Sanei. The period beginning in 1885 and stretching to 1907 came to be considered the first Issei period, followed by the second Issei period, which began in 1908. Whereas the earliest Issei had been happy to accept work in mining, lumber, and agriculture, the second wave of Issei sought more sophisticated employment by purchasing their own small farms or businesses. As more women were allowed by the Japanese government to immigrate to the United States, family life began to develop, especially up and down the West Coast.

In 1913, the state of California passed legislation forbidding aliens from certain nations to own land because they were deemed ineligible for citizenship. The California Alien Land Act prohibited all Asians from owning land. This was followed by the Immigration Act of 1924, which blocked immigration by any groups that were not eligible for citizenship.

In the face of an increasingly hostile environment, Buddhist churches began to model themselves on Christian churches, incorporating communal prayer, sermons, and social activities. While the community worshiped on Saturday night, with lectures on Sunday, Monday nights were set aside for educational talks for non-Asians who expressed an interest in learning more about Buddhism. What were more rightly called temples began to call themselves "Buddhist associations" or "Buddhist churches." However, most socialization remained within the Japanese community, because discrimination during the period prevented the mixing of the races.

The Issei period came to an end with the attack on Pearl Harbor by Japanese forces. The Federal Bureau of Investigation arrested many of the priests associated with the temples and imprisoned them. With the older Japanese-speaking generation abruptly removed, religious leadership passed into the hands of the next generation, the American-born and English-speaking Nisei. But by spring of 1942, it was determined that all Japanese represented threats to national security, and Japanese citizens were rounded up, stripped of their property, and relocated to isolated inland internment camps, far from the coast, in areas such as Owens Valley in California. Many of the accoutrements that supported Buddhist practices, such as books or sutras, were lost. Imprisoned, Buddhists reconstructed the lost articles. Some Nisei sought to prove their loyalty by joining the U.S. military in segregated units.

After World War II, Japanese Buddhists were permitted to return to the West Coast. Temples had to be rebuilt from scratch. Jobs had to be secured in a still-racist and discriminatory job market, and many Japanese Americans were dramatically underemployed. The temple became the source of social and cultural support, as well as religious practice. Nisei encouraged their Sansei children to learn of their Japanese heritage through participation in temple-based cultural activities.

Many of the immigrant's children, more distant from their Japanese heritage and more Americanized by growing up in the United States, drifted from traditional Buddhist practice. Some Sansei seem to be reversing this trend and returning to the temples, showing a new appreciation for their rich cultural and religious heritage. With this return to religion has come the development of new forms of culture that have sprung exclusively from Japanese Americans, such as Taiko. In some ways, this echoes the experience of Judaism in American, where the third generation embraced its heritage.

Buddhists were not pristine, however, but incorporated more and more interracial marriages, especially in California, where the rate of interracial marriage has reached as high as 50 percent. The American Buddhist landscape has become correspondingly more complex. In addition to Japanese Buddhist traditions, subsequent waves of immigration have brought the Buddhist traditions found in Thailand, Tibet, Vietnam, Cambodia, Burma, Korea, Laos, Malaysia, and Sri Lanka. Maintenance of cultural and religious identity becomes even more difficult as diversity increases.

Today, more and more people who identify themselves as Buddhist do not have an Asian heritage but an American or European background. Consistent writing on Buddhism by such figures as Herman Hesse, Friedrich Nietzsche, Albert Einstein, C. S. Lewis, and G. K. Chesterton, along with a perception of Buddhist practice as chic or hip, has greatly increased the number of non-Asian converts. Many of these, though, engage in Buddhist practice on a private level and are not necessarily formally connected to temples or associations.

Many Americans, when asked what image comes to mind when they think of the word "Buddhist," would describe the orange-robed followers of Tibetan Buddhism or their leader, the Dalai Lama. Legend has it that Buddhism was introduced to Tibet by two princesses, a Chinese princess and a Nepali princess, who married the king of Tibet, Srongtsen Gampo, in the seventh century. Now, historians believe that it came to the area through the work of an Indian monk, Padmasambhava, who founded a Buddhist monastery near Lhasa in approximately 750. Three hundred years later, a reformer named Atisa (982–1054) brought greater unity to the Tibetan priesthood, eliminated excessive practices, and achieved greater conformity between the rules that governed the various monasteries.

Another reformer, Tsong-Kha-pa (d. 1419), strengthened the discipline of the monastic orders even more, instituted celibacy, and created more systematic methods of practice for confessions and retreats. His influence spread to Mongolia, where a prince handed over civic and spiritual control of Tibet to the fifth grand lama, Ta-lai, or Dalai, Lama. Dalai Lama translates roughly to "teacher of wisdom as vast as an ocean." Thought to be a reincarnation of the Bodhisattva, the Dalai Lama became the temporal ruler of Tibet, while the Panchen Lama, the abbot of the Tashi Lumpo monastery, became the chief spiritual authority of the land.

Sequential Dalai Lamas have ruled Tibet ever since. Since the selection of a new Dalai Lama is dependent on reincarnation, the death of a sitting Dalai Lama necessitates a long and arduous search for the infant or young child who reincarnates the dead leader. Complex testing is done by monks entrusted with the process of finding and recognizing the new Dalai Lama, who is then removed from his family for specialized training that will enable him to be a just, wise, and holy leader.

Belief in the divinely directed leadership of the Dalai Lama is one of the beliefs that set Tibetan Buddhism apart from other schools of Buddhism. Other distinct beliefs include the belief that lost scriptures can be recovered by individuals with high spiritual development and the idea that certain individuals can reincarnate the Guatama Buddha. Padmasambhava, who brought Buddhism to Tibet, is believed to have been one such reincarnation of the Buddha.

Tibetan Buddhism emphasizes the use of meditation. Meditation is sometimes combined with the construction of elaborate sand paintings known as *mandalas*, or the symbolic use of handbells and daggers to reflect spiritual passages. Those who seek the blessings of the monks may participate in special dances, while the monks provide musical accompaniment. They are also encouraged to make pilgrimages, give offerings, and offer prayers.

The current Dalai Lama was born on July 6, 1935 in a farming village named Taktser. He is the fourteenth Dalai Lama to serve his people. Discovered when he was two years old, he was renamed Tenzin Gyatso, emphasizing gentleness, compassion, and wisdom, and taken to Lhasa, where he was installed in 1940.

The success of the Communist Revolution in China in 1949, however, brought profound changes to Tibet. In 1950, the nation was seized by China. Rather than serve as a puppet ruler for the Chinese, the Dalai Lama escaped to India and has ruled in exile, in Dharamsala in northern India, since 1960. Throughout the decades of his exile, he has worked in the hope of reestablishing the independence of Tibet and was awarded the Nobel Peace Price in 1989 for his efforts. His efforts to "Free Tibet" have brought many Tibetan monks to America to educate Americans about various aspects of Tibetan Buddhism, to attempt to garner additional political support for his cause, and to establish centers for the study of Tibetan Buddhism.

Four main schools of Tibetan Buddhism are recognized. One is called Nyingma(pa), or the Ancient Ones. It was established by the reincarnation of the Bodhisattva, Padmasambhava. The second is known as Kagya(pa), or Oral Language, and has numerous subsects. The third, Salkya(pa), or Grey Earth, was founded by Sakya Pandita (1182–1251), born the same year as Francis of Assisi. The fourth school is Geluk(pa), or the Way of Virtue, also known as the Yellow Hats.

Two of the best-known texts of Tibetan Buddhism are *The Tibetan Book of the Great Liberation* and *The Tibetan Book of the Dead. The Tibetan Book of the Great Liberation,* which first came to the attention of many Westerners when it was translated and edited by W. Y. Evans-Wentz in 1954, gained even wider readership when psychologist Carl Gustav Jung agreed to write a psychological commentary for the volume. The book seeks to school the reader in the process of moving toward nirvana through the systematic cultivation of coming to know the mind. *The Tibetan Book of the Dead,* which also boasted a commentary by Jung in the Evans-Wentz translation, introduces the reader to Tibetan Buddhism's complex understanding of the world after death and the transitions the human makes through planes, known as *bardos*, on the way to reincarnation.

Today, as interreligious dialog grows and deepens, and more and more Americans demonstrate an ongoing thirst for spiritual guidance, the belief systems that were once almost exclusively associated with specific Asian populations have become widely known and practiced. In addition, as more and more Westerners have learned of the mental and physical benefits of meditation, more and more have turned to Eastern schools for training in the rudiments of the practice.

The Japanese scholar of Buddhism, Daisetz Teitaro Suzuki (1870–1966), contributed immensely to the bridging of East and West through his accessible and widely published works in English. Educated at Tokyo University, Suzuki had studied in the United States from 1897 to 1909. He later came to teach in numerous universities in Japan, Europe, and the United States. His introduction to Zen Buddhism, simply entitled *Zen Buddhism,* helped bring many Americans to an awareness of the religion and helped them to understand its basic tenets and beliefs. Among those who favorably received the volume was the Trappist monk Thomas Merton, perhaps best known for his own autobiography of his spiritual journey, *Seven Storey Mountain*. The exchange between Merton and Suzuki opened the way for subsequent interaction between Buddhist and Christian beliefs. Perhaps most prominent among later developments in this interaction is the practice of Centering Prayer, developed by Basil Pennington and Thomas Keating. Centering Prayer uses Eastern meditation techniques in a Christian framework and has spread widely across the United States since its early development.

Developments such as these make more and more Americans willing to explore the riches found in Eastern religious practices such as Buddhism. They have also helped to dispel stereotypes and promote greater intercultural understanding between widely disparate cultural traditions. From the first tentative Chinese miners who headed for Gold Mountain, to the workers who risked and lost their lives working for the Central Pacific Railroad, the influence of Chinese religion has steadily worn away the stone of American resistance. From the bitter racial and economic discrimination practiced against Japanese Buddhists to the Japanese army unit in World War II that became the most decorated in history, Japanese Americans have proven themselves committed to America as a nation and enriched it with their understanding of Buddhism. From the dramatic history of Tibetan Buddhism, to the patience, wisdom, and nobility of the Dalai Lama in his ongoing pursuit of the peaceful recovery of his lost homeland, Tibetans have taught Americans how to find nobility in loss and profound beauty in the transient.

Today, the American religious landscape is absorbing and integrating the impact of more and more diverse forms of Eastern thought and religion, with immigrants from China, Vietnam, Laos, Cambodia, Burma, Singapore, Taiwan, Japan, Thailand, Bhutan, and other nations. No one piece of writing could summarize the diversity of their traditions and contributions. Only one thing can be assured. With the continuing growth of economic trade across the Pacific, the rich trade envisioned by those who built the transcontinental railroad is finally becoming a reality, and the rich heritage and many gifts of Asian religious traditions that enrich the American religious landscape are certain to increase.

20

PLURALISM AND PERIPHERY

A merican religious history has never been a sedate one marked by peace and harmony. Instead, periods following the arrival of large numbers of new groups or encounters with groups of widely different backgrounds have been marked by violent resistance and a slow, painful process of social integration. In the last few decades, the painful costs and legacy of such violence have been increasingly addressed by historians, scholars, and writers. But in spite of these periods of shadow, the American religious history is not simply a dark one. Rather, periods of shadow create a chiaroscuro effect, alternating with periods of remarkable altruism and a steady trend toward growing tolerance. Increasingly, in terms of both religion and race, America is developing a workable pluralism that honors diverse paths and histories, yet asserts a unified identity as a nation.

No one individual or group can be given credit for the emergence of this growing tolerance and functional pluralism, but certain individuals have stood as bellwethers, promoting a pluralistic vision long before it was popular to do so or widely recognized as politically correct. Among those are William James and W. E. B. DuBois, who could be considered architects of a new age of pluralism in America.

In terms of philosophy, perhaps no other figure is associated more strongly with the term pluralism than William James (1842–1910). James is somewhat of a paradox in American religious history. He penned what is arguably the best-known book on the subject of religion ever written by an American, his 1902 *Varieties of Religious Experience*. He admitted that religion was the greatest interest in his life. Yet, James never became a member of any religious congregation and never committed himself to a single religious tradition. Even more ironically, those who knew him said that entering his house was like entering a church. James served as a critical figure in the development of one of the few distinctly American philosophical systems, yet never identified himself solely as a philosopher. Even his own career was pluralistic; he was alternately a medical doctor, a psychologist, a philosopher, and a scholar of religion.

James's interest in pluralism is most pertinent to this study. His pluralism emerged from his larger philosophical project and was emblematic of his views of both science and religion.[1] James anticipated the turn to the phenomenological in the twentieth century and anticipated many of the elements familiar to us today as postmodern thought. He was determinedly opposed to what was arguably the dominant intellectual perspective of his day, a worldview informed by Enlightenment philosophy and emphasizing a positivistic approach to science and a monistic perspective that enshrined a single objective "truth." From that perspective, reason could resolve all, and everything in the world could be understood and controlled by the power of the rational mind. All the world was mechanical, subject to understanding and manipulation by rational mechanics.

James favored a return to the experiential and, as his book title suggests, to the varieties of experience as they confront the human being. Coining the phrase "stream of consciousness," he explored how alterations in states of consciousness produced differing perceptions and different truths. James responded to positivism with his own form of empiricism, which he termed "radical empiricism." He developed a three-part philosophy composed of pragmatism, pluralism, and radical empiricism. From a Jamesian perspective, all explanations of reality are based on a metaphysical system, whether consciously or not. Positivistic science, rather than being free of metaphysics or religious perspectives, is based on a form of monism and a metaphysic that elevated the position of the physical. By demanding that all information be framed in terms of availability for observation and reason, positivistic science mandates a metaphysical truth based on those elements.

The idea of radical empiricism, posited by James, entails a return to experience. It includes the same empirical data allowed in the scientific approach but also allows one to make use of subjective realities that lie outside the narrow tracts of reason and sight. This perspective is inherently pluralistic, as it widens the gate through which one can interpret reality, and by allowing subjective elements, it allows widely disparate elements of personal experience. Additionally, since experience is constantly changing, as posited in the idea of the stream of consciousness, no perspective can encompass all of reality for any length of time. The return to experience, promulgated by James, also means a return to the pragmatic. Theories must be tested by experience, and lived experience becomes the primary means of determining the utility of any theoretical approach.

This combination of pragmatism, pluralism, and radical empiricism creates a framework that allows for fundamentally different experiences in life and for different conclusions to be drawn based on those differing experiences. Validity of action shifts away from a competing system of claims about ultimate truth to a system in which the value of religious belief (or any other belief) is determined by outcomes, by the actions generated by that belief system, rather than by adherence to a specific form of doctrine.

James provided support for this perspective in greater detail in his widely read *Varieties of Religious Experience.* True to his own beliefs, he proposed a typology of differing types of religious experience, rather than advocating a specific doctrinal or dogmatic approach to religious belief and practice. But James went on to promote a vision of American pluralism in a way that many American scholars fail to recognize. James's pluralistic vision was not limited to religion and philosophy but also played an important part in furthering the process of racial pluralism in the United States and the process that culminated in the civil rights movement. He did so, in part, through his relationship with William Edward Burghardt DuBois (1858–1963).

DuBois was the first African American to receive a doctoral degree from Harvard University. James mentored DuBois through the process, serving as the chair of his doctoral committee as he pursued his Ph.D. The James family had a long association with the abolitionist movement. Living in Boston, Massachusetts, which was the center of much of the abolitionist activity in the North, the James family knew many of the leaders of the abolitionist movement. James's brothers, Robertson and Garth Wilkinson James, studied in an abolitionist school run by John Brown, who later led the armed slave revolt at Harper's Ferry. The two James brothers also served as adjutants to the officers leading all-black regiments in the Civil War. Garth Wilkinson was adjutant to Col. Robert Gould Shaw in the highly lauded 54th Regiment.

W. E. B. DuBois's obvious talent found expression in a doctoral dissertation titled "The Suppression of the African Slave Trade." James's own views on the value of experience would encourage and validate DuBois in the decision to pursue studies that addressed African American experience and history.

DuBois was born in Great Barrington, Massachusetts, in 1868. Very few African Americans lived in Great Barrington, and although many areas of Massachusetts were racially tolerant, DuBois was exposed to racist re-marks and attitudes throughout his early life. Academically gifted, DuBois was offered a scholarship to Fisk College in Nashville, Tennessee. With the scholarship and the help of family and friends, he was able to pursue col-lege studies. During his studies at Fisk, DuBois was shocked and saddened the by extent of the discrimination he experienced in the South. Spending his summers teaching, he was also exposed to the struggles of poor blacks in rural areas.

After graduation from Fisk, DuBois studied history and philosophy at Harvard, where James was a professor of philosophy. After completing his master's degree, DuBois received funds to study abroad and spent two years at the University of Berlin. He entertained completing his doctoral studies there, but problems with additional funding required his return to Harvard, where he completed his doctorate under James's direction.

It was after the completion of his doctorate that DuBois plunged into greater racial activism. He taught for two years at Wilberforce University in Ohio, then accepted a research project that would take him deep into the black slums of Philadelphia, Pennsylvania. DuBois began a study of Philadel-phia's impoverished black population that incorporated history, statistics, an-thropology, and sociology. It culminated in a report entitled *The Philadelphia Negro.*

Publication of the report was followed by DuBois teaching and re-searching for thirteen years at Atlanta University. DuBois explored the im-pact of urbanization on blacks, their morality, their church, and their rela-tionship to crime. He advocated social reform and became embroiled in political and ideological debates. DuBois argued for the recognition and support of the "Talented Tenth," the 10 percent of African American youth who might pursue higher education and serve as guides and advocates for the rest of black society. In 1903, he published what is probably his most widely known work, *The Souls of Black Folk.*

DuBois also became known for his public disagreements with another widely known African American leader of the time, Booker T. Washing-ton, founder of the Tuskegee Institute. Many considered Washington the most powerful black man in the United States, and his voice held tremen-dous influence in terms of funding and political support. Washington ar-gued that blacks should work toward self-sufficiency and the preservation of personal dignity and self-respect. Rather than concentrating on higher education and political advocacy, he felt black communities should stress industrial education that would quickly secure better-paying jobs. When DuBois published *The Souls of Black Folk,* he devoted an entire chapter to an analysis and critique of Washington's ideas. It earned him Washington's lifelong enmity.

Shortly thereafter, in 1905, Washington addressed a rally in Boston. William Monroe Trotter, a friend of DuBois's from his studies at Harvard, verbally attacked Washington at the rally. Trotter was subsequently jailed on nebulous charges that were thought to have stemmed from supporters of Washington. In an angry reaction to the event, DuBois sent out a call to other African American men who supported "freedom and growth" for the American Negro.

Those responding to the call, twenty-nine men from fourteen states, gathered together to meet not far from Niagara Falls in January 1906. They were not permitted to meet within the United States, so they gathered on the Canadian side of the border. Those attending came to be known as the Niagara Movement and jointly agreed to advocate for greater civil justice for blacks and to work toward the abolishment of racial discrimination. But DuBois had little expertise in managing groups. His friend from Harvard, Trotter, became increasingly divisive in terms of his views on whites. The group began to dissolve after accusations of fraud were raised against it, although these charges may well have been the result of individuals loyal to Washington and seeking a means to discredit the group.

Out of the ashes of the Niagara Movement came a new organization. When the remnants of the movement joined forces with a group of white liberal thinkers, the resulting organization was named the National Association for the Advancement of Colored People (NAACP). DuBois served as director of publications and research and editor of their flagship journal, *Crisis* magazine, for twenty-five years.

By 1919, DuBois was serving as the NAACP observer at an overseas peace conference when he decided to organize a conference devoted to the problems of Africans worldwide. Although one pan-African congress, as it had been called, was held in 1900, he decided to hold a second in 1921. After his experience abroad, DuBois became increasingly disenchanted with the American response to racism and increasingly impatient with the policies of the NAACP. In the 1930s, he left the organization he had helped to found and returned to teaching and writing, producing two more books.

DuBois maintained his interest in pan-Africanism however and participated in several subsequent congresses. The fifth congress elected him international president and dubbed him the father of pan-Africanism. But DuBois's increasing alienation from American foreign policy and advocacy on behalf of the proletariat made him a political target in a political climate that became increasingly intolerant during the cold war. After being ordered to register as an agent of a "foreign principal," DuBois refused and left the United States, settling in Ghana as an expatriate. In the last years of his life, he developed the *Encyclopedia Africana* and became a citizen of Ghana.

Although DuBois elected to leave his native country, he left behind a powerful legacy that argued for racial equality and pluralism in the United States. The NAACP went on to become the best-known organization lobbying for improved standing for African Americans. DuBois's pioneering work, along with that of his old adversary Booker T. Washington, provided alternate streams for African Americans to explore in their movement toward greater social, economic, and racial equality. DuBois in particular served as an inspiration to many of those black leaders who would later come together to form the core of the civil rights movement. And the organization he helped to found, the NAACP, played a critical role in galvanizing the nation in support of the civil rights movement.

The return to experience and the refusal to accept monistic perspectives in philosophy and religion, advocated by William James at the turn of the twentieth century, were channeled through the work of W. E. B. DuBois into the growing racial tolerance and movement toward racial equality that developed in the aftermath of the civil rights movement. The pluralism and phenomenological approaches advocated by James over a century ago have found fruition in postmodern approaches that validate lived reality from a variety of perspectives. Together, these elements have helped to create an increasingly tolerant religious subcurrent in America, one in which we increasingly see other religious views and perspectives as sources of enrichment rather than as threats or heresies.

Numerous political movements have sought to marry specific religious perspectives with certain political goals, and some have been successful to varying degrees. But regardless of the "moral majority" proposed decades ago or the vocal assertions of some religious groups that their own religious perspectives characterize the religious views of the entire nation, their assertions are undermined by an ever-increasing level of complexity and diversity in the American religious landscape. Rather, in these assertions, we see yet another manifestation of the ongoing tension between center and periphery that has so long characterized the American religious experience. Those whose numbers currently allow them to claim their own positions as central or dominant in American thought or culture would be well advised to review their nation's history. They should pay special attention to the ways in which smaller peripheral groups in America's past have grown to be central players in this dynamic and ever-changing landscape, and some who assumed their dominance would last forever have found their traditions withering away, relegated to the sidelines themselves.

Surveying the American religious experience one is struck by the dynamic, ever-changing nature of religious life in the United States. A nation that boasts perhaps the greatest religious diversity in the world is a nation constantly interacting with that larger world. New faith traditions continually arrive as unregistered passengers, stowaways in the souls of the immigrants they accompany. Multiple tensions are sustained by this dynamic, moving landscape—cultural tensions, racial tensions, tensions between different religions, and tensions between different denominations of the same religious tradition. Often as not, religion in America has contributed to these tensions rather than mediated them. But one of the tensions that can be seen most often in a survey of American religious history is that tenacious tension between center and periphery that still colors today's religious landscape.

America is a land of immigrants, and as soon as one group of immigrants becomes firmly established on American soil and develops a distinctly American identity, it is confronted with another wave of immigrants. The new wave challenges that newly established identity, bringing different cultural values, different religious beliefs, and different assumptions about the nature of the spiritual world. The growth of smaller groups, the resistance of larger groups, and the tension between religious center and periphery can be seen time and time again in American history. So many religious traditions have started out as small groups on the periphery of the larger American culture. It might be the Methodists dissenting from established Anglican values. It might be the Baptists challenging accepted views of baptism and predestination. It might be the first group of Mormons embracing a new religious tradition. It might be the holiness movement's unsettling challenges to the larger Methodist tradition. But many peripheral groups, seen as radically divergent in their own times, have eventually found themselves well established in the center of American religious thought and belief, boasting millions of believers and supporting hundreds or thousands of churches nationwide. Once their dominance in the central stream of religious acceptance in America has been established, they, in turn, find themselves challenged by newer groups, by splinter groups within their own traditions, and by newly imported religious traditions emerging from radically different cultural climates.

The collision of cultures that has formed the New World continues to shape American religious history. Today, arguably more than ever, American religion is intrinsically multicultural. An ever-growing number of nations is represented in the American religious landscape, and immigrants are no longer willing to dispense entirely with the culture of their homelands and ancestries. They want to retain their own family and cultural histories and still participate fully in American life. The interplay of cultures is accelerated by globalization and the ever-increasing role of communication technologies in facilitating international interaction.

But an honest survey of American religious history finds that it has never been exclusively American. In fact, it has always had a global dimension—one that has often been underestimated or underrecognized in terms of shaping contemporary American beliefs. Whether one looks at the deep roots of African traditional religions in the black church or examines the Spanish legacy in America's burgeoning Hispanic population, the echo of distant lands is there. It is there in John Calvin's Swiss experiment in Geneva, which shaped the future of Calvinism. It is there in the English roots of Methodism, when John Wesley began to push against the constraints of his own Anglican faith. It is there in the deep histories of India, China, and Tibet, which frame and inform American Buddhism. Thus, in many ways, the increasing global interaction that characterizes American religious life today may be more of a circular return to its roots than an innovation.

Similarly, interdenominational understanding in America continues to grow. In the wake of the ecumenical movement in the latter part of the twentieth century, more and more denominations hold regular exchanges with members of other denominational groups. Movements such as the charismatic movement, which grew out of the Pentecostals and holiness movement, have created worship approaches that cross denominational boundaries and provide a fruitful common ground for exploration of other differences. Active engagement in ongoing ecumenical dialog continues to develop documents that clarify shared positions and views, similarities and differences between denominational affiliations.

Common ground is also being found between different religious traditions. Widespread exposure to meditation and other techniques common in religious traditions of the East have increased the interest and receptivity of Americans to religions other than Christianity. The adoption of meditation techniques by health professionals as a means of dealing with stress-related disorders has increased American appreciation for the validity of such approaches from across the Pacific. From across the Atlantic, the significant progress made in Catholic-Jewish relationships under the papacy of John

Paul II encourages a new receptivity and tolerance for different faith traditions and for exploration of common roots in differing streams.

But while Americans become increasingly willing to explore the depths of other denominations and other religious traditions, they retain one of their most singular characteristics in terms of religious participation. Americans continue to demand that religion cannot be limited to abstract intellectual ideas or restrictive dogmatic certainty. Instead, American religion demands a vibrancy that recognizes the importance of personal religious experience and creates channels through which the individual can share that religious experience with others. Perhaps this results from the historical distrust of the politics that accompanied the national churches the European Americans left behind in the Old World. Perhaps it is the deep vein of anti-intellectualism that colors the American perspective. Whatever the reason, Americans have long sought emotionalized, unmediated contact with their God. That unmediated contact can be achieved by dance, in traditions that descended from African traditional religions or Native American traditions. It can be achieved by great preaching, such as that pursued in the Baptist or Methodist traditions. It can be achieved by deep forms of contemplative prayer, such as that found in Buddhism and Zen or in the monastic orders of Roman Catholicism and Anglicanism. It can be found in the inner voice that speaks to one in a Quaker prayer meeting or in the simple way of life that has sustained the Amish and the Mennonites. Or it can be felt in the movement of the Spirit in the churches of the holiness movement, Pentecostalism, or the charismatic movement.

American religion is determinedly experientially oriented in a way that continues to frustrate and perplex scholars of religion, but that keeps it vibrant and alive, infused with an energy that seems only to expand and grow. From the emotionalized preaching of the Great Awakening to the camp meetings and revivals of the nineteenth century, Americans want to experience God first hand and to do so in the framework of a religious perspective that honors their experience.

America consistently has some of the highest percentages in surveys of religious belief or belief in God. But the American God must be one that is constructed like a hologram, where a million small reflections join together to create a composite image. The incredibly diverse American religious landscape poses its own set of problems in terms of religious identity. For one must construct a religious identity without the support of a uniform national identity in religion or culture. This thought brings us to the final tension that comes along with the richness of the American religious experience, the challenges our diverse heritage presents to today's believer in terms of forming and sustaining religious identity.

The American religious landscape is unlike any other. Jefferson's separation of church and state has had far-reaching implications for the development of religious groups in American society. While many nations still retain a monistic religious culture, or a religious tradition that is so deeply ingrained in the culture of the country as to be emblematic, America is decidedly, determinedly diverse. In that sense, William Penn's "holy experiment" continues to be played out across twenty-first-century America.

But the very breadth of the American religious scene brings its own set of challenges to today's believer. How can one know that one's own faith is normative and still accept the right of others to pursue radically different faith traditions? If other religious or denominational traditions are valid and worthy of respect, what makes one's own faith worthy of even greater respect and loyalty? Is one in danger of becoming a serial monogamist in terms of religious belief, simply converting from one tradition to another, over and over, in an lifelong search for grace?

Perhaps instead of answering these difficult questions, the American religious believer is forging a new way to be religious in the world. Rather than unthinkingly accepting a tradition practiced by their ancestors or handed down through a national church, many American believers are bringing both heart and head to their own religious affiliations and commitments. They are challenging their religious leaders to provide theological depth, challenging their historians to know more about the ways in which the tradition was preserved in the past, and challenging their pastors to help them find ways to live that tradition in a meaningful way in the present.

When the American Roman Catholic Church moved westward in the nineteenth century and began to build the infrastructure of the church today, it did not lead the explorers in the manner often depicted, with Spanish conquistadors and Franciscan monks. Instead, the Roman Catholic Church followed the ever-growing stream of settlers further and further to the west, playing catch-up as it struggled to build churches and schools for growing Catholic populations in newly established towns and cities. Perhaps, on the American religious frontier of the twenty-first century, a similar shift will occur, and traditional churches will find themselves following their own believers into new territories in terms of interreligious dialog, ecumenical exchange, and enrichment through engagement with other religious traditions. Perhaps the widespread success and enthusiasm of the Charismatic Renewal will lead mainline denominations into greater appreciation and acceptance of the experiential forms of worship embraced by so many Americans today. Perhaps we will begin to see a landscape emerge in which the growing voice of the laity balances the traditional power of the clergy in newly collaborative structures and missions.

It is such a rich landscape. In the process of exploring other religious traditions and the histories that formed and shaped them, one has the opportunity to explore traditions that lay far outside one's own family or geographical inheritance. In real engagement with American religious history, one has the opportunity to immerse oneself in the search for religious purity demonstrated by the Puritans. One can witness the excitement and enthusiasm of the Great Awakening. One can see the curious blend of the Ephrata Cloister and know the beautiful, profound faith of the Moravians. One debates the differences between Wesley's justification and sanctification and the sudden and gradual ways in which God works in the heart of the individual believer. One hears the resonant preaching that gave birth to the evangelical tradition or peers into the unique lifestyle Amish on their quiet Pennsylvania farms. One can join the Shakers and cultivate the ability to produce beautifully wrought furniture and houses or sit with the Quakers in respectful silence until the inner voice speaks. One engages with the long reach of Henry David Thoreau, from his transcendentalist roots to his influence on Mahatma Gandhi's and Martin Luther King Jr.'s nonviolent resistance movements.

American religious history offers us the Sephardic and Ashkenazi immigrants and the growth of American Judaism and sees the Anglican Church transformed into the Episcopalian tradition in the aftermath of the Revolutionary War. It brings Scandinavian and German Lutherans to some of the richest farmland in the world. We witness the evolution of the Black Church and the emergence of Santería. We find Baptist missionaries and Southern Baptist preachers and watch the holiness movement give birth to Pentecostalism. We bring the tragic history of the Native American people into dialog with the powerful sanctity of Hispanic Catholic tradition. We stand by as the Mormons establish one of the world's newest and fastest-growing religious traditions in the high desert of Utah, and we feed on streams of American Buddhism as they weave their way into the religious beliefs of thousands of Americans.

Through the work of determined pluralists like William James and W. E. B. DuBois, America has been moved into an unparalleled world of diverse religious traditions, of rich religious heritages, and of increasing tolerance in the face of religious difference. But the development of the American religious landscape is far from over. The rate of growth and diversity is not diminishing, but ever expanding. Through sun and shadow, through altruism and anger, through certainty and disillusionment, the American religious landscape continues to grow and is arguably the richest in the world.

NOTE

1. For this section, I am indebted to and deeply influenced by the work of Eugene Taylor in his masterful work *William James on Consciousness beyond the Margin* (Princeton, NJ: Princeton University Press, 1996), see 112–14.

RESOURCES FOR
FURTHER READING

CHAPTER 1: INTRODUCTION

Comblin, José. *Called for Freedom: The Changing Context of Liberation Theology.* Maryknoll, NY: Orbis Books, 1998.

Elliott, J. H. *Imperial Spain 1469–1716.* New York: Penguin Books [1963] 1990.

Gaustad, Edwin, and Leigh Schmidt. *The Religious History of America: The Heart of the American Story from Colonial Times to Today.* San Francisco: Harper San Francisco, 2002.

Taylor, Eugene. *Shadow Culture: Psychology and Spirituality in America.* Washington, DC: Counterpoint, 1999

CHAPTER 2: CALVIN IN NEW ENGLAND

Bouwsma, William J. *John Calvin: A Sixteenth-Century Portrait.* New York: Oxford University Press, 1988.

Campbell, John. "The Word of Righteousness: The Perseverance of the Saints." *Affirmation and Critique* VIII, no. 1 (April 2003): 54–68.

Gaustad, Edwin, and Leigh Schmidt. *The Religious History of America: The Heart of the American Story from Colonial Times to Today.* San Francisco: Harper San Francisco, 2002.

Marsden, George M. *Jonathan Edwards: A Life.* New Haven, CT: Yale University Press, 2003.

McGrath, Alister E. *A Life of John Calvin.* Oxford: Blackwell Publishers, 1993.

McNeill, John T., ed. *The Library of Christian Classics, Calvin: Institutes of the Christian Religion.* Vols. XX and XXI. Philadelphia: Westminster Press, 1960.

CHAPTER 3: PIETY IN PENNSYLVANIA

Gaustad, Edwin, and Leigh Schmidt. *The Religious History of America: The Heart of the American Story from Colonial Times to Today.* Rev. ed. San Francisco: Harper San Francisco, 2002.

Gordon, Ronald J. "The Ephrata Cloister: Conrad Beissel and His Communal Experiment." Available at Church of the Brethren Network, www.com–net.org/cloister.htm (accessed January 22, 2005).

Taylor, Eugene. *Shadow Culture: Psychology and Spirituality in America.* Washington, DC: Counterpoint, 1999.

CHAPTER 4: JOHN WESLEY AND THE METHODISTS

Collins, Kenneth J. *A Real Christian: The Life of John Wesley.* Nashville, TN: Abingdon Press, 1999.

Collins, Kenneth J., and John H. Tyson, eds. *Conversion in the Wesleyan Tradition.* Nashville, TN: Abingdon Press, 2001.

Wynkoop, Mildred Bangs. *A Theology of Love: The Dynamic of Wesleyanism.* Kansas City, MO: Beacon Hill Press of Kansas City, 1972.

CHAPTER 5: JONATHAN EDWARDS, CONGREGATIONALISM, AND THE EVANGELICAL TRADITION

Edwards, Jonathan. *The Religious Affections.* Carlisle, PA: The Banner of Truth Trust, 2001.

Marsden, George M. *Jonathan Edwards: A Life.* New Haven, CT: Yale University Press, 2003.

CHAPTER 6: THE AMISH AND THE MENNONITES

Generich, Rev. Eli, interview, cited in Leonard Gross, "Background Dynamics of the Amish Movement." Available at www.goshen.edu/facultypubs/GROSS.html (accessed February 19, 2005).

Yoder, Paton. *Tradition and Transition: Amish Mennonites and Old Order Amish, 1800–1901.* Scottsdale, PA: Herald Press, 1991.

CHAPTER 7: THE QUAKERS AND THE SHAKERS

Fox, George. *Autobiography of George Fox*. Edited by Rufus Jones. Richmond, IN: Friends United Press, 1971.

Stein, Stephen J. *The Shaker Experience in America*. New Haven, CT: Yale University Press, 1992

CHAPTER 8: BACON, SWEDENBORG, AND TRANSCENDENTALISM

Menand, Louis. *The Metaphysical Club: A Story of Ideas in America*. New York: Farrar, Straus, and Giroux, 2001.

Swedenborg, Emanuel. *Emanuel Swedenborg: The Universal Human and Soul-Body Interaction*. Edited and translated by George F. Dole. Classics of Western Spirituality. New York: Paulist Press, 1984.

Taylor, Eugene. *Shadow Culture: Psychology and Spirituality in America*. Counterpoint: Washington, DC, 1999

CHAPTER 9: CATHOLIC–ANTI-CATHOLIC

Billington, Ray Allen. *The Protestant Crusade: 1800–1860*. Chicago: Quadrangle Books, 1964.

Ellis, John Tracy. *American Catholicism*. Chicago: University of Chicago Press, 1956.

Morris, Charles R. *American Catholic*. New York: Random House, 1997.

Wade, Richard C. *The Urban Frontier*. Chicago: University of Chicago Press, 1959.

CHAPTER 10: AMERICAN JUDAISM

Sarna, Jonathan D. *American Judaism: A History*. New Haven, CT: Yale University Press, 2004.

CHAPTER 11: ANGLICAN TO EPISCOPAL

Holmes, David L. *A Brief History of the Episcopal Church*. Harrisburg, PA: Trinity Press International, 1993.

CHAPTER 12: LUTHERANS, GERMANS, AND SCANDINAVIANS

Blayney, Ida Walz. *The Age of Luther: The Spirit of Renaissance-Humanism and of the Reformation*. New York: Vantage Press, 1957.

Dillenberger, John, ed. *Martin Luther: Selections from his Writings*. Garden City, NY: Anchor Books, 1961.

Luther, Martin. *Martin Luther's Basic Theological Writings*. Edited by Timothy Lull. Minneapolis: Fortress Press, 1989.

Noll, Mark A. "The Lutheran Difference." *First Things* 20 (February 2992): 31–40.

CHAPTER 13: EVOLUTION OF THE BLACK CHURCH

Murphy, Joseph M. *Santería: African Spirits in America*. Boston: Beacon Press, 1993.

Raboteau, Albert J. *Slave Religion: The "Invisible Institution" in the Antebellum South*. Oxford: Oxford University Press, 1980.

Smith, Theophus H. *Conjuring Culture: Biblical Formations of Black America*. Oxford: Oxford University Press, 1994.

Wilmore, Gayraud S. *Black Religion and Black Radicalism: An Interpretation of the Religious History of African Americans*. 3rd ed. Maryknoll, NY: Orbis Books, 1998.

CHAPTER 14: BAPTISTS AND BAPTISM

Helwys, Thomas. *A Short Declaration of the Mystery of Iniquity*. Edited with an introduction by Richard Groves. Macon, GA: Mercer University Press, 1998.

Leonard, Bill J. *Baptists in America*. Irvington, NY: Columbia University Press, 2005.

Lumpkin, William L. *Baptist Confessions of Faith*. Valley Forge, PA: Judson Press, 1969.

McBeth, Leon. *The Baptist Heritage*. Nashville, TN: Broadman Press, 1987.

Tull, James E. *Shapers of Baptist Thought*. Valley Forge, PA: Judson Press, 1972.

CHAPTER 15: PENTECOSTALS AND THE HOLINESS MOVEMENT

Synan, Vinson. *The Holiness-Pentecostal Tradition: Charismatic Movements in the Twentieth Century*. Grand Rapids, MI: William B. Eerdmans Publishing Company, 1997.

———. *The Century of the Holy Spirit: 100 Years of Pentecostal and Charismatic Renewal, 1901–2001*. Nashville, TN: Thomas Nelson Publishers, 2001.

CHAPTER 16: THE CALIFORNIA MISSIONS AND THE HISPANIC SOUTHWEST

Bridgers, Lynn. *Death's Deceiver: The Life of Joseph P. Machebeuf.* Albuquerque: University of New Mexico Press, 1997.

Johnson, Paul C., ed. *The California Missions: A Pictorial History.* Menlo Park, CA: Lane Book Company, 1964.

Simmons, Mark. *NM: An Interpretive History.* Albuquerque: University of New Mexico Press, 1989.

———. *The Last Conquistador: Juan de Onate and the Settling of the Far Southwest.* Norman: University of Oklahoma Press, 1991.

CHAPTER 17: RAIDS, GHOSTS, AND RENEWAL

Brown, Dee Alexander. *Bury My Heart at Wounded Knee: An Indian History of the American West.* 30th anniv. ed. New York: Henry Holt and Company, 2001.

Deloria, Vine, Jr. *For This Land: Writings on Religion in America.* With an introduction by James Treat. New York: Routledge, 1999.

Holler, Clyde. *Black Elk's Religion: The Sun Dance and Lakota Catholicism.* Syracuse, NY: Syracuse University Press, 1995.

Ward, Geoffrey C. *The West: An Illustrated History.* Boston: Little Brown and Company, 1996.

CHAPTER 18: MORMON COUNTRY

Palmer, Spencer J. *The Church Encounters Asia.* Salt Lake City, UT: The Church of Jesus Christ of Latter-Day Saints, 1970.

Smith, Christopher. "Unearthing Mountain Meadows Secrets." *The Salt Lake Tribune,* March 14, 2000.

Smith, Joseph, trans. *The Book of Mormon: An Account Written by the Hand of Mormon Taken from the Plates of Nephi.* Salt Lake City, UT: The Church of Jesus Christ of Latter-Day Saints, 1990.

Walker, Ronald W., David J. Whittaker, and James B. Allen. *Mormon History.* Urbana: University of Illinois Press, 2001.

CHAPTER 19: GOLD MOUNTAIN

Evans-Wentz, W. Y., ed. *The Tibetan Book of the Great Liberation.* With a psychological commentary by C. G. Jung. London: Oxford University Press, 1954.

———, ed. *The Tibetan Book of the Dead*. With a psychological summary by C. G. Jung. London: Oxford University Press, 1960.

Houston, Jeanne Wakatsuki, and James D. Houston. *Farewell to Manzanar*. New York: Bantam Books, 1974.

Kitagawa, Joseph. *Religions of the East*. Philadelphia: Westminster Press, 1968.

Prebish, Charles S., and Kenneth K. Tanaka, eds. *The Faces of Buddhism in America*. Los Angeles: University of California Press, 1998.

Seager, Richard Hughes. *Buddhism in America*. New York: Columbia University Press, 2000.

Ward, Geoffrey C. *The West: An Illustrated History*. Boston: Little Brown and Company, 1996.

Yang, C. K. *Religion in Chinese Society*. Berkeley: University of California Press, 1961.

CHAPTER 20: PLURALISM AND PERIPHERY

DuBois, W. E. B. *The Oxford W. E. B. Dubois Reader*. Edited by Eric J. Sundquist. Oxford: Oxford University Press, 1996.

———. *The Suppression of the African Slave Trade*. Baton Rouge: Louisiana State University Press, [1896] 1965.

James, William. *William James: Writings 1878–1899*. Edited by G. E. Meyers. New York: Library of America, 1992.

———. *William James: Writings 1902–1910*. Edited by B. Kucklick. New York: Library of America, 1987.

Lewis, David Levering. *W. E. B. Dubois: Biography of a Race, 1868–1919*. New York: Owl Books, 1994.

Perry, Ralph Barton. *The Thought and Character of William James*. Vol. 1. Boston: Little, Brown, 1936.

———. *In the Spirit of William James*. New Haven, CT: Yale University Press, 1938.

Taylor, Eugene. *William James on Consciousness beyond the Margin*. Princeton, NJ: Princeton University Press, 1996.

INDEX

abolitionists, 46, 55, 146, 150, 152, 163

Achomawi, 183

Acoma, 3, 187

activism 55–56

A.E.L.C. (*see* Association of Evangelical Lutheran Churches)

African Methodist Episcopal church (AME), 31–32, 47, 150

African Methodist Episcopal Zion church (AME Zion), 11, 150–51

African traditional religions, 1, 3, 6, 145, 153, 155, 236, 237

Aldersgate, 29, 40, 169

Algonquian, 17

Allen, Richard, 47, 149–50, 152, 156, 172

A.M.E. (*see* African Methodist Episcopal)

A.M.E. Zion (*see* African Methodist Episcopal Zion)

American, defined, 12n1

American Baptist Churches in the United States, 167

American Baptist Home Mission Society, 162

American Baptist Publication Society, 162

American Friends Service Committee, 78

American Home Missionary Society, 52

American Interdenominational Evangelical Alliance, 137

American Republicans, 105–6

Amish, 31, 35, 61, 65–67, 68–69, 237, 239

Ammann, Jakob, 65–66

Anabaptists, 22, 31, 61–62, 68, 157

Anglican Church, 49, 52, 123–24, 239

Anglicanism, 4, 30–32, 41–42, 51, 61, 124–25, 147, 235, 237

Anglo-Catholicism, 128, 163

Anthony, Susan B., 77

anti-Catholicism, 5, 100–108

anti-Chinese sentiment, 221–22

anti-intellectualism, 7

Anti-Romanist, 5

anti-Semitism, 110, 115–16, 120

Apache, 3

Arapaho, 194–96

Arius, 91

Arminianism, 21–24, 29, 56–57, 59

Arminius, James or Jacobus, 21–22

Arndt, Johann, 26

Asbury, Francis, 43, 44, 47, 150

Ashkenazic, 109–111, 119, 239

Ashkenazim, 109–111, 119, 239

Association of Evangelical Lutheran Churches (AELC), 144

Asuza Street Revival, 175–76, 178
Augsberg Confession, 135, 137
Augustine of Hippo, 14, 21, 56–57, 61,
    134, 142, 157

Baca, Cabeza de, 1
Bacon, Francis, 85
baptism of the dead, 216
baptism of the Holy Spirit, 53, 170
Baptist, 23, 31–32, 45, 52, 55–57, 59,
    147–48, 150, 157–168, 235, 237,
    239
Baptist General Tract Society (*see also*
    American Baptist Publication
    Society), 162, 167
Baptist Missionary Society, 162
Baptists, General, 158–59
Baptists, Particular, 158–59
Bebbington, David, 55–56, 59
Beissel, Johann Conrad, 32–36
believer's baptism, 61, 157, 160, 168
Benedict of Nursia, 35
Benedictines, 35, 108
biblicism, 55–56
Bight of Benin, 146
Bight of Biafra, 146
Black Kettle, 194–95
blue laws, 15
Board of Home Missions, 143
Bohler, Peter, 29, 40
Bohme, Jakob, 33
Book of Common Prayer, 121
Book of Mormon, 206–7, 209–210
Brainerd, David, 17–19
de Brebeuf, Jean, 1–2
Bridger, Jim, 210–11
Brown, John, 94, 231
Buddhism, 4, 11, 222–25, 236, 239
Bunyan, John, 160

Cabazon, 183
California, 181–86, 191, 217–18, 224
California Alien Land Act, 224

California Gold Rush, 217–18
California missions, 182–86
California Synod, 143
Calvin, Jean (*see* Calvin, John)
Calvin, John, 13, 24, 56, 61, 157,
    236
Calvinism, 13–16, 19–22, 24–25, 41,
    47, 50, 236
Cambridge Platform, 50
camp meetings, 44, 52, 170, 237
Cane Ridge, 45, 170
Catholicism, 2, 4, 6–7, 10–11, 27,
    31–32, 35, 49, 55, 62–63, 147,
    152–54, 237, 238
Centering Prayer, 228
Central Conference of American
    Rabbis, 112
Central Pacific Railroad, 220–21
Channing, William Ellery, 91
Charismatic Renewal, 179–180,
    238
Charles I, 38
Charles II, 30, 75–76
Charles V, 109
Chauncey, Charles, 58
Chemehuevi, 183
Cherokee, 143
Cheyenne, 194
Chinese Exclusion Act, 221–22
Chinese immigration, 218, 228
Chippewa, 126
Chivington, John, 194–96
Christian Brothers, 108
Chun Ming, 217
Church of England, 4, 43–44, 49,
    61–62, 122–24, 135, 158
Church of God, 175
Church of Jesus Christ of the Latter-
    Day Saints (*see also* Mormons), 5
Church of the Nazarene, 48, 173
Church of Religious Science, 8
Clarke, John, 161
Cochiti, 3

Coffin, Catherine, 78
Coffin, Levi, 78
College of New Jersey (*see* Princeton University), 19
College of William and Mary, 129
Comanche, 3, 194–96
Comblin, José, 8–9, 12n2, 35
Concordia Seminary, 138
Concordia Theological Seminary, 138
Confucius, 218
Confucianism, 218–20
Congregationalism, 4, 11, 17, 20, 24, 49–60, 61
Congregationalists, 46
Conservative Judaism, 112, 117
Conversion, 18, 29, 40, 42, 44–45, 54,148
Conversionism, 55, 59
Coptic Christians, 145
Coronado, Francisco Vásques de, 186–87
Costanoan, 183
Cotton, John, 16, 49, 51
Cranmer, Thomas, 121
Crocker, Charles, 220–21
Cromwell, Oliver, 75
Crucicentrism, 56
Custer, George Armstrong, 202

Dalai Lama, 225–26
Deaconesses, 130–131
Debois, W. E. B., 229, 231–34, 239
Delille, Henriette, 153
Deloria, Vine, Jr., 199–200
Doctrine of Correspondences, 88
Drake, Sir Francis, 181
Duchemin, Marie Almaide Maxis, 153
Durham, William H., 177–78
Dutch Reformed Christians, 15

Eddy, Mary Baker, 8
Edwards, Jonathan, 7, 8, 17–19, 41, 49–50, 55, 58–59

Egypt, 145
Eliot, John, 16
Elizabeth I, 182
Emerson, Ralph Waldo, 89–92, 95
empiricism, 85
enthusiasm, 8, 58
Ephrata Cloister, 8, 31, 33–6, 239
Episcopal, 10, 121
Episcopal Church, 123
Episcopalian, 22
Esselen, 183
Ethiopia, 145–146
evangelism, 148
Evangelicalism, 55, 58–59
experiential, 2, 6–7, 44, 230–31, 237–38

Ferdinand of Spain, 109, 181
Finished Work controversy. 177–78
Finney, Charles G., 53–54, 55, 57, 100, 170
Fire-baptized Holiness Church, 174
First Great Awakening (*see* Great Awakening)
Five Classics, 218
Five Dissenting Brethren, 50
Fletcher, John, 23–24, 35, 134, 169, 174
Franciscans, 4, 182–85, 188, 238
Frederick I of Denmark, 135
Frederick IV of Denmark, 142
Frederick William III of Prussia, 138
Free Africa Society, 47, 149–50
French Huguenots (*see also* Huguenots), 15
French Revolution, 185
Ford, Henry, 116
Forsyth, James W., 201–202
Forty-two Articles, 121–22
Four Books, 218
Fox, George, 73
Fulford, W. H., 174
fundamentalism, 58–59

Gandhi, Mahatma, 239
Gautama Buddha, 222–23
General Assembly, 160
General Missionary Convention, 162
General Synod, 139
General Synod of Lutheran Churches, 137
General Synod of the Confederate States, 139
General Theological Seminary, 130
George III of England, 16
Ghost Dance, 196–201
Gingerich, Eli E., 69–70
glebe, 122
Gold Mountain, 217, 220, 228
grace, 134–35
Graves, J. R., 163
Gray, Asa, 95
Great Awakening, 8–17, 18, 40, 51–52, 58–59, 148, 177, 237, 239

Half-Way Covenant, 18
Hahnemann, Samuel, 88
Hare, William Hobart, 127
Harper's Ferry, 94, 231
Harris, Barbara C., 132
Hasidic Judaism, 118
Haygood, Atticus Greene, 173
Hebrew Union College, 112
Helwys, Thomas, 22–23, 158
Henry VIII, 121, 132, 157
Hensley, George, 179
Hicks, Elias, 77
Hicksites, 77
Hinckley, Gordon B., 213
Hispanic, 1, 236, 239
Hobart, Henry, 125
Holiness Movement, 22, 169–180
Holocaust, 117, 119
Home Mission Society, 164–65
Hooker, Thomas, 15–16, 51
Hopkey, Sophia, 39
Hopkins, Mark, 220

Hsun-tzu, 219
Huguenots, 19
Huntington, Collis P., 220
Huron, 2
Hus, John, 27

Inskip, John 171–72
Institutes of the Christian Church, 14
interdenominational, 4–5
interreligious, 3–4
Invisible Institution, 147, 156
Iowa Holiness Association, 174
Iowa Synod, 139
Iroquois, 126
Irwin, Benjamin Hardin, 174
Isabella of Spain, 109, 181
Isleta, 3
Israel, 119
Issei, 224

James I of England, 158
James, Henry Sr., 90
James, William, 90, 229–30, 234, 239
Japanese immigration, 224
Japanese interment, 224
Jefferson, Thomas, 5, 98, 238
Jemez, 3
Jessey, Henry, 159
Jesuit (*see also* Society of Jesus), 4, 98, 102–3, 108, 152
Jewish immigration, 114–15
Jewish Theological Seminary of America, 112
John Paul II, 236–37
Jones, Absolom, 149, 151
Jones, Charles Colcock, 148
Judaism, 2–3, 11, 109–120, 145
Julian of Eclanum, 21
Jung, Carl, 218, 227
justification, 40, 43, 134

Karok, 183
Kearny, Stephen Watts, 189

Keble, John, 127
Kemper, Jackson, 125–26
Kempis, Thomas à, 38
Keres, 3
King, Martin Luther, Jr., 156, 239
Kiowa, 3, 194–96
Know-Nothing Party, 107
Krauth, Charles Porterfield, 139
K'ung Fu Tzu, 218

L.C.M.S. (*see* Lutheran Church
   Missouri Synod)
Laguna, 3
Lakota, 197, 201
Lamy, Jean Baptiste, 190–192
Landmark movement, 163
Lasuén, Fermín, 183
Lathrop, John, 159
Lee, John D., 212
Lee, Mother Ann, 73, 79
Leeser, Isaac, 111
Leo XII, 99
van Leyden, John, 63
Little Big Horn, 202
Luther, Martin, 13, 26, 29, 32, 35, 61,
   133, 157
Lutheran Church Missouri Synod
   (LCMS), 142
Lutheran missionaries, 143
Lutheranism, 11, 26, 31, 41, 61,
   133–144, 167, 239

Machebeuf, Joseph, 190–91
Magdeburg history, 97
Malcolm X, 156
Manifest Destiny, 193
Marianists, 108
Martin, Joel, 199
Martínez, Antonio Jose, 190–91
Massachussetts Bay Company, 14
Massasoit, 2
Mather, Cotton, 51
McLaughlin, James, 200

Meachum, Joseph, 80
meditation, 226, 236
Melancthon, Philipp, 26, 35, 134–35
Mencius, 219
Mennonite Mission Network, 70
Mennonites, 22, 31, 35, 61, 63–65, 158,
   237
Merton, Thomas, 228
Methodism, 4, 10–11, 21–24, 37–48,
   52, 55–57, 59, 147, 169–70, 235–37
Methodist Church in America, 44–48
Methodist Episcopal Church, 149
Mexican Revolution, 184–85, 191
Midwest, 141
Modoc, 183
Mohawk, 19, 126
Mohicans, 19
monasticism, 8, 35
Monk, Maria 102–103
Moravians, 27–29, 35, 39, 40–41, 57,
   239
Mormon missionaries, 209, 213–14
Mormons, 5, 205–216, 235, 239
Mott, Lucretia, 77
Mountain Meadows Massacre, 212–13
Mt. Saint Mary's, 107
Muhlenberg, Frederick, 137
Muhlenberg, Henry Melchior, 136–37
Muir, John, 94–96
multicultural, 2, 5–6, 236
Munzer, Thomas, 62–63

N.A.A.C.P. (*see* National Association
   for the Advancement of Colored
   People)
Nambe, 3
National Association for the
   Advancement of Colored People
   (NAACP), 233–34
National Camp Meeting Association
   for the Promotion of Holiness, 171
Native Americans, 2–3, 6–7, 11, 16–18,
   31, 39, 46, 52, 57, 193–204, 237

nativism, 4, 98
naturalism, 86, 96
Nazarenes, 22
New Light Schism, 57–58
New Light Stir, 79
New Jerusalem, 89
New Mexico, 181, 193
New World, 1–2, 21, 235
Newman, John Henry, 127
Niagara Bible Conference, 59
Niagara Movement 233
Ninety-Five Theses, 133, 135
Nisei, 224–25
No-Popery, 97
Northern Baptist Convention, 167

Oberlin College, 53, 170
Oblate Sisters of Providence, 153
Oglethorpe, James, 39, 124
Ohlone, 183
Okwanachu, 183
Old Order Amish (*see* Amish)
Old World, 2, 237
Oñate, Juan de, 187
Original Sin, 134
orishas, 154
Orthodox Judaism, 113, 117
Oxford Movement,127

pacifists. 75
Palmer, Phoebe, 170–71
P.C.U.S.A. (*see* Presbyterian Church in
   the USA)
Pelagianism, 21–22
Pelagius, 21
Penn, William, 4, 15, 30–32, 76, 123,
   238
Pennsylvania, 4, 29, 31, 36
Pennsylvania Dutch, 67
Pennsylvania Ministerium, 142
Pennsylvania Synod, 137
Pentecostals, 8, 22, 48, 169–180, 239
periphery, 2, 10–11, 229, 235

Philadelphia Baptist Association,
   160–62
pietism, 5, 25–27, 30, 32, 35, 61
pluralism, 5, 229–231
polygamy, 5, 63, 208, 214
Popé, 188
pragmatism, 7, 231
predestination, 14
Presbyterian Church in the USA
   (PCUSA), 20
Presbyterian Rebellion, 16
Presbyterianism, 19, 24, 31, 45, 50–52,
   57, 61
Presbytery of Philadelphia, 20
Priesthood of All Believers, 26
Primitive Holiness Mission, 172
Princeton University, 19, 58, 104, 137
Protestant, 4, 7, 10, 14, 27, 35, 44, 46,
   55
Protestant Vindicator, 5
Protocols of the Learned Elders of
   Zion, 116
psychology of religion, 19
Pueblo, 3, 188
Pueblo Revolt, 188–89
Puritanism, 1–2, 4, 11, 13–16, 21–22,
   30, 49, 98, 239
Pusey, Edward Bouverie, 127

Quakers, 30, 31, 46, 52, 73–79, 106,
   150, 237, 239
Quorum of Seventies, 215
Quorum of Twelve, 209–210

radical empiricism, 230–31
Reconstructionist Judaism, 118
Reed, Rebecca, 101
Reform Judaism, 112–13, 117
Reformed Society of Israelites,
   110–111
religious authority, 8–10
religious experience, 7–9, 11, 17, 19,
   148

Religious Society of Friends (*see also* Quaker), 74
revivals, 18, 44–45, 58, 237
Roman Catholicism (*see* Catholicism)
Rowe, Peter Trimble, 127

Salesians, 108
Salinan, 183
Salt Lake City, 211
Salvation Army, 48
San Felipe, 3
San Ildefonso, 3
sanctification, 42
Sand Creek Massacre, 194–96
Sanei, 224
Santería, 153–56, 188, 239
Sarna, Jonathan, 119
Saybrook Platform, 51
Scandinavian immigration, 140
Schleiermacher, Friedrich, 138
Schmucker, Samuel Simon, 137–38
Scottish Presbyterians, 15
Seabury, Samuel, 125
Sephardic, 109–111, 119, 239
Serra, Junipero, 182–83, 185–86
Seymour, William Joseph, 175
Shakers, 79–84, 239
Shoshone, 3
shunning, 62, 65, 69
Sierra Club, 96
Simons, Menno, 63–64, 72, 158
Sioux (*see also* Lakota), 194–96
Sisters of Charity, 108
Sisters of Loretto, 108
Sisters of Mercy, 108
Sitting Bull, 200–201
slavery, 7, 28, 46, 55, 75, 94, 106, 146–47, 152, 155, 165
Smith, Hyrum, 208
Smith, Joseph, 5, 205–208, 213
Smyth, John, 22, 158–59
snake handlers, 179
Society of Jesus (*see also* Jesuits), 103, 152

sola scriptura, 13
Soule, Silas, 195–96
Southern Baptist Convention, 164, 166–7
Southern Methodist Church, 47
Spangenberg, Augustus, 28
Spener, Philipp Jakob, 25–28, 32
Stanford, Leland, 220
Stanton, Elizabeth Cady, 77
State of Deseret, 211
Stoddard, Soloman, 18
stream of consciousness, 230
Sulpicians, 10
Sutter, John, 217
Sutter's Mill, 217
Suzuki, Daisetz Teitaro, 227–28
Swedenborg, Emanuel, 85, 87, 96

Taoism, 4
Taylor, Eugene, 34, 36n1, 89
Taylor, Jeremy, 38
Thoreau, Henry David, 90, 92–94, 96, 239
Tennent, Gilbert, 57–58
Tennent, William, 57–58
Tewa, 3
Tibetan Buddhism, 225–27
Tichenor, Isaac Taylor, 165
Tiwa, 3
Tolow, 183
Towa, 3
Tractarians, 127, 129
Transcendentalism, 19, 85–96
Transcendentalist Club, 90
Trappist, 35
T.U.L.I.P., 20
Turner, Victor, 9

Underground Railroad, 55, 78, 150
Union of American Hebrew Congregations, 112
Unitarians, 18, 20, 52, 58, 91, 110
University of Pennsylvania, 32

Ursulines, 5, 101, 152
U.S. Conference of Catholic Bishops, 10

Vargas, Don Diego de, 189
Varick, James, 172
Vasa, Gustavus, 136
vestry, 122
visionary traditions, 2, 10–11
voudou, 153, 156

Walden Pond, 93
Walther, Carl Ferdinand Wilhelm,
    138–39
Wampanoag, 2
Warner, D. S., 175
Wesley, Charles, 23, 29, 38–9, 42
Wesley, John, 4, 21–23, 27–29, 35,
    37–44, 55, 124, 134–35, 169, 180,
    239
Wesley, Mary, 42
Wesley, Samuel, 37
Wesley, Susanna, 37–38
Wesleyan Methodists, 46
Westminster Assembly, 20, 50
Westminster Confession of Faith, 19, 50

Whipple, Henry, 127
White, William, 125
Whitefield, George, 8, 28–29, 38,
    40–41, 44, 51, 55, 58, 148
Widney, J. P., 173
Williams, Roger, 15, 161
Willis, Joseph, 151
Wisconsin vs. Yoder, 68
Wise, Isaac Mayer, 112
Women's Home and Foreign
    Missionary Society, 143
Women's Missionary Union, 166
Wounded Knee, 200–203
Wovoka, 197, 200
Wynkoop, Ned, 194–95

Yoruba, 154–55
Yosemite, 95
Young, Brigham, 209–215
Yurok, 183

Zen Buddhism, 4, 223, 228
von Zinzendorf, Count Nikolas
    Ludwig, 27–28, 41
Zuni, 3

ABOUT THE AUTHOR

Lynn Bridgers holds a Ph.D. in Religion from Emory University and is assistant professor of Pastoral Ministries and Religious Education at the Institute for Pastoral Ministries, St. Thomas University, Miami. Winner of 1998 Spur Award, Best Nonfiction–Biography, from the Western Writers of America, she teaches history and practical theology with a focus on religious experience. Her most recent book was *Contemporary Varieties of Religious Experience: James's Classic Study in Light of Resiliency, Temperament & Trauma*.